THE RYDER CUP

THE
RYDER CUP

GOLF'S GREATEST EVENT

Bob Bubka
and
Tom Clavin

Crown Publishers
New York

Published by Crown Publishers, 201 East 50th Street, New York,
New York 10022. Member of the Crown Publishing Group.

Random House, Inc. New York, Toronto, London,
Sydney, Auckland
www.randomhouse.com

Crown is a trademark and the Crown colophon is a registered
trademark of Random House, Inc.

Printed in the United States of America

Design by Rhea Braunstein

Library of Congress Cataloging-in-Publication Data

Bubka, Bob
The Ryder Cup : golf's greatest event / by Bob Bubka and
Tom Clavin. — 1st ed.
1. Ryder Cup—History. I. Clavin, Thomas. II. Title.
GV970.B83 1999
796.352'66—dc21   99-12131

ISBN 0-609-60404-X

10 9 8 7 6 5 4 3 2 1

FIRST EDITION

To my Mom and Dad, Sister and Brother,
and my wife, Donna.
—B.B.

To Robert H. Hamma
—T.C.

CONTENTS

ACKNOWLEDGMENTS

Near the top of our list of people to thank are the players and others whom we interviewed who gave generously of their time. We would like to think they went out of their way to help us, and in a few cases that provided some motivation, but for the most part these very busy people participated in the creation of this book because of their respect for the Ryder Cup and how honored they feel to be connected to it.

In particular, we want to express our appreciation to: Ben Crenshaw, who gave us more than could be expected from a man with a very full plate; our agent, Nat Sobel, who took a chance on this book and found it a home; our editors at Crown, Steve Ross, Sue Carswell, and Rachel Kahan, for their expertise, determination, and patience; Helen Casey, not only for her wonderful photographs but also for her enthusiastic research; Rees Jones, who should be appreciated as much for being a gentleman as for being one of the world's best golf course designers; Carla O'Donoghue and Kitty Merrill, for their painstaking help during the writing process; Danny Peary, for his constant interest and advice; Mary Schuck, for creating such a lovely book jacket; the folks at The Independent Newspaper Corp., for putting up with us during the writing process; and the many people we encountered along the way who thought a book on the Ryder Cup Matches was a terrific idea and kindly encouraged us to push on.

We also want to recognize NBC sports and the many fine publications that over the years have covered the Ryder Cup Matches. *Golfweek, Golf Digest, Golf Magazine, Sports Illustrated,* and numerous daily newspapers have been particularly useful sources of information, and we look forward to their reporting on the Battle of Brookline.

At the very top of our list are our families and friends who gave us much-needed support in addition to tolerating the time we had to devote to *The Ryder Cup*. Thanks from Bob to his mother and father, who have always been there for him; Robin, Robert, Lane, and Noah, who were always there when needed; Bob Joyce and Sonny Rhodes, who beat Bob to death on the golf course but better friends no one has; his brother, Tom, and sister, Nancy, for their love; and to his wife, Donna, whose courageous, winning battle with cancer convinced him never to quit. And thanks from Tom to his wife, Nancy, and his children, Katy and Brendan, for coping with both golf and writing.

With these wonderful people, at the end of every day we wind up way under par.

FOREWORD BY JACK NICKLAUS

Any time I have the honor of representing my country, golf has taken on a greater significance. The Ryder Cup is certainly no exception. I have had the privilege to play in six Ryder Cup Matches and to captain two United States teams, and each opportunity had provided many special memories.

Every two years, the Ryder Cup brings to the golfing world excitement, pressure, emotional highs and lows, a long and continuing tradition of sportsmanship, and some of the most brilliant shot-making in golf. The players and captains represent their countries without pay, because there is little more special than winning as a team and bringing the Ryder Cup home.

The combination of a challenging golf course, some of the most talented players in the world, the honor of representing one's country, the unique heritage of the event, fair play, and working as a team toward a common goal has made the Ryder Cup one of golf's greatest international events.

Since that first official Match in 1927, some of the finest golf courses of the world have served as host to a Ryder Cup competition. I've played at Muirfield in Scotland, and I've captained at my own course of Muirfield Village in Columbus, Ohio. Scioto

Country Club in Columbus, the course on which I learned the game as a small child, has also had the honor of hosting a Ryder Cup. My father was even in the gallery for that 1931 Ryder Cup Match.

But the element that has provided the Ryder Cup a rich history, steeped in drama, are the players. I've had the privilege to call some of the greatest players in history my teammates and my competition. To this day, I am still asked about my first Ryder Cup in 1969, when I conceded a two-foot putt to Tony Jacklin on the final hole of the final Match that led to the first tie between the teams in the event's history. Today, they consider my decision "memorable," but at the time, I simply considered it the right thing to do in a competition founded in sportsmanship.

There has been a lot written about the Ryder Cup Matches, and I am pleased to see there is a book that chronicles the entire history of the event. Samuel Ryder might be the name behind the Ryder Cup trophy, but it has been the players, captains, PGA of America officials, and fans that have made the Ryder Cup the event it is today. This book shows you how they did it, and why the Ryder Cup should continue to be one of the world's great golfing events well into the twenty-first century.

INTRODUCTION

The first official Ryder Cup Match took place in Massachusetts in 1927. Seventy-two years later, for many millions of people, it has become the world's most riveting sports event. Each Match is more exciting, more intensely played, more pressure-packed, and more dramatic than the one before. All of this was evident in 1997, when the Americans were on the verge of a miraculous comeback. No Ryder Cup team in the previous thirty-one Matches had overcome such a large deficit on the final day, and as Sunday dawned at the legendary Valderrama course in Spain, the United States was down 9–4.

But, as shadows lengthened, after clawing back in the singles matches and with just two matches left, the United States needed only these two wins to tie their European opponents. Several Ryder Cups in the last decade had been decided in the final match. This one in September 1997 would be no different. Could the United States team members show their hosts that they were truly invincible, as their fans believed them to be?

Even in Spain, thousands of miles away from their fan base, the Americans had their supporters. The night before, former President George Bush had given a rousing speech to raise the spirits of the shell-shocked team. They were also visited by Michael Jordan, a golf addict who knows a few things about winning championships. Sunday began with a firm resolve to at least go down swinging.

Once Bernhard Langer, for the Europeans, sank his putt to defeat Brad Faxon in their singles match, and with the score

14–11, Europe was assured of at least a tie. But there's nothing like soundly beating your longtime rival, and with three matches left the home team could really pile it on.

Sorry, folks, the Americans wouldn't allow it. They charged back big-time. Jim Furyk downed the imposing Nick Faldo to make the score 14–12. Lee Janzen, a controversial pick by U.S. team captain Tom Kite, was down two holes to Jose Maria Olazabal with only three holes to play, and the crowd was screaming for their countryman. Then, playing the best he ever has under pressure (well, excluding two thrilling U.S. Open victories), the young American took the last three holes and the match. To everyone's amazement, the score stood 14–13, with one match left. A tie would take a lot of wind out of the European squad's sails.

That pivotal match pitted Colin Montgomerie of Scotland, the leading European money-winner five years in a row, against Scott Hoch, who at 41 was the oldest rookie to make a Ryder Cup team. Courageously, Hoch birdied the seventeenth hole to draw even. If he could just do it again . . .

But his tee shot on 18 went astray. He tried to recover, but Montgomerie's approach shot landed within fifteen feet of the hole. His birdie attempt ended up close enough that Hoch conceded. Then, showing the sportsmanship that is typical of the Ryder Cup, he conceded Hoch's eight-foot par putt, not wanting to risk him or the Americans further embarrassment.

It was a bitter 14½-to-13½ loss for the United States. Who would have believed that the trio of Woods, Leonard, and Love—who had won the Masters, the British Open, and the PGA Championship that year—would win only one of thirteen Ryder Cup Matches between them? There was no next week, no next month for the United States to avenge its stunning defeat, its second Ryder Cup loss in a row.

The Americans would have to wait two years—until September 1999 at Brookline, Massachusetts—to have another shot at winning the Ryder Cup. The world will be watching.

* * *

The Ryder Cup has become the most prominent and prestigious international prize in golf, yet it had a very modest origin in its founder, Samuel Ryder, the son of a Manchester corn merchant. A successful self-made businessman, he enjoyed playing and watching golf.

A match Ryder observed in 1926 pitted a group of visiting Americans against a British squad, all of whom were simply practicing for that year's British Open at Royal Lytham and St. Annes. The British won easily, 13½–1½. Ryder enjoyed the friendly competition so much, he didn't want to see it end there.

Samuel Ryder put his money where his heart was, providing a trophy—a gold cup—for 250 pounds. It was decided that the next year's competition for what was immediately known as the Ryder Cup would be in the United States, at the Worcester (Massachusetts) Country Club (a forty-minute drive from where this year's Match will be held). Captained by Walter Hagen, the U.S. team triumphed there, 9½–2½.

Except for the years spanning World War II, the Ryder Cup has been contested every two years, with sites alternating between the United States and Great Britain (until 1997, when the matches were held for the first time on the Continent).

Unlike the stroke play to which the American golf audience is more accustomed, and with individuals competing against each other for one winner, the Ryder Cup Matches include best ball, alternate shot, and match play (in other words, what counts is winning holes, not fewest strokes), and no matter how well or badly any individual does, the winner is determined by which team scores the most points—today, it's 14 to successfully defend, 14½ to wrest the Ryder Cup from the defender.

Despite some unfamiliar factors, this event has become as popular as, if not more so than the four major golf championships: the Masters, the U.S. Open, the British Open, and the PGA Championship. According to Jim Awtrey, CEO of the PGA of America, "This has become our preeminent event." Each competition contains more emotion, brilliant shot-making, pressure, ecstasy, agony, controversy, and courage than any dozen tournaments put together.

"It's the biggest happening in golf," stated Curtis Strange, a five-time Ryder Cup competitor. "And for a player, it's like making the all-star team."

With TV ratings soaring, spectators battling for tickets, every form of media reporting on the competition, revenue surging, and most of the best players in the world fighting for berths on the teams, it is clear why the Ryder Cup Matches have become the preeminent contest in golf—and why in 1999 it will be *the* major international sports event.

One reason is that the Ryder Cup offers one of the few opportunities, and certainly the best one, for well-known professionals to play for their own countries. Any pro golfer who has experienced it will tell you that the pride of bringing the Ryder Cup home is equal to or better than the pride of winning a tournament, no matter how big the paycheck. No one is paid to play on a Ryder Cup team; they do it for pride, honor, and love of country. How often are those words associated with pro sports these days?

Another reason for the unprecedented anticipation of this September's event is that after having dominated the event from its inception, the Americans have been in a slump, losing the last two Matches. The stakes are very high: No U.S. team has lost three times in a row—and you can bet the Americans will fight tooth and nail not to lose on their home course.

Things are looking up for the U.S. side, though. In Tiger Woods, Justin Leonard, Phil Mickelson, Jim Furyk, and David Duval (the first four with much-needed experience under their belts), the United States has the potential for the mightiest quintet ever to anchor a twelve-man Ryder Cup team. These five playing together for one of the most coveted prizes in the world of sports will take interest in the Ryder Cup to new heights.

Other players are in the running for U.S. and European team berths, such as Mark O'Meara (winner of two majors in 1998), Tom Lehman (British Open winner), Davis Love III (PGA

Championship winner), Lee Janzen (two-time U.S. Open winner), Fred Couples (Masters winner), Paul Azinger (PGA Championship winner), a reinvigorated Tom Watson (the last successful Ryder captain and a multimajor winner), and other clutch competitors. With them the United States may well be fielding its best squad in more than twenty years. Colin Montgomerie, Nick Faldo, Bernhard Langer, Ian Woosnam, Jose Maria Olazabal, Lee Westwood, and Jesper Parnevik are waiting to take on the best the Americans have to offer and throw it right back at them, to make up for all those decades of American domination.

This book offers the full story of the Ryder Cup: the players, organizers, captains, and commentators, the competitions, the great shots, the heartbreaking twists of fate, the funny and startling anecdotes, the personal feuds, the amazing displays of sportsmanship, and the very thin line between failure and triumph. All this and more are in the pages to follow. Among those interviewed for this book are the finest players from both sides of the Atlantic: Gene Sarazen; Byron Nelson; Arnold Palmer; Jack Nicklaus; Tom Watson; Max Faulkner; Jack Burke, Jr.; Raymond Floyd; Jose Maria Canizares; Gene Littler; Brian Barnes; Fred Couples; Curtis Strange; Billy Casper; Nick Faldo; Lee Trevino; Larry Nelson; Neil Coles; Mark James; and Ben Crenshaw.

What do we hope you will get out of *The Ryder Cup: Golf's Greatest Event*? Well, fun and reading enjoyment would be nice. An understanding of the format and rules of the Ryder Cup. A ton of information. And certainly an appreciation of what the Ryder Cup Matches have been and are and will likely be.

However, most satisfying for everyone concerned, especially our readers wherever they may be, is to come to respect and admire the wonderful tradition, heritage, and special qualities of the Ryder Cup. It is unlike any other sports event in the world. Those who have participated in a Match have memories that last a lifetime. Those who have watched know they have witnessed the best drama in sports. Those who one day dream of competing for the Ryder Cup—well, this book gives you more reasons to cherish that dream.

And for those who have had the privilege of writing about the Ryder Cup, it doesn't get any better than this.

BOB BUBKA
TOM CLAVIN

THE
RYDER
CUP

Chapter 1

DRAMA AT VALDERRAMA

It wasn't supposed to end this way.

Tiger Woods, Justin Leonard, Jim Furyk, Fred Couples, Davis Love III, Mark O'Meara, and the rest of the U.S. Ryder Cup team could only stand helplessly exposed in front of a worldwide audience as Seve Ballesteros held aloft the much-coveted gold cup, a gesture of victory in what had become golf's premier international event.

The Ryder Cup isn't that big or heavy a trophy, though it is made of gold. But Seve seemed to be straining a bit, almost as if he were holding up not only the cup but the large, gray, cloud-filled sky above it. Despite his imposing strength, his arms quivered slightly. Ballesteros, the Atlas of Europe, could not hold up the Ryder Cup forever—but the wide, sparkling grin on his olive-skinned face implied that he would sure try.

Surrounding him were his fellow team players, their hair pasted back or flattened on their heads by rain and their clothes disheveled from literally jumping for joy; a few were already tipsy from champagne. At that moment no amount of money could have increased their ecstasy. It was impossible not to notice the contrast between the European team and the chanting, umbrella-holding, gleeful crowd behind them—and the dour, despondent U.S. squad.

The appearance of the stunned and frustrated Americans that September evening in Sotogrande was almost a mirror image of the scene at the 1995 Ryder Cup two years earlier. At Oak Hills, outside Rochester, New York, the U.S. contingent was forced to witness the European players and captain celebrate their triumph, taking back the cup the Americans had won under Tom Watson in 1993.

But 1997 should have been different. The Americans were favored, even with the treacherous winds of Valderrama. They simply could not lose a Ryder Cup Match twice in a row. They fielded a team of players that was perhaps the strongest since the 1981 squad. That now-legendary team had included Jack Nicklaus, Lee Trevino, Johnny Miller, Raymond Floyd, Ben Crenshaw, Tom Watson, Larry Nelson, and Tom Kite, among others. They had not only beaten the Europeans but had humbled them 18½–9½ at Walton Heath in England, the margin of victory so wide that it was reasonable to believe that Europe would never take back the Ryder Cup. And the 1997 team had Kite as its captain. He was a proven winner—nineteen PGA Tour events, the U.S. Open in 1992—and no American had earned more money on tour.

"The United States team assembled for the Valderrama Match was one of the strongest ever assembled," stated Neil Coles, chairman of the PGA European Tour, who had played on eight British Ryder Cup teams.

That Sunday in Spain the U.S. players staged a furious, Arnold Palmer–like charge to try to wrest the Ryder Cup from Europe's grasp. It had almost been the greatest single-day comeback since the Ryder Cup Matches officially began in 1927.

Still, as they watched their rival's euphoria and the start of a celebration that would last well into the warm, salt-aired night, that comeback couldn't wash the bitter taste of defeat from the Americans' mouths. They had no choice but to wait two long years for another stab at the Ryder Cup. At least this time it would be on their own turf, in Brookline, Massachusetts.

In 1967 the American team captain, Ben Hogan, had introduced his U.S. team by saying that "these are the best golfers in the world." At the time this was not hyperbole but the honest truth. And up to the 1980s any U.S. Ryder Cup captain could have made the same proclamation without much argument.

But in September 1997, as the shell-shocked Americans looked on—with the Battle of Brookline and the possibility of redemption an eternity away—the U.S. players knew that as far as millions of golf fans around the world were concerned, what Hogan had said in 1967 was no longer true.

Part of the reason the U.S. so badly wanted to win the Ryder Cup in 1997 was that the tournament that year was receiving an unprecedented amount of media attention. If the Americans were going to avenge their loss of 1995, there was no better time to do it than when a hefty portion of the world population was watching, listening, and reading about it.

What was the big deal about the Ryder Cup? After all, to some it was little more than an exhibition match, a fairly friendly outing among Americans, Englishmen, Scotsmen, Irishmen, and Spaniards, with a Swede or Italian or German thrown in. And, for goodness' sake, there wasn't even any prize money involved. These millionaire athletes were congregating every two years to scrum over a cup that, if sold, would retail for less than the round-trip airfare used to get to the Ryder Cup course. Fortunately, golf fans and the participants and officials involved knew what was at stake.

Television rights had been purchased at prices that were unthinkable a decade earlier: over $4.5 million. The number of trees felled to produce coverage in newspapers and magazines probably made a big dent in the Brazilian rain forest, and passes to the competition were as valued as winning lottery tickets. Around the globe the match was referred to as the "Drama at Valderrama."

The golf course itself was a big part of the story. Known as the "Augusta National of Europe," Valderrama had been designed in 1975 by Robert Trent Jones, the patriarch of an American course-design dynasty. In the 1940s Jones had remodeled several of the holes at Augusta, where the Masters is played. Now 90 years old, he would be on hand for the 1997 Ryder Cup Matches at a course that, like Augusta in Georgia, had been created out of a former tree plantation.

Portions of Valderrama, in the Andalusian region of Spain, overlook the Mediterranean Sea, and its most impressive view is of the Rock of Gibraltar and the north coast of Africa. In another direction were the Sierra Blanca Mountains. To prepare for the 1997 matches Valderrama's owner, Jaime Ortiz-Patino, who doubled as head greenskeeper, had attended to every detail, including having Seve Ballesteros redesign the seventeenth hole with Augusta-like characteristics. The entire course would be in excellent shape.

"It's the best-conditioned golf course I've ever seen," marveled Tom Kite.

The event at Valderrama confirmed Patino's status as one of the most important figures in the growing international golf scene. His passion for the sport began in 1956, during the Italian Open. The Welshman Dai Rees had to replace his caddy for the final day, and up stepped a young man from South America. After the final round Rees, instead of offering Jimmy Patino money, gave him two tickets to the following year's Ryder Cup at Lindrick in England.

Patino went to it. Rees was the captain of Great Britain's team, which defeated the United States for the first time in twenty-four years. Patino was hooked. He vowed that one day he would host a Ryder Cup.

There was a special excitement to having the Ryder Cup event in Spain, a clear indication of the global expansion of golf. In the previous seventy years, the Matches had been held only in the United States and Great Britain. That Jimmy Patino, born in Bolivia and the heir to a tin-mining fortune, had persuaded the European PGA to hold the event in Spain allowed other countries on the Continent to hope that they too could host an international sports competition in the twenty-first century.

Valderrama would present formidable challenges. The course is filled with cork and olive trees. The combination of these relatively short trees and the shifting winds coming off the sea made it difficult to control shots lofted high into the air, and club selection would be crucial. Though very smooth, the greens were also well protected by bunkers, so precision would be required. The 6,734-yard, par-71 course would play longer and tougher than expected.

Then there was the redesigned seventeenth. Many observers expected that quite a few of the matches would be decided on that 511-yard, par-5 hole. It had fairway mounds and rough stone walls bordering either side, and a small green surrounded by sand traps and more mounds. Former Ryder Cupper Sam Torrance of Scotland called it "sadistic." European PGA Player of the Year Colin Montgomerie referred to it as "hideous." This from the guys who had played the course. What about the players coming from America, only three of whom had been on the course before?

Davis Love III said of the course, "It's a patience test, and you must putt well." It sounded like an understatement, but it turned out to be a wise prediction.

Another reason for the unprecedented attention was the composition of the European team. It was led by Nick Faldo, who was playing in the Ryder Cup for a record-setting eleventh time even though he was only 40 years old. The precocious Englishman of 20, who looks barely out of grade school in the 1977 team photo, had become the winningest player in Ryder Cup history, an imposing presence whose tight-lipped glare could reduce opponents to jelly. Though he wasn't winning quite as much as he used to, he had captured his third green jacket at the Masters only seventeen months before. Coming into Valderrama, Faldo had twenty-one Ryder Cup victories—the entire 1997 U.S. team *combined* had twenty.

The rest of the European squad was a curious mix, and observers wondered how they would coexist. There were longtime Ryder Cup veterans Bernhard Langer of Germany, a 40-year-old two-time Masters champion; the Welshman Ian Woosnam, also the owner of a green jacket; Jose Maria Olazabal of Spain, a Masters champion who was recovering from a debilitating foot injury; and Costantino Rocca of Italy, who had nearly won the British Open two years earlier and in 1996 had won the Volvo Masters—the equivalent of the season-ending Tour Championship on the PGA Tour—at Valderrama. Indeed, in the previous nine years, Faldo, Langer, and Montgomerie had each won a Volvo Masters at Valderrama.

This grizzled group was joined by Thomas Bjorn, 26, of Denmark; Darren Clarke, 29, of Northern Ireland; Ignacio Garrido, 25, of Spain; Per-Ulrik Johansson, 30, and Jesper Parnevik, 32, of Sweden; and Lee Westwood, 24, of England. None were exactly household names—though Parnevik, the son of a comedian, was known even on the American tour for wearing his hat with the brim up, like a comic-book schoolboy. The bridge between these two groups of golfers was the husky, red-haired Colin Montgomerie.

A Scotsman whose father was general manager at Royal Troon, Montgomerie was an international match-play veteran and, at only 34, was in the prime of his career. In 1997 he would be the European PGA Tour's leading money-winner for the fifth straight year (he would repeat in '98). He had played on the Europeans' '91, '93, and '95 Ryder Cup teams (with a 6–5–2 record) and had participated in the Walker Cup and World Match Play competitions. He was big and strong and hungry for greater (and deserved) recognition.

Still, Monty had also failed in more than a dozen attempts to win one of the four major championships, three of which are held on American soil. Several times, especially in the 1997 U.S. Open that was won by Ernie Els, he had self-destructed, and some golf fans questioned his ability to withstand the intense pressure of performing in Ryder Cup Matches.

This motley mix of aging veterans, a volatile Scotsman who couldn't win when competing with Americans, and youngsters who seemed to have gone directly from sandboxes to sand saves, was the follow-up to the team that had beaten the Americans in '95. This was not the most formidable force ever to walk a Ryder Cup fairway, and the world sensed that the cup was soon to sail back across the Atlantic.

The world? Yes, well, the event that was watched by only a few hundred spectators in 1927 would in 1997 be followed—via television, radio, still photography, and the Internet—by more than 700 million. That, more than anything else, was why the "Drama at Valderrama" would be *the* sports event of the year, especially for fans who relish international competition.

The World Cup of soccer was not played in 1997; the Super Bowl that January, in which Green Bay had dominated, was not much of an eye-opener; and the World Series that would pit the Florida Marlins against the Cleveland Indians wasn't exactly a thrill a minute. Certainly for those sports fans who could see beyond their borders, the Ryder Cup was *it*.

Probably the biggest reason for the '97 Ryder Cup's huge audience was the American team's roster. It too had Ryder veterans who were household names: Fred Couples, Mark O'Meara, and the captain, Tom Kite, but most of the attention was focused on the young marquee players who had won three of the four major championships that year: Tiger Woods (the Masters), Justin Leonard (the British Open), and Davis Love III (the PGA Championship). Since his professional debut one year earlier at the Milwaukee Open, Woods had become a dominant player and perhaps the best-known golfer worldwide since the heyday of Palmer, Player, and Nicklaus.

"If they asked me who I would like to play, it would be Tiger," said an obviously unintimidated Lee Westwood. "I would love to beat him. He's just a very good player. He is not phenomenal."

Leonard, although much less flashy than media darling Woods, wasn't too far behind on the money list, and Love had both previous Ryder Cup experience (a 5–4 record in '93 and '95) and the positive momentum of winning his first major only the month before. There was speculation that these three gunslingers alone could account for the winning total of 14½ points the Americans needed.

Rounding out the U.S. team was a collection of up-and-comers and proven pros. Jim Furyk, at 27, and Scott Hoch, at 41, were also playing in their first Ryder Cup; both were in the midst of big-money seasons. Lee Janzen, a captain's pick like Couples, and Tom Lehman had played on Ryder Cup teams (in '93 and '95, respectively) and each had won a major—Janzen the U.S. Open (which he would win again in '98), Lehman the British Open. Phil Mickelson, a player on the '95 Ryder Cup team, was only 27 yet had won eleven PGA titles; until Woods and Leonard came along, he was the hottest young golfer on the pro scene. Jeff Maggert and Brad Faxon were solid pros, both two-time Ryder Cup veterans. Faxon, in fact, had shot a 65 in the final round of the PGA Championship a month earlier to lock up a spot on the team.

The '97 team captain was Tom Kite, who had briefly considered picking himself to play but decided not to deny a spot on the team to a player higher on the Ryder Cup points list. Though 47, he was still a strong performer (the previous April, he had finished second to Woods at the Masters) and the leading American career money-winner. His nineteen PGA Tour victories placed him high on the list of active U.S. pros. Kite had long been known as a "grinder"—a player who works especially hard to get the most out of his abilities—and seemed to have the detail-oriented, nose-to-the-grindstone personality that would get the most out of a more-than-able U.S. team.

Various factors would likely affect the outcome. For the U.S. team, the primary goal was to avenge the startling loss two years earlier at Oak Hill, only the second time since 1927 that the Americans had lost on their own turf. And while many U.S. pros had become unaccustomed to match play, the Ryder Cup team this year had players who had excelled at it in the 1990s: Mickelson had won the 1990 U.S. Amateur Championship, Leonard had won that title in 1992, and Woods had won it three years in a row, 1994–96, twice with dramatic comebacks. Because of this match-play domination, these players—Woods in particular—salivated at the prospect of going one on one against Europe's finest.

On the European side, Seve's squad had the home-field advantage. All of the players, even if they hadn't won it, had played in the Volvo Masters Championship held at Valderrama every fall and thus knew more about overcoming the course's powerful winds. With the exception of a small percentage, the crowd would overwhelmingly favor the Europeans, a pleasant switch for players like Faldo, Langer, and Olazabal, who had not been greeted enthusiastically when participating in PGA Tour events in the States.

It had to enhance the home-field advantage that there were three Spaniards on the squad. Jose Maria Olazabal, at only 31, had already been on four Ryder Cup teams, and he had won the Masters in 1994. Ignacio Garrido, 25, was a Ryder rookie, but his father, Antonio, had played on the first European Ryder Cup team in 1979, and thus Ignacio knew something of what to expect. Then there was Seve Ballesteros.

Ballesteros, along with Faldo, had been the most consistently feared Ryder Cup competitor of the last two decades. He had played on eight European teams since 1979 and had compiled a brilliant 20–12–5 record. Since 1976 he had earned seventy-two tournament titles worldwide, including five majors: two Masters and three British Opens. And there was nothing he enjoyed more—especially at this stage of his career, which had been slumping—than beating the Americans. It would be close to ecstasy to do it in the first Ryder Cup Match held in Spain, where he was perhaps the country's best-known athlete.

Seve certainly looked the part of the strong, determined sports star. Though of average height, he was solidly built. His black hair gleamed in sunlight, and his dark eyes could flash with anger or study a tricky putt with such focused intensity that one might expect it to move toward the hole without being touched. His sharp-featured, olive-complected face, especially when hosting a wide grin, was movie-star handsome. The press in Spain regularly referred to Ballesteros as the "matador of the fairway."

"This is the moment I've been waiting for," Ballesteros said before play began at Valderrama. "It will be a tremendous thing. If we win—and I feel very positive we will—I will be on top of the world."

Faldo, though just as feared and admired, and blessed with roguish good looks, was not put out by being overshadowed in Spain. Graciously, he stated about his captain, "He is our Arnold Palmer."

Few doubted that having Ballesteros at the helm would be an advantage to the European team. His passionate partisanship, high energy, and volatile personality would, at the very least, provide inspiration. It remained to be seen if Ballesteros's presence in the stressful caldron of Ryder Cup competition would be too much of a good thing.

That sure seemed possible earlier in the month. With the European squad set, Ballesteros booted Angel Miguel Martin off the team, contending that the younger Spaniard was physically unable to play. That summer Martin had injured his wrist and undergone surgery. He insisted that he would be recovered in time for the Ryder Cup, and having played his way onto the team, he believed he shouldn't be denied the opportunity. Ballesteros believed otherwise and wouldn't risk a weak link in the lineup, so he sent Martin packing and replaced him with Olazabal.

The media in Europe and a few players contended that such turmoil was an unnecessary distraction to a relatively inexperienced team. Ballesteros ignored the complaint. This was *his* team. As it turned out, Martin had to withdraw from another tourney in mid-September because of his wrist, which seemed to confirm Seve's decision that he was not fit to play.

Kite was quoted as saying that he had complete confidence in his team members, that there wasn't one player he would hesitate to send out on the course. Ballesteros was equally confident. With five of the last six Ryder Cup Matches having been decided by two points or less, there was every indication that the 1997 contest would also go down to the wire.

Inevitably, because of the elevated attention it had achieved and the worldwide expansion of the sports media, the 1997 Ryder Cup would be subjected to all sorts of distractions before the first shot was even fired.

As the Europeans were trying to leave the Martin episode behind, the Americans found controversy when Earl Woods, Tiger's father, announced he was upset because he wasn't allowed on the team plane. Declaring that he had made more of a contribution to Tiger's career and the team than "all the wives and girlfriends combined" (who were allowed to travel with the players), the elder Woods said that he would stay home.

The U.S. team shrugged off such sulking. The captain and the players met with President Clinton in New York City, and then on the Sunday before the Ryder Cup, they left JFK Airport on a chartered Concorde for Spain, with Tiger Woods traveling alone.

Though Woods kept a low profile and concentrated on practicing, that week he was part of another distraction when several of the European players singled him out as the one to beat. Then Colin Montgomerie took a different tack. European newspapers quoted Monty as saying that Valderrama did not suit Woods's game and that the youngster wasn't the player the home team should be worried about. This was only five months after Monty boasted that he had more experience in major tournaments than Tiger, but then in the final round of the Masters, the great Scot had shot a 74 while Woods won the major with a 65.

Monty kicked up even more dust by ruminating on the personal woes of Faxon, who was in the midst of a divorce: "I don't think Brad Faxon will be straight enough for Valderrama. His divorce will also mean that he's not with it." He then took a swipe at another U.S. team member, saying, "You're not going to be frightened by Jeff Maggert." Then about Hoch, who had missed a short putt in 1989 to give Nick Faldo the Masters, Monty mentioned, "If it comes down to holing the last putt, from our point of view we'd like it to be Scott Hoch because he's been there and done that."

Clearly, golf was losing some of its luster as a gentlemen's game. Faxon had missed a key putt in the 1995 Ryder Cup, and it remained to be seen if Montgomerie's off-the-cuff comment would rattle him or strengthen his resolve. Maggert and Hoch—well, how would they respond? Privately, veterans like Couples, Love, and O'Meara angrily deplored Monty's comments, but publicly the team offered a calm and united front.

During the week of practice rounds at Valderrama, celebrities began to appear, confirming that this event was the real deal in sports. On the American side, former President George Bush and his wife, Barbara, arrived to encourage the squad, as did Michael Jordan and Michael Douglas. For the Europeans, Prince Andrew of Great Britain was in attendance, as was Sean Connery.

And of course there was the crush of media. The European PGA had never before experienced the demand for access credentials that they did in the days leading up to and during that September. As expected, a horde of American and European print and broadcast journalists crowded the event, but added to the throng were crews from other parts of the world, especially Asia. On that continent the Ryder Cup was infinitely more interesting than the World Cup and truly rivaled the Olympics in popularity.

With all this media hoopla and hundreds of spectators straining the town's resources, wasn't this the perfect time for a strike by the local police? That's what happened, adding to the traffic turmoil and no doubt giving Jimmy Patino a pounding headache. On the first full day of the Ryder Cup, the players were strolling onto the golf course, but everyone else was left outside because no police were available to handle the crowd, check tickets, and the like. Patino pulled some strings with the local politicians and reached an "understanding" with the police, who soon returned to their posts.

Some of the media were close to going on strike too because the hotel where they stayed cost an outrageous $5,000 a week. It had quite a few amenities, including staff who spoke English, but the guests needed over an hour to get to the action. On the other hand, yours truly, Bob, was directed to a hotel in Los Barrios by Patino where no one spoke English but a room was only $60 a night and was only fifteen minutes from the Valderrama course. (Shhh, don't tell anyone!)

All this ratcheted up the pressure on the players, especially those who were thousands of miles from home. Even experienced Ryder competitors like Faldo, Ballesteros, Kite, Couples, Love, Woosnam, and O'Meara had to contend with constant requests for interviews in various languages, foreign food, and a different electrical system. And in a very short amount of time, the Americans had to learn the intricacies and eccentricities of an unfamiliar golf course.

Fred Couples in particular struggled to keep focused—both his father and his girlfriend were battling cancer. Couples had the reputation of being a cool customer, and in Sotogrande he had tried to live up to it, giving interviews and practicing as hard as his teammates. But it was clear that it took all of his strength of character to stay focused on an event that had diminished in his personal priorities. If both his father and girlfriend hadn't repeatedly urged him to be part of America's team, Couples would never have boarded the Concorde.

Finally, on Thursday night the participants gathered for the traditional pre-Match dinner. Ballesteros and Kite made remarks and offered a toast to good sportsmanship and mutual respect. Autographs were signed, dinners were downed, and the players slipped away to hit the sack to prepare for the early-morning start. Instead of telling them a good-night story, Kite, not one for much public speaking himself, had his players watch a video of past captains making inspirational speeches.

With both Ballesteros and Kite all set to go, with a golf course that was one of the Continent's jewels, and with the number of potential spectators covering close to a quarter of the planet, the biggest international golf showdown in history was set to begin. Ready or not, it was time for the thirty-second Ryder Cup Match.

Someone should have told the weather to cooperate. For three hours on Friday, beginning at 5:30 A.M., the skies over Sotogrande wept, forcing a delay in the start time. (There hadn't been any rain in the region in at least four months, which reinforced the old adage, "If you want rain in a particular place, schedule a major golf tournament there.") The delay was a harbinger: For the U.S. team, everything would be off schedule this weekend.

Jimmy Patino had prepared Valderrama so well that not even torrential rain could prevent play. According to a veteran Ryder Cup photographer Helen Casey, Patino is "a committee of one who uses his own golden rule: 'I have the gold, I make the rules.' He had the course up and running after only an hour-and-forty-minute delay. Educated in agronomy, fine wine, art, and elegant living, he used skills familiar to a Captain of Industry. 'Team Jimmy' included ground crews, staff, volunteers, bus drivers, the Spanish Golf Federation, and local officials. And got the job done."

Shortly after ten A.M., once the rain had stopped and all the sweeping of greens and draining of fairways were done, the first fourball match began. Kite was not taking any chances with rookies—for the first two better-ball contests of the morning, the captain was teaming Davis Love III with Phil Mickelson and Fred Couples with Brad Faxon.

Ballesteros countered with two veterans, Jose Maria Olazabal and Costantino Rocca, but he took a risk with his second duo, pairing Nick Faldo and first-timer Lee Westwood. This would prove to be brilliant strategy, combining the only two Englishmen: Faldo, the soon-to-be all-time Ryder Cup winner, and Westwood, the 24-year-old with little match-play experience and who, with his gap-toothed grin and copper curls, looked like he belonged carrying suitcases back at the media's high-priced hotel.

Faldo would be as tough and steady as expected, while Westwood, to match his newfound mentor, would raise his game to a new height.

For the Americans, the first fourball match (in which on each hole the best score by each player is counted as the team's score) began auspiciously. On the first hole Love drained a twenty-footer to give his team the early lead. As they teed off on the twelfth hole, Love and Mickelson were up by two. The Europeans' slow start could indicate that Olazabal wasn't fully recovered from his foot ailments and Rocca's best matches were in the past.

For the American team, it might as well have kept raining. The two Europeans recovered and won the match. A sign from the golf gods of how this day and the next would go for the Americans came on the eighteenth when Mickelson, who had birdied the tenth and eleventh holes, missed a five-foot putt that would have tied the match.

Things were looking better elsewhere. Faldo was vulnerable after all, and maybe Westwood wasn't ready for the enormous pressure of international competition. The team of Couples and Faxon emerged from that match-up with a victory, 1-up. This was sweet redemption for Faxon. Aside from having to endure public comment about his marital problems, he had missed that seven-foot putt on 18 on Sunday at Oak Hill that had returned the Ryder Cup to Europe. In this match on Friday at Valderrama, with the outcome in the balance, Faxon sank an identical putt to ensure the win.

The third contest looked like a breeze for the Americans: the unflappable Tom Lehman and the hot-streaking Jim Furyk against Per-Ulrik Johansson and Jesper Parnevik. The former was virtually unknown in the United States; the latter was probably just as well known for eccentricities like eating volcanic ash during tournaments for strength. Parnevik walked around with the brim of his hat up, looking like a schoolboy, especially when he smiled, which he did often because like his father he enjoyed performing in front of an audience.

Any doubts about the duo were dispelled by early afternoon. Team Sweden won 1-up, with Parnevik birdieing both the seventeenth and eighteenth holes. It was Europe 2–1, not the most promising start for the guests.

Before Friday morning ended, it was time for Tiger's Ryder debut. He was paired with his best friend on the PGA Tour, Mark O'Meara. Despite their nineteen-year age difference, or perhaps because of it, the steady O'Meara had taken Woods under his wing during the past year, and Woods, who could afford to live anywhere, had bought a house only a 7-iron away from O'Meara's place in Florida. The two often played practice rounds together, and to ward off nerves, the unlikely couple pretended that their match against the formidable Colin Montgomerie and Bernhard Langer was just another walk in the sun.

Here was Monty's opportunity to back up his bold words, and Langer still sought redemption for missing a six-footer on the last hole in the 1991 Ryder Cup on Kiawah Island, South Carolina, that had given the cup to the Americans. But this was not to be the time for either the Scotsman or the German. While Woods was a bit erratic, for O'Meara it was business as usual, and the U.S. team won easily, 3 and 2, with O'Meara dropping a thirty-footer into the hole at 16 to seal the victory.

The Americans were warmed up: It was time for them to show that the 2–1 favorites that the oddsmakers had them was no fluke. Then darkness fell—literally.

In the afternoon foursomes (where players on each team alternate shots), Montgomerie and Langer avenged their loss by smoking Woods and O'Meara 5 and 3. Kite, wanting to get everyone involved, paired Scott Hoch and Lee Janzen against Olazabal and Rocca. The gamble worked, with the United States eking out a win, 1-up. Next Kite paired Justin Leonard and Jeff Maggert, pitting them against Faldo and Westwood, and then he tried the combination of Lehman and Mickelson on Johansson and Ignacio Garrido.

One can speculate whether the 1997 Ryder Cup would have turned out differently if these last two matches had been completed on Friday. The American teams were matched up well, and Lehman and Mickelson were certainly expected to prevail against their no-name opponents. However, because of the rain delay and the fact that it was late September, both remaining matches were suspended by darkness. It was time to call it a night, with the Americans and the Europeans tied at 3–3.

Captain Kite had one more bit of strategy. Again he went to the video file, and that night he showed his troops *Simply the Best*, a compilation of 207 great golf shots set to music by Lee Greenwood and Carly Simon. As it turned out, early-to-bed might have been a better idea.

For the Americans, Saturday looked promising. Most of the team had already played, allowing them to get the kinks out of their game. They had almost a full day of competitive experience with the golf course under their belts. Kite was confident, terming Friday's action "neat" and feeling more positive about pairings. His team had gotten a good night's rest so that they could . . .

. . . face another rain delay, this one nearly two hours long. Again, though, the resilient course was ready for play as soon as the rain stopped, and the two suspended matches were resumed. Leonard and Maggert lost with Westwood, of all people, sinking a six-footer to ice it. Worse, the best Lehman and Mickelson could do was halve their match against Garrido and Parnevik. The Americans sure didn't find Jesper funny.

As it turned out, the first action of Saturday morning was the good news. For Tom Kite and the U.S. team, the rest of the day was like watching a train wreck in slow motion.

In the first fourball match, Couples eagled the par-4 eighth hole, and it looked like he and Love were in command. Then Montgomerie and rookie Darren Clarke of Northern Ireland birdied five of the next seven holes and wound up winning 1-up. More agonizing was that Ian Woosnam, 39, who should have been stiff from sitting on the bench, and 26-year-old Thomas

Bjorn, a Danish rookie with scant match-play experience, stuck it to Leonard and Faxon 2 and 1. (Woosie, by the way, has more Ryder Cup fourball wins than anyone, with ten victories.)

Crash. Faldo and Westwood earned their second triumph of the day by downing Woods and O'Meara 2 and 1. It certainly did seem that Valderrama, and how it had been prepared for the Ryder Cup (especially with narrow fairways lined with trees), had clipped Tiger's claws, particularly in taking away his long-hitting advantage.

"I'm not saying he can't play [Valderrama], it's that it makes Tiger just another player," commented NBC broadcaster and former Ryder Cupper Johnny Miller. "When he's hitting 2-irons and the rest of the players are hitting woods as straight as his iron shots—he's a good iron player but not a great one."

The only consolation was that Mickelson and Lehman halved their match with Olazabal and Garrido, saved by Lehman sinking a tricky four-footer on the last hole after Olazabal had sent home a scintillating putt from fifteen feet. "I was never more nervous over a putt in my life," said Lehman—this from a man who had survived Q School, won the British Open, and had a second and third place in the U.S. Open the previous two years.

Johnny Miller warned, "The Americans on paper have an advantage in singles, but if they get too deep in a hole, they will have to go crazy on Sunday to have a chance."

The visitors apparently weren't listening, and there was more mayhem in store. Montgomerie and Langer reteamed in an afternoon foursome match and got revenge for Friday's loss by beating the peach-fuzz duo of Janzen and Furyk 1-up. What had been a 3–3 tie at the end of yesterday had turned into a 9–4 European stampede. This time darkness was a friend to the United States— the three remaining foursome matches were suspended before further blood was shed.

Kite was in as tight a spot as any American captain had ever been. His players had been thoroughly set back on their heels. While the teams were not playing for money, the adage "drive for show, putt for dough" still applied: You can't win if you don't put the ball in the hole. Time after time, the U.S. players' putting had failed at crucial moments.

On Sunday, the final day, the lively partisan crowd would be hoping for a slaughter. Ballesteros, who for two days had seemed to be everywhere on his fast-moving cart, would not let his team relax, even though no Ryder Cup team in seventy years had come back from anything close to as huge a deficit as the United States now faced. The big guns had fired mostly blanks—Woods had 1 point, but between them Love, Leonard, and Couples had only 1. Tomorrow would not be pretty.

On Saturday night, as the stunned Americans tried to regroup, Kite knew it was time for a "win one for the Gipper" speech. With the Gipper not available, Kite reached for the next-best thing: He invited George Bush in to address the troops. The former president delivered a stirring speech, and chins lifted.

The captain outlined the strategy. The first goal was to win at least two of the three suspended matches, to make the tally 10–6 Europe. Then they would tackle the twelve singles matches, typically an American strength. But going 8–4 wasn't good enough, because Europe needed only 14 points to retain the cup it had won at Oak Hill. The United States had to win three out of every four singles matches to win 15–13.

Mission impossible? Maybe. But as the Americans sank into troubled sleep that night, they vowed to come out swinging.

And they *almost* did the impossible.

Sunday dawned clear and dry—the first piece of good news all weekend for the American squad. A better bit of news was that in the first resumed foursome, in which the Europeans had been 3-up, Scott Hoch and Jeff Maggert rallied to win 2 and 1. (So much for Monty's harsh remarks about their abilities.) Next!

What came next wasn't good enough, although the comeback the Americans staged on Sunday, September 28, was a more valiant effort than had been seen in any previous Ryder Cup.

A crucial match was the young-gun tandem of Woods and Leonard against Parnevik and Garrido. If the Americans could only win this one . . . but they didn't. The match was halved, a golden opportunity lost. In the third suspended match—another pivotal one, pitting steel-jawed veterans Couples and Love against Olazabal and Rocca—the Europeans came out on top, 5 and 4.

All right, it was 10½–5½: not quite the best-case scenario, but not exactly the Alamo either. Captain Kite had a smart, simple idea: In the first singles matches, he would put the best players out there, the ones who ate pressure for breakfast, and if they caught fire, the rest of the U.S. team would be swept along.

Kite looked like a genius in the first match, giving Fred Couples center stage. Ballesteros countered with Masters champion and eight-time Ryder Cupper Ian Woosnam. There was plenty of carnage for the Welshman. Couples had five birdies and an eagle, and the match, at 8 and 7, was over after the eleventh hole.

Now it was up to Love, Woods, and Leonard, the three major winners, to add more steam to the train Couples had set on the track. Instead, it derailed.

Johansson defeated Love 3 and 2. Rocca, who had gone into golf from a box-factory assembly line, pasted Woods 4 and 2. And Bjorn withstood the best Leonard could dish out to halve the match. "I feel like I aged about five years out there on the back nine," Leonard sighed.

The score was 13–7. With Europe needing only one more point and with eight matches to play, wasn't it time for the U.S. squad to pack up and go home?

The Americans didn't think so. They staged a fast and furious rally that came close to resulting in the Ryder Cup's greatest comeback. It began with Mickelson downing Darren Clarke 2 and 1—a double loss for the Irishman, because his sponser had promised him a new Ferrari if he remained undefeated in the '97 Match.

Then O'Meara, with seven birdies in fourteen holes, pummeled Parnevik 5 and 4. This was followed by an especially courageous effort by Lee Janzen. Down with only two holes left and knowing a loss meant his team was finished, the former U.S. Open winner birdied those holes to overcome Olazabal.

Now it was time to tame that pup Westwood, who didn't have Faldo to protect him any longer. Texan Jeff Maggert took care of that, dusting the youngster 3 and 2. And what about Faldo, who the day before had established new Ryder records for victories, with twenty-three, and points with 25? It would be fitting if he put the final nail in the Colonists' coffin. But Jim Furyk wasn't about to allow three losses on his rookie Ryder record; he beat the surprised veteran 3 and 2. Tom Lehman also took care of business, scoring six birdies on twelve holes to spank Garrido, 7 and 6.

An astonishing recovery? The sports story of the year back in the States? Well, it was a great story anyway, a true exhibition of never-say-die spirit, and the partisan crowd wasn't nearly as chipper as it had been since Saturday morning. But a couple of European players weren't standing around composing their team's obituary. Two of the toughest competitors of the past decade stood firm to turn back the charge of the Yanks.

The most fitting ending involved Bernhard Langer, who had lived for six long years with the painful memory of missing a putt on the last hole at Kiawah Island. All the money and titles he had won in the interim—he would finish second to Montgomerie on the European money list in 1997, and he counted two Masters victories among fifty-one first-place finishes worldwide—couldn't quite erase the shame of letting down an entire continent with one missed putt. On the final day of the Ryder Cup, there is no tomorrow or next week.

But sometimes there is two years later, two years after that, or in Langer's case, six years later. Langer and Faxon, who had his own demons to exorcise, dueled in the Andalusian sun as the shadows—even those of the squatty olive trees—lengthened and dark clouds approached. When Faxon birdied the twelfth hole, one of only two birdies in the entire match, he pulled even with Langer.

Alas, that was the pinnacle for Faxon. He bogied 13, then 14, while Langer steadily marched ahead, par after par. With rain falling and the last putt conceded, Langer had won 2 and 1, and with 14 points the Europeans had the score they needed to retain the Ryder Cup.

The spectators erupted in wild cheers. The European caddies began to sing. Rocca started to cry, then Olazabal pinched his cheeks. Everywhere there were hands shaking, hugs exchanged, shoulders shuddering.

Too early to celebrate, though. It's one thing to barely cling to the cup, having come within a whisker of losing it. It's another to win it outright with a score higher than what's needed for a tie.

This offered Montgomerie the opportunity, finally, to monopolize the spotlight and support his brash comments. It was him versus Hoch, one of the men he had dissed in the press. Hoch, the taciturn 41-year-old rookie, was the only American with two victories, and he hadn't yet tasted defeat. Montgomerie, who had carried the European squad on his broad shoulders, was 3–1 on the weekend and would play a marathonlike eighty-five holes. Could Hoch add to U.S. pride by knocking off Europe's big gun?

He tried his best. Hoch bogied the sixteenth to go 1-down, then birdied the seventeenth. It came down to the final hole. Hoch and Monty were tied. Then those darn cork and olive trees appeared taller and wider than they really were. Hoch's drive on 18 found branches, as did his second shot. Meanwhile Monty was hitting the fairway, then hit an approach shot to only eighteen feet from the hole. To have any chance at winning, Hoch had to hole his third shot.

His third shot was a very good one—but not good enough. It landed eight feet from the eighteenth hole. As he and Montgomerie strode up to the green at 18, thousands of blue-and-white umbrellas bobbed behind them, carried by rushing spectators who chanted, "Monty . . . Monty!" The Scotsman was oblivious to the pummeling rain. He sized up perhaps the biggest putt of his life and gave the ball a ride.

Montgomerie's putt didn't go in, but it was close enough that Hoch had to concede, ensuring that the match would be halved. Now if Hoch missed, he would lose the match outright.

Most fitting of all is that the 1997 Ryder Cup Match ended with a generous gesture of sportsmanship. Though Hoch had an easily missable putt, Montgomerie conceded it, meaning the match would be no worse than halved for the United States. Europe, the gracious winner, had triumphed, winning the overall Match 14½–13½.

To viewers, listeners, and Internet users around the world, the final result must have seemed incredible. On that final Sunday in Sotogrande, the Americans had captured 9½ points—but it wasn't quite enough. Europe's troops had beaten back the invaders with 5½ points, just enough and then some. For the fifth time in the last seven Ryder Cup Matches, the fellows from Great Britain, Ireland, Italy, Sweden, Germany, Denmark—and most important this year, as the huge crowd went wild—Spain, were soon to go their separate ways as the victors.

Now it was time to watch Seve kiss the cup, and the rest of the closing ceremonies.

"It's very special playing the Ryder Cup in Spain for the first time and being the captain," said Ballesteros, who became the first European to win as a player and a captain. "I've won a lot of matches around the world, but there's nothing like the Ryder Cup."

As the Americans, in their sharp-looking blue blazers, stood to the side to allow their rivals to bask in glory, they analyzed what had gone wrong and pondered what it would take to win in 1999.

"I'm convinced that we still have the best players," said Lehman. "We proved that today. But put their guys together, and they have magic at their fingertips. They are greater than their parts."

"I lived at Valderrama for eight years on the eighteenth tee, and I know that golf course intimately," said Tony Jacklin, who owns the best record of any European captain. "The Americans didn't know that course and really had no idea how to play it, especially when the wind picked up. I'm sorry, but in golf it doesn't matter who you are or what your accomplishments have been—if you can't play the course you are not going to win. Let's never forget the essential relationship we as players have with the golf course; it's one that can't be faked, and the competitive levels are so close now that the golf course will make a significant difference. The Americans should have prepared a bit more."

Falling on his sword, Tom Kite took the blame. "I should've been more forceful in having the [U.S.] players come to Valderrama before or after the British Open to become familiar with the course," he said. "That made a difference."

It should be pointed out that Kite was in an excruciatingly difficult position—in the seventy-year history of the Ryder Cup, you could count the previous losing U.S. captains on one hand. Kite was probably right about Valderrama, but maybe not as much as he thought. After all, of the twelve Americans on the team, three—O'Meara, Love, and Woods—had visited Valderrama in July, and only O'Meara ended up with a winning record.

And the major-winning trio? It didn't deliver in Spain. Between them Woods, Leonard, and Love were 1–9–3. And in the No Good Deed Goes Unpunished category, the democratic Kite made sure that every one of his players competed at least twice, while Ballesteros not only went repeatedly with his main horses—Montgomerie, Faldo, Langer, and Olazabal—but got an astonishing 8 points out of his Ryder Cup rookies: Westwood, Parnevik, Bjorn, Garrido, and Clarke.

At Oak Hill in '95 the U.S. team had seemed a bit too confident going into Sunday with a 2-point lead and had been overtaken by the upstart Europeans. In '97 the problem was that the Americans were far away from home, lauded as the favorites, and didn't get back on track until it was a matter of too little, too late. Only their pride was salvaged.

No one, however, was prouder than Ballesteros. "What we have done, it's unbelievable," he said on Sunday evening. "All my wins have been wonderful, but this—this is a moment I will never, ever forget."

"He hasn't been so much a captain as a father to us," said Ignacio Garrido about Spain's hero. "Every time I was thinking,

'What can I do here?' he'd appear out of nowhere and tell me what to do. We put our hands on the clubs, but Seve's the one who played the shots."

Now all eyes are on the Battle of Brookline in '99, the last Ryder Cup event of the century. For both teams, the core group of players may well remain the same. Having turned the tables victory-wise, the Europe squad may be considered cocky.

"We have nothing to prove until 1999," Westwood said. "And then we can prove we're the best again."

Could Samuel Ryder ever have envisioned such a hotly contested rivalry when he founded the competition?

Chapter 2

"WE MUST DO THIS AGAIN"

In our advertising-driven sports world, some people may assume that the Ryder Cup, the event held every two years either in the United States or in Europe, is named after the truck-rental company. They'd be wrong—*that* tournament is the Doral-Ryder Open on the PGA Tour, held every March in Florida. The Ryder Cup Matches, now seventy-two years old, don't carry a corporate name in America yet—, though for many years, up through the 1997 Match, the event was called the Johnnie Walker Ryder Cup in Great Britain and Europe.

The international competition bears the name of Samuel Ryder, an English seed merchant. However, he didn't exactly originate the contests between British and American players that eventually became the Ryder Cup Matches. Those seeds were first planted in 1921 in Scotland. Or was it Ohio? It depends on whom you talk to.

First the Scottish version. In 1920 *The Glasgow Herald* sponsored a tournament at the Gleneagles King's Course with the total purse equivalent to around $1,250. When the same tournament was held for the second time, in 1921, there was a sudden influx of competitors from the United States. The British Open that year was being held at nearby St. Andrews, and the Americans viewed the Gleneagles tourney as an opportunity to tune up for the major and perhaps collect a few quick pounds while doing so.

After the British Open was held, and before the U.S. contingent boarded the boat back home, an exhibition match was organized between British and American players. This informal joust ended with the local lads defeating their guests 10½–4½. (Some accounts claim the score was 9–3.)

Now hold on—let's not give Scotland all the credit. Another version says that in 1921 Sylvanus Jermain, president of the Inverness Club in Toledo, proposed the concept of British and American teams of golfers going head to head. There is, however, no reliable information about who participated, how many golfers played, or who won.

There is even a third story, that James Hartnett of *Golf Illustrated* originated the idea in 1920 for a tournament that later became the Ryder Cup. Supporting this theory is the fact that the PGA of America did vote that year to allocate a small amount of funds to explore the concept of a Britain-versus-America tournament.

What golf historians do agree upon is that the next time the two teams went at it was in 1926. This time the British Open was to be held at Royal Lytham and St. Annes in England, and the Americans were again "over there" early in full force, including Walter Hagen, one of the first stars of U.S. golf.

Hagen, born in Rochester, New York, was a charismatic and dynamic figure, a stocky, slightly balding man with an oval face who dressed impeccably. Despite having only the usual two hands, he always appeared to be comfortable holding a drink, a cigarette, and a golf club simultaneously.

Hagen was a charter member of the PGA of America and is credited with greatly increasing the popularity of golf in the United States after World War I. While his game was unpredictable, he always put on a good show and loved to party afterward. He crisscrossed the country during the 1920s to participate in exhibition matches and fledgling tournaments, drawing bigger and bigger crowds with his larger-than-life gestures and talents. He was the first American player to make money solely from golf, and he did very well at it—at the height of his career, he made close to $1.5 million in today's dollars, much of which he spent having fun: fast cars, plenty of parties at speakeasies, and picking up checks for friends.

With Hagen all fired up for international combat in 1926, another exhibition match was arranged, this one at the golf course at Wentworth, and the British routed the visitors 13½–1½. Certainly for the Americans, such get-togethers didn't appear to have much potential.

Samuel Ryder, who had helped arrange the exhibition, was quite delighted with the match he had just witnessed. He joined British team members George Duncan and Abe Mitchell and American teammates Hagen and Emmett French for tea afterward. They recounted the competition between the two squads and mourned that it might be a one-time event. They then headed for a pub, and after more discussion Ryder stated, "We must do this again."

What may have just been a heartfelt remark turned into serious business when Ryder was asked to put his money where his mouth was. He agreed to pay 250 pounds (in today's dollars, about $1,250) for a gold cup that would go to the winner of a tournament between British and U.S. teams. The trophy that would be known as the Ryder Cup was crafted by the Mappin & Webb Company. It stood seventeen inches tall and weighed four pounds—not all that impressive, but it would come to represent one of the finest competitions in international sports.

Why would Samuel Ryder care so much? Well, by this time in his life he was very passionate about golf and was devoting more attention and energy to it than to his business. Having a competition named after him, even if it turned out to be a one-time event, was the next-best thing to being a professional.

Ryder was a wealthy man who had literally made his fortune penny by penny. He had grown up in Manchester, England, the son of a corn merchant and one of five children. Like most young men of the time, his main sports interest was cricket, a hobby to pursue while he completed his education and prepared to enter his father's field of business.

Then came a detour. Ryder had the bright idea of selling flower seeds in packets for a penny each. At the time seeds for flowers and other plants were purchased in bulk amounts by large estates. Sam Ryder thought that working-class folks who wanted to have small gardens would buy seeds if they were made very affordable. His father, however, disagreed. Not only did the elder Mr. Ryder not approve of the idea of penny packets, considering it rather lowbrow, but as a practical matter he doubted people in the middle and lower classes would actually spend money.

The son struck out on his own, moving with his wife and three daughters to St. Albans in 1895. The young Ryder turned out to be right. The penny packets—he and his wife produced and mailed their own catalogs and packaged the seeds for shipping themselves—proved to be hugely popular, and Sam made a bundle. His slogan, "Everything at one penny from orchids to mustard to cress," while not exactly up to the catchy phrases of modern-day Madison Avenue, caught the public's attention.

Ryder's business boomed, and he became very involved in his adopted hometown. He was elected to the city council, then ran for mayor of St. Albans and won in 1905. In addition to his business and political pursuits, Ryder became known for underwriting numerous charitable organizations and for his vast collection of flowers from all over the world.

Golf replaced cricket as Ryder's favorite pastime when, upon his fiftieth birthday in 1908, he began taking lessons as a way to get fresh air and exercise and recover from work-induced exhaustion. By the 1920s Ryder was paying a top British professional, Abe Mitchell, an annual salary of about a thousand pounds to be his personal tutor. (Mitchell, not Ryder, is the figure who stands atop the Ryder Cup.)

Ryder's home course was Verulam, and he played golf assiduously six days a week. (A very religious man, he wouldn't play on

Sundays.) He became captain of the Verulam Club in 1911, and again in 1926 and '27. As he grew older, he got better, his handicap shrinking to six. He became active in organizing and staging a variety of tournaments. So it was no wonder, then, that the old man was overjoyed at the prospect of coordinating an event with an international flavor.

Putting up a cup was one thing; underwriting the entire event was another. Ryder, Hagen, and the other organizers decided that the first Ryder Cup Match would be held in the United States, in Worcester, Massachusetts. (This is little more than a musket shot from where the thirty-third Ryder Cup Match will be held in September 1999.) A few of the participants had played at the Worcester Country Club before, and some of the club members were wealthy manufacturers and merchants who did business with their British counterparts.

Unfortunately, the British Professional Golfers Association didn't have the funds to pay the related expenses. A campaign by the British magazine *Golf Illustrated* raised $2,500 of the $3,000 sought, with contributions coming in from throughout Great Britain as well as the United States, Canada, and even such far-flung locations as Ceylon, the Transvaal, Australia, and Nigeria. Ryder made up the difference, and additional expenses—such as uniforms—were paid for out of Hagen's pocket.

Certainly Ryder and the players were excited. There hadn't previously been a match-up between professional golfers in Great Britain and the United States. The press in Great Britain became very interested and saw the first Ryder Cup Match as an opportunity to spank the impertinent Americans who had "borrowed" the sport from its home country. The U.S. press was also intrigued and saw this first "Ryder Cup" as an opportunity for the U.S. players to show they were no longer poor relations of the fairway. It is difficult to say if the press in the Colonies would have made an even bigger deal of the Match if they hadn't been a bit distracted—the month before the competition was set to begin, Charles Lindbergh took off to cross the Atlantic to Paris, and very little else mattered.

For the contest that was to take place June 3–4, 1927, the British squad arrived by ship. Samuel Ryder was accompanied by Aubrey Boomer, Archie Compston, George Duncan, George Gadd, Arthur Havers, Herbert Jolly, Ted Ray (the captain), Fred Robson, and Charles Whitcombe. Ironically, the great Abe Mitchell was there in gold only—he could not participate in the first Ryder Cup Match because of appendicitis. Without him, the Brits were to face a formidable U.S. team.

Events leading up to the first Match didn't help the British team at all. Crossing the Atlantic on occasionally storm-tossed seas took six days, and the Brits were a bit woozy when they arrived. To their credit, the U.S. team offered to delay the Match until their opponents recovered, but the visitors declared themselves ready to go.

It didn't help either that their hosts were a tad too hospitable—the U.S. team insisted on taking their guests out on the town to celebrate the first official competition. According to G. A. Philpot, the manager of the 1927 British team, after disembarking on the Manhattan docks and being greeted by "a great crowd that had assembled to give us welcome," including Walter Hagen and PGA officials, the team was taken by cars up to a Westchester County golf club for a cocktail party, dinner, vaudeville performance, and impromptu competition on the links. (Surprisingly, the $100 prize for best score was won by the bleary-eyed Brit Aubrey Boomer.)

The next day it was more fun and games. Members of the British team were brought to watch their first baseball game. They went to Yankee Stadium, where the home team was playing the Washington Senators. " 'Babe' Ruth, of course, was the chief 'star' of the New York team, and he was cheered wildly by the crowd whenever he came out to bat," Philpot reported. Alas, though Ruth was in the midst of his record-breaking sixty-homer season, the Yankees lost 3–2. Perhaps this boded well for another team trying to defeat the Yanks.

Hagen was the American captain, and he was still at the peak of his abilities—that year he would win his fourth straight PGA

Championship. Also on the team were Leo Diegel, Al Espinosa, Johnny Farrell, Johnny Golden, Bill Mehlhorn, Joe Turnesa, Al Watrous, and a man who would become one of the true legends of golf, Gene Sarazen.

Apparently inspired by the prospect of repelling the Brits on Massachusetts soil—no doubt what the U.S. squad would like to imitate this year—once the Match began the Americans won easily.

Despite their long journey and the exhausting entertainment provided by their hosts, the British started out well, down by just a bit when the foursomes concluded. "Then came the singles, and the British rout was complete," reported *Golf Illustrated* in its June 10, 1927, issue. "Charles Whitcombe, too, managed to hold his own against Sarazen, but try as he would, he could not finish on top. The American, as a matter of fact, was five holes in arrears at one point in the game, but one by one he pulled the holes back and ultimately finished level. And there the British success ended."

There were few pats on the back among the British players. On the first day Boomer and Whitcombe had won a foursome 7 and 5 over Diegel and Mehlhorn, but the second day, after Sarazen bounced back against Whitcombe and by the time George Duncan defeated Joe Turnesa, the Ryder Cup had taken on an American look.

The 9½–2½ victory for the "locals" sent the visitors packing. Ryder had paid for the cup, but he sailed home across the Atlantic empty-handed.

"The 'Ryder' Cup has gone the way all good cups in golf seem to go—it has gone to America for a year," lamented *Golf Illustrated*.

A total of twelve matches were played at the '27 event, four foursomes and eight singles. This time the result had been very different from the previous informal competitions. Hagen led the way, winning both matches he played.

Despite their loss, or perhaps because of it, the British were keen on doing it again, and Ryder was more enthusiastic than

ever. However, it would be too much of an intrusion on the players' careers and too expensive to be crossing the Atlantic every
year. The British PGA and the PGA of America agreed to continue
the competition but to hold the Ryder Cup Matches every other
year and alternate between Great Britain and the Colonies.

A tradition was born.

Let's take a time-out to discuss how and why the method of play,
format, and selection process of the Ryder Cup separates it from
other golf events. Being familiar with this background information, how it all evolved from 1927 to the present, helps to really
appreciate the Ryder Cup and understand why the high-stakes
competition is so intense.

First of all, to be on a Ryder Cup team, you must have been
born in the United States or Europe. It doesn't matter if you've
played on the PGA Tour or European Tour for twenty years—if
you're not a native, you're not eligible. That's why you don't see
top players like Vijay Singh, Greg Norman, Nick Price, Ernie Els,
and others in the Ryder Cup. However, there has been some discussion among PGA of America officials to relax the rule, which
could benefit players such as Brian Watts, an American citizen
born in Canada, who finished second in the 1997 British Open
and thus earned a stack of Ryder Cup points.

To the casual American golf fan, the way Ryder Cup Matches
are played may seem odd because in the States spectators are used
to medal, or stroke, play. With few exceptions—such as the various
amateur championships sponsored by the U.S. Golf Association
and some club tournaments—American audiences are not confronted with match play.

Stroke play, in which a player's score is determined by how
many strokes he/she requires to complete an eighteen-hole round,
is used in all the major professional tournaments and (except for
the PGA Tour's Sprint International in September) in all PGA Tour
tournaments. Thanks to the telecasts of significant amateur events
and the Ryder and Solheim Cups, Americans are exposed to

match play, but the vast majority of viewers and those who attend PGA tournaments see only stroke play.

To win in stroke play, a player must have required fewer strokes during the three- or four-day tournament than the rest of the field, which can include thirty or fifty or seventy or more players. For example, a player who is 6 under par needed two fewer strokes than a player who ended at 4 under par. Being under par doesn't automatically mean victory—in last year's U.S. Open, Lee Janzen won at even par, which was the best score on a very tough Olympic Golf Club course in San Francisco. Each course has its own par for a professional tournament, anywhere from 70 to 73 per round.

At the completion of the fifty-fourth or seventy-second hole, if there is a tie, there is a sudden-death playoff—except in the U.S. Open tournaments, when there is an eighteen-hole playoff the next day. The winner receives a big check, ranging from around $100,000 to $1 million, depending on the tournament's total purse.

Match play is quite different and quite exciting. In the Ryder Cup groups of two play against each other for two days, and then individuals compete on the final day, with every outcome scoring points for the overall team.

The Ryder Cup is composed of two sessions—one on Friday and the other on Saturday—of *fourball,* meaning each member of the two-man team plays his own ball on each hole, but only the lower score of the two counts toward winning or halving the hole. There are also two sessions of *foursomes,* or alternate shot, meaning the players on a two-man team take turns hitting the same ball, until it drops into the cup; one player tees off at the odd-numbered holes, the other on the even-numbered ones.

In a sense this format asks players used to medal or stroke-play tourneys to flex different muscles. And it truly inspires teamwork. In foursomes, for example, a good shot by one player can be followed by a bad one by his teammate, and vice versa. Ordinarily in stroke play each player is responsible for his own shots and his own score.

During the first two days of the Ryder Cup, the two players on a team must depend on each other, and collectively the outcome of the matches determines how the entire team is doing entering the final day. A total of 16 points is up for grabs during the first two days of play.

On Sunday are the singles matches, twelve in all. The one-on-one match-play rounds begin in the morning and conclude in the late afternoon. The winner of the hole is the player with the lowest score on that hole; for example, if Fred Couples birdies the hole and Ian Woosnam pars it, Couples wins the hole. If there is a birdie, par, or bogey for both players, the hole is halved, no points. A player wins the match when his lead in holes won exceeds the number of holes left to play. For example, if Woosnam leads by three holes after the sixteenth hole, the match is over and he wins 3 and 2, and earns 1 point for his team.

The higher the score, the bigger the drubbing: In the first singles match on Sunday in Valderrama, when Couples beat Woosnam 8 and 7, that means Couples was up by eight holes won with seven still to play—a real in-your-face triumph.

An intriguing element of match play is that it doesn't matter how much you win (or lose) a hole by. In stroke play let's say you're tied for the lead at 2 under par. At the par-4 sixteenth hole your ball goes in the water, you have all kinds of other problems, and you score a 7. Suddenly you're now 1 over par, and if your opponent shoots par on the final two holes, you have to shoot an almost-impossible 4 under par to win.

In match play you win a hole whether or not you played it one stroke or five strokes better than your opponent. Indeed, to save time and effort, your opponent would concede the hole if he cannot or has only a minuscule chance of tying you for a halve. If your ball is in the cup (or the short putt was conceded) in four strokes and your opponent has taken four strokes and his ball is still ten feet away, you've won the hole, whereas in stroke play the other competitor is required to finish out the hole even if it takes ten strokes.

The singles matches are very high-pressure because they are one on one, eyeball to eyeball, as opposed to a typical tournament, when several players are jockeying for the top spot on the leader board and you're playing the course as much as the rest of the field. Remember, in such a tourney on the PGA Tour, a second place can still be worth a couple of hundred thousand dollars. In a Ryder Cup singles match, only first place counts.

The 12 points won on Sunday bring the total number of points available in a Ryder Cup Match to 28. Half-points are earned when a fourball, foursome, or singles match ends in a tie. To defend the Ryder Cup, a team needs to tally 14 points. For Europe in '97, if the score had ended 14–14 (instead of 14½–13½), Seve's squad still would have wound up with the cup because Europe had won it in '95 and was defending. To take the cup away, a team needs 14½ points. This is what the U.S. team will have to total, at minimum, in Massachusetts in 1999 to keep the cup from staying across the Atlantic. And unlike in the tourneys most Americans are accustomed to watching, if you don't win one week there is no next week—the next crack at the Ryder Cup is two years away. This, obviously, is another reason why the three days of competition are so intense.

These Ryder Cup rules have changed, or evolved, since 1927. Through 1959 the format was four foursomes on one day and eight singles matches on the second day, for a total of 12 points. In 1961 there were eight foursomes on one day and sixteen singles the second, for 24 points. Two years later a third day and eight fourball matches were added, boosting the total to 32 points. In 1977 there was a retrenchment, with five foursomes the first day, five fourball matches on Saturday, and ten singles matches the final day, for 20 points. The format we have today was instituted two years later. There have been discussions on changing the format again, but that won't happen before the 1999 Ryder Cup.

There have been two other significant changes. One is the inclusion of European players (discussed in detail in Chapter 5). The other is the method by which the two teams have selected players.

For the American team initially eight players were selected based on the previous three years of performance. Well, that's the "official" version. As Gene Sarazen—who is 97 now and the only surviving player from the first Ryder Cup in 1927—told us, "The first few Matches, Hagen put who he liked on the team."

Since 1927 there have been nineteen changes in the selection process, and the number of players varied. The method used today was developed in 1993: Ten players earn berths on the U.S. team based on points awarded for placing first through tenth in PGA Tour events from January 11, 1998, through the PGA Championship the month before the Ryder Cup. The PGA Championship will be held this year August 12–15 at the Medinah Country Club in Illinois. Points in the second year are worth twice the first year, and a win in a major championship is worth three and four times as much in the first and second years, respectively.

Confused? Let's use an example, with our friend Mr. Couples again. In May 1998 he won the Memorial at Muirfield Village, which earned him 75 points. (Second place in a tourney is worth 45 points, and each place down through tenth is worth 5 points less.) If Fred had won that same tournament in 1999, it would have been worth 150 points. If he had won the U.S. Open (or the Masters, British Open, or PGA Championship) in '98, that would have been worth three times as much as a "regular" tourney, or 225 points. Winning the U.S. Open or any other major in 1999 results in 300 points.

Wisely, the PGA of America, which oversees the U.S. Ryder Cup team, set up this method because it increases the chances that "hotter" players will make the team. David Duval had a tremendous 1998 season, but a stone-cold season in 1999 means he may not end up with enough points to be in the top ten in total points. (Yeah, we know, how likely is that?) Conversely, Brad Faxon had what for him was an ordinary '98; if in '99 his game takes off and he wins two or three tournaments and the PGA Championship, with double and quadruple points, he will rack up enough points and make the Ryder Cup team while playing superior golf.

Whoever developed this method at the PGA deserves a big pat on the back.

Okay, there are ten players—but twelve spots on the team. This is where the captain plays a crucial role. He has two picks. He can select the fellows who are number 11 and number 12 in points, but he doesn't have to—he can pick anyone he wants, even Bob and Tom if he really goes off the deep end. Usually, the captain will look to add experience to the squad, a player who has a winning Ryder Cup record, and/or a man who has been playing well that summer and can be expected to go into September with good momentum.

In 1989 the U.S. captain, Raymond Floyd, went for both experience and a winning record by choosing Lanny Wadkins and Tom Watson. In '91, Dave Stockton went with experience by choosing Raymond Floyd and a hot player by selecting Chip Beck. Not surprisingly, in '93, for the last victorious American team, Tom Watson went with Raymond Floyd and Lanny Wadkins. As will be discussed further in Chapter 8, this very difficult decision that the captain makes can and often does have a major impact on how a team fares.

Amazingly, since the selection process was first established in 1927—when a committee of Harry Vardon, James Braid, and J. H. Taylor did the picking—the process of composing the British and then European team has been changed twenty-four times. Don't worry, we won't explain the particulars here, but we will tell you how this year's team will be chosen.

The European team selection is also determined by a point system—and is to some extent dependent on competition in the United States. The Order of Merit, or the top golfers on the European PGA Tour, is determined by the amount of money earned. Also included is what a player earns by winning one or more of the three major championships held in the United States: the Masters, the U.S. Open, and the PGA Championship. Included too is the outcome of the three World Golf Championships, played for the first time in 1999. Out of this tossed salad come the top ten players, and the captain has two picks.

Clearly in the play, format, and selection process, many, many factors can influence the outcome of each Ryder Cup Match. It certainly makes the typical tourney seem simple by comparison—there you show up, pay your entry fee, try to make the cut, then try to win the event, and even fifteenth place can mean a nice payday. If you're out of luck, you head to the next tourney. In the Ryder Cup there are almost two years of preparations, and everything involved is focused on three days, with only the winner left standing.

Despite the British team's inaugural defeat, Sam Ryder remained enthusiastic about the every-other-year competition, and no event could bear a more golf-loving name.

A good and careful businessman, Ryder arranged for the drawing up of a Deed of Trust, which set up the format and rules of play of the Matches. According to Thomas Anderson Davis, Ryder's nephew (son of Sam's youngest sister, Marie), who as a solicitor drew up the document, it was agreed to by the Ryder family and the respective PGAs and was signed on December 8, 1929. The Ryder Cup Matches were official.

During the early Matches the home team won. The British took the cup back in 1929, 7–5, in Leeds, England. When the two captains matched up, even Hagen couldn't overcome his revenge-minded hosts. According to the English reporter in the May 3 issue of *Golf Illustrated:* "The Duncan-Hagen match took a huge gallery. Before he went out [George] Duncan said to me, 'This guy has never beaten me in a serious match and he never will.' That was Duncan's mental attitude, and his golf reflected it. Duncan was round in 68, to secure a 5 holes lead. In the afternoon he just went mad with 31 for the outward half, and finished off with a 10 and 8 victory. It was a Captain's touch—superb."

Apparently Hagen was unprepared for the beating he would suffer. According to Sarazen, "Hagen and myself were in the men's room, and he told me, 'I know George Duncan is playing in number-two place. I'll put myself number two—I know I can knock him off.' Well, it happened that Duncan beat him badly, and at the dinner that night, we told the story and it was very funny. Afterward it occurred to me, though, that you had to sit in the men's room on the toilet to get the lowdown on the American Ryder Cup strategy."

Two years later the Ryder Cup returned to the Americans, who triumphed in the intense summer heat in Scioto, Ohio. During this event Hagen, captain for the third time, more than lived up to his reputation as a reveler: As he and the British captain, Charles Whitcombe, stood on the first tee to begin their singles match, a waiter strolled onto the course carrying a tray and offered a cocktail to Hagen, who promptly drained the glass, then sent his drive down the middle of the fairway. (He won the match 4 and 3.)

Thanks to advances in technology, Samuel Ryder had been able to broadcast a message to America before the Match began, one that was heard on radios in England, too. He praised all the players and the U.S. hosts, then added, "I look upon the Royal and Ancient game as being a powerful moral force that influences the best things in humanity. I trust the effect of this Match will be to influence a cordial, friendly, and peaceful feeling throughout the whole civilized world."

Ryder left off with, "I have done several things in my life for the benefit of my fellow men, but I am certain I have never done a happier thing than this."

The old man was right that sportsmanship and mutual respect were priorities—but no one wanted to lose, either. "Oh yes, there was a great rivalry at that time," recalled Sarazen, who among many other accomplishments remains the youngest winner of the PGA Championship—he won at the age of 20 in 1922—and won both the British and the U.S. Opens in 1932. "It was very tense when we got together. We wanted to beat the British in the worst way. They looked upon us Americans as no more than a bunch of caddies."

The British retook the Ryder Cup in '33 at Southport and Ainsdale. It was Samuel Ryder's last time as a spectator. The locals had really meant business this time. In preparation the team's captain, J. H. Taylor, hired a physical training specialist and had his players on the beach at 6:30 every morning for a brisk run. The endurance training, though resented by the players, must have done the trick because, with a crowd of 15,000 watching, the home team won when Syd Easterbrook holed the last putt to beat Densmore Shute 1-up. (Shute would console himself by winning the British Open that year.)

On hand to award the cup was the Prince of Wales, later King Edward VIII, who said, "In giving this trophy I am naturally impartial, though we over here are very pleased to have won."

The cup went back to the Americans in '35 in Ridgewood, New Jersey, and as far as anyone knew, the matches could seesaw indefinitely. But things were getting ready to change, because increasingly the U.S. teams comprised players who were emerging not just as the best in America but as the best in the world.

Sarazen and Hagen were on the squads that competed from 1927 through 1935, and that last year they started to be joined by more top-gun talent. Henry Picard helped the United States win 9–3 in '35 despite the Brits' strategy of placing three brothers— Reg, Ernest, and Charles Whitcombe—on the team. Also competing on the squad, for the fourth time, was Percy Alliss, father of Peter Alliss, who became a highly regarded player and broadcaster.

This was the last Match bearing his name that Samuel Ryder followed, by telegram. He had personally witnessed the ones in 1929 and 1933 in England. But he had become too old to make the arduous journey across the Atlantic. He looked forward to the return of the competition to Great Britain in 1937, but he didn't see it: On January 2, 1936, while he was with his family in London for the holidays, he suffered a massive hemorrhage and died at 77.

The family carried on. His youngest daughter, Joan, was present for all the Ryder Cup Matches for the next half-century played in Great Britain. The last one where she was an honored spectator was the one at the Belfry in 1985 when, at 81, she saw the home team defeat the U.S. squad for the first time in twenty-eight years. Not long after that, she died at her home in Sussex.

In 1937 Walter Hagen dropped off the player roster (he remained captain, though), but Sarazen and Picard were joined by Byron Nelson and Sam Snead. For the first time, in 1937, the visiting team won, with the Americans on top 8–4 at Southport and Ainsdale. A pivotal match was Sarazen's 1-up win over Percy Alliss.

"Caught a heck of a break in that one," Sarazen recalled. "I hit one too hard on the fifteenth hole, and the ball sailed clear over the green. But it landed in a lady's lap. She wasn't too happy about a Yank treating her like that, so she tossed it away. Well, it landed close to the hole, and I made birdie."

On a regrettable note (especially for bartenders and hotel concierges), after being captain of six teams and playing on five, this would be Hagen's last "official" Ryder Cup appearance. He finished his Cup career with a strong 7–1–1 record.

The 1937 Match was just the beginning, though, for Byron Nelson. Nelson had been working as a junior assistant for the PGA in Ridgewood, New Jersey, in 1935 when the Ryder Cup was held there. "I got to see these great players, and I made up my mind then and there that I wanted to be on the Ryder Cup team," recalled Nelson, now 87.

"I was just a young whippersnapper then, and it was a lot to think I'd be good enough to make a Ryder Cup team, but fortunately my game was starting to gel at that time," Nelson continued. "The main thing was, I won the Masters in 1937, and that put me on the team. Made me feel like I'd really arrived."

Of course, we can assume that the Brits wanted revenge on American soil the next time around, but there wouldn't be a next time for ten years. Thanks to the outbreak of World War II, the Ryder Cup stayed in the States. Aside from other pressing concerns, it was too dangerous for the U.S. and British teams to cross the ocean to play.

The cancellation of the 1939 Match created a crisis for the decade-old competition: Would it survive World War II? At the time, of course, no one knew how long the war would last or who and what would be left standing. As important as an international golf event was to its fans and players, clearly it paled in comparison to the enormous loss of life and destruction that was taking place. Given that the Ryder Cup was barely established, it was conceivable that there wouldn't be sufficient interest in reviving the Matches when the smoke cleared. The Ryder Cup, and the traditions it had established, might well have been played for the last time in 1937.

"We didn't forget about the Ryder Cup at all, but there was a lot more going on here to pay attention to," said Max Faulkner, one of the top British golfers of the 1940s and 1950s. "Even when the war ended, that didn't mean the competition would be on again. It looked rather bleak."

Was a tradition about to die?

Chapter 3

THE WAR YEARS:
KEEPING THE CUP ALIVE

There have been two crises that threatened the continuation of the Ryder Cup Matches. Together they came very close to killing off the contest. But the Ryder Cup stayed alive, thanks to groups of people on both sides of the Atlantic Ocean who kept the candle burning—and because of a fruit grower in Portland, Oregon.

World War II officially began on September 1, 1939, just after the Ryder Cup Match would have taken place that year, in America. No doubt the British would have sent over a team hungry to avenge the '37 loss at home by giving the Yanks a taste of their own medicine.

Unfortunately, well before the official start of the war, it was clear that little time and attention was available for golf, with the Nazi threat looming over the British Isles, and it was not a good idea to take transatlantic ship voyages unless absolutely necessary. By mutual consent the respective PGAs suspended the 1939 match. Surely no one involved envisioned that the time lapse between Ryder Cups would grow to ten years.

The Battle of Britain virtually put an end to golfing activities. It's rather difficult to line up a putt when you know you could be strafed, or that the bunker your ball just landed in might actually be a bomb crater. Most of the Brits who would have participated in the Ryder Cup in some fashion were serving in the military or dedicating themselves to the war effort.

On the other side of the dangerous sea, the Americans were preparing for war, yet there was still room for some golf. While Americans might have had much less time and resources to devote to the game, some, especially those who had competed before, refused to let the Ryder Cup become history.

Beginning in 1939, the U.S. players organized "Ryder Cup teams" as if there still were to be competitions. The teams didn't pretend to be United States versus Great Britain, but a similar spirit was there. The bottom line was to keep the United States ready for the next Ryder Cup Match—whenever that was.

"The team for 1939 was already chosen, then it seemed like we'd done that for nothing because any moment the whole world was going to war," recalled Byron Nelson, who was on the U.S. team. "But there were a lot of people interested in the Ryder Cup, not just the pros but people interested in golf and its future. Okay, if we couldn't play the English fellows, let's figure out a way to play among ourselves."

A ten-member "Ryder Cup" team played challenge matches against ad hoc teams every year through 1943, winning four of the five matches. For the restless Walter Hagen, the war offered an exciting opportunity. He returned from retirement to captain the '39, '40, and '41 squads. Proceeds from these matches went to the Red Cross.

Looking back from the perspective of more than half a century and knowing what followed, it is clear now that the matches held during the war years paved the way for the subsequent American domination of the Ryder Cup. Not only were the unofficial Ryder Cup teams strong, but they matched up against some pretty darn good challengers. And just the fact that many of the top American players were able to compete at all, while in Great Britain the players were busy being soldiers and factory workers and bond salesmen, contributed to the big shift in golfing power after World War II.

None of this would have mattered, of course, if the Ryder Cup didn't survive the war, and no one was sure at the time that it would. "We heard the fellows in America were going at it, trying to keep it going," recalled Max Faulkner. "But there was too much else going on, and we were rather distracted. The issue of the survival of the Ryder Cup was not a priority."

The British did make some efforts to keep it going. With the hope that life would somehow remain "normal," in 1939 the PGA of Great Britain selected a group of players—Jimmy Adams, Dick Burton, Sam King, Alf Padgham, Dai Rees, Charles Whitcombe, and Reg Whitcombe—and appointed Henry Cotton as captain. The team did not stay active, especially after the war began in September of that year, and the players went on their own war-related ways.

Ironically, given the expanding talent in the United States, the exhibition "Ryder Cup" matches organized in the States pitted the finest American players against each other. The keenest competition was in America, and unfortunately for the British, who endured so much in the 1940s, when the Ryder Cup resumed, they were rusty and far outmatched.

In 1940, for example, Hagen could put Nelson, Picard, and Snead out on the Oakland Hills Country Club in Bloomfield, Michigan. They won, but the challengers included Sarazen, Jimmy Demaret, and a very young Ben Hogan. The following year in Detroit Hagen's troops were vanquished 8½–6½ by a team of challengers led by none other than the legendary amateur Bobby Jones. This was to be Jones's last appearance on the center stage of competitive golf.

In 1942 Hagen was out as captain (replaced by Craig Wood, which has to be the equivalent of Wally Pipp replacing Lou Gehrig). Undaunted, Hagen formed his own group of challengers. They weren't enough, though, as they lost to a powerful squad that included Sarazen, Demaret, Hogan, Lloyd Mangrum, and Nelson. Essentially the same teams (without Hogan) met up the next year and produced the same result.

It became very difficult, however, to keep even unofficial matches going, as rationing increased and the fate of the world far beyond fairways and greens literally hung in the balance. Most sporting events were scaled back or canceled, and golf was no exception. The PGA Championship, for example, was not played in 1943. Not even an exhibition Ryder Cup Match was played in 1944. Once again the Ryder Cup was in danger of being discontinued.

The next Ryder Cup Match would have been in 1945, but with the war not ending until August, it was impossible to coordinate a contest. Quite possibly, if the Ryder Cup was not held the next time around, the event would not survive a layoff in excess of ten years—the same amount of time it had existed in the first place.

"It didn't look good," Sarazen said. "Once the war was over, there was some room for hope, but who knew what would happen, what kind of shape everyone was in. There was very little to be sure about."

Barely breathing, the Ryder Cup was heading toward being little more than a footnote in golf history. Then the passion of a man in Portland made the difference.

Robert A. Hudson has not gotten his full due in the annals of golf. While Samuel Ryder founded the Ryder Cup, Hudson was the man who saved it from extinction.

The good news in 1947 was that there was genuine interest in resuming the Ryder Cup Matches. The bad news was that with the terrible price Great Britain paid to beat the Axis powers, and with finances and other resources at low ebb, gathering a team and sending it into competition would be just about impossible. Even so, the PGAs in Great Britain and the United States wanted to give it a go.

It was decided that the revived Ryder Cup, should it happen at all, would be held at the Portland Golf Club in Oregon. For the British, this was almost the same as saying the competition would be held on Mars, because the British PGA had no funds and couldn't possibly underwrite a team trip to the United States. Enter Robert Hudson.

While only a decent amateur player, Hudson, a fairly success-ful Oregon fruit grower, deeply loved the game of golf. He was more than willing to volunteer his time to improve the sport, and to that end he had just become a member of the PGA Advisory Committee. (He would serve until 1968.) He was delighted that an attempt to resurrect the Ryder Cup would take place in his backyard—if it took place at all.

Opening his wallet, Hudson offered to pay all the British team's traveling expenses. In addition to that, he would take care of whatever else they needed and escort them to the playing site.

After paying for their passage, Hudson met the visitors when they stepped off the *Queen Mary* in New York and threw a cele-bratory party for them at the Waldorf Astoria Hotel. He then paid for and accompanied them on the four-day train trip across the country to Portland. "It was a marvelous trip, to see America up close like that, but not the best way to prepare to play golf," Max Faulkner recalled. "We were rather stiff and worn out by the time we stepped off the train."

Once in Portland, Hudson paid for the British team's meals, caddies, and all other costs.

That he was essentially leading the lambs to the competitive slaughter didn't diminish Hudson's good intentions and the cru-cial role he played in preserving the Ryder Cup. It's not unreason-able to think that his passion and generosity meant as much to the event as Samuel Ryder's.

"What he did was marvelous," said Faulkner, who was part of an official Ryder Cup team for the first time in 1947. "Hudson did everything he could and would not accept a penny back, nothing more than a thank-you. We wouldn't be talking here about the Ryder Cup today if it wasn't for him."

"I felt sorry for the British players because they hadn't been able to play golf or do anything since fighting the war over there," Byron Nelson said. "But they were very nice and everyone treated them well and they had a good time."

The 1947 U.S. team was stacked; among the players were Ben Hogan, Jimmy Demaret, Lloyd Mangrum, Nelson (who two years earlier had set a record by winning eleven straight tourneys), and Sam Snead. (Snead and Nelson were the only holdovers from the 1937 team.)

"I think that when Snead, Nelson, and Hogan came into the Ryder Cup, that team became too strong for the British," Sarazen said. "Look at all those three have done, and they were at their prime. How could any team match up against them?"

The two-day Match began on November 1, and it rained . . . and rained . . . and rained. Still, after all this effort, no one was backing out. Onto the drenched course in the soaking rain the players went for thirty-six-hole foursomes the first day and thirty-six-hole singles the second.

It was still raining when the last putt was sunk, and the U.S. team won 11–1. It must have been a long and somber trip back home for the British. On the other hand, the Ryder Cup was still alive, and with the world recovering from war, it was expected to continue.

To fully honor him, we want to point out that Robert Hudson's generosity and goodwill went far beyond the golf course. At Christmas that year and every Christmas for ten years after, members of the British Ryder Cup teams received large gift baskets stuffed with fruit and other food.

"It was an unbelievable and lovely thing to do," Faulkner said. "You have to remember, for many years after the war, food was still scarce here, and we certainly weren't making much in the golf business. Every holiday, though, was made quite a bit brighter that my family and the other families had this big basket from Hudson. It's very gratifying and appropriate that that generosity of spirit is associated with the Ryder Cup."

It's one thing to bring a group of opponents to America, treat 'em well, then send 'em packing, fruit or no fruit. The fact that there had been an official match in 1947 did not guarantee that the Ryder Cup would continue. Could Great Britain host a Match when its turn came? If so, could they be competitive?

As it turned out, the Brits could, and they battled the Yanks valiantly. However, just as when they marched on Bunker Hill, the British didn't know what was in store for them. After the home team won at Southport and Ainsdale in 1933, it would be twenty-four years before the British team would win again—and this fact only hints at the thoroughness of the American domination from the late 1940s to the early 1980s.

The good news for all concerned was that the Ryder Cup was back in business, though still gasping a bit. As part of the effort to recapture the cup, the Professional Golfers Association of Great Britain endeavored to raise its own funds to underwrite the team. By persevering and leaning on national pride, the organization was able to scrape up enough money to put its team on a steady footing.

There was more good news for the British in 1949. The visiting U.S. team would be at half-strength. The captain, Ben Hogan, could not play because he hadn't fully recovered from a devastating car accident that February, and Byron Nelson had decided to retire. How nice it would be to get back to the old pendulum nature of the Ryder Cup, with the host team winning every two years.

However, the international golf scene was changing. While the sport remained very popular in Great Britain and was emerging in other parts of the world—the appearance in the 1960s of such winners as Gary Player of South Africa, Bob Charles of New Zealand, and Isao Aoki of Japan was evidence of more widespread appeal—the focus shifted primarily to the United States. As the Ryder Cup results demonstrated, America was consistently producing the finest players in the game.

One reason for the superiority of the U.S. players is that some veterans who had started to win in the late 1930s and through the 1940s, like Hogan and Snead, continued to earn victories and be competitive in the two decades after World War II. They had established a standard of excellence and performed their roles in maintaining it. Another reason was the across-the-board depth of American players. They were coming out of colleges and country clubs with strong fundamentals and feeding off the competition with each other.

More than any other tournament or event, the Ryder Cup Matches were representative of the shift in talent. Beginning in the late 1940s, a U.S. loss was an aberration—from 1947 through 1983, the Americans won seventeen of the nineteen Matches (retaining the Ryder Cup once via a tie).

A clear indication of the strength of the U.S. Ryder Cup teams is the names on their rosters in the 1950s, '60s, and '70s. Among the members were Ben Hogan, Sam Snead, Jimmy Demaret, Jack Burke, Jr., Lloyd Mangrum, Cary Middlecoff, Tommy Bolt, Dow Finsterwald, Julius Boros, Billy Casper, Arnold Palmer, Gene Littler, Bob Goalby, Tony Lema, Don January, Gay Brewer, Gardner Dickinson, Al Geiberger, Miller Barber, Jack Nicklaus, Raymond Floyd, Lee Trevino, Dave Stockton, Hale Irwin, Johnny Miller, Tom Watson, and others who were winning tournament trophies, including the four majors, by the armful. Most of these players were household names, and some of them are now viewed as legends.

It was difficult for Great Britain to gather a team to match the Americans' star power and depth. Dai Rees, Arthur Lees, Fred Daly, Peter Alliss, Christy O'Connor, Sr., Max Faulkner, Ken Bousfield, Bernard Hunt, and Harry Weetman were good, hard-nosed players, but they just didn't give off the same wattage. Things really didn't begin to change for the better for the Brits until Tony Jacklin began to make the team in the late 1960s.

Why was the United States in its golden age of golf in the 1950s through the 1970s? One factor was the economy. The post-war years were financially heady times in the States, and prosperity allowed for more private and public courses to be built and for more people to devote time to the sport. With more families having access to golf, inevitably more good players were produced.

Another factor was that an increasing number of players could devote themselves to being full-time professionals. Until Walter Hagen demonstrated in his brash way (with the help of his personal PR person) that one could make a living at golf, most players kept their day jobs and tried to win tournaments on weekends. But by the 1950s the pros were at it full time, thanks to the rising amount of total purses and to the fact that the thousands of rounds the pros played every year resulted in a higher level of play.

A third factor was technology. Today we may take for granted that every year there is a better club, a better ball, a new way to grow grass, and so on. Before World War II golf equipment didn't change very much. There were always innovations, but the pace was slow. Part of the stepped-up research and industrial vigor of the postwar United States was advances in sports equipment and sites. The best American professionals—the ones who made it onto Ryder Cup teams—had the most access to and could afford to use the best equipment and the finest courses.

One more factor: the growing popularity and higher visibility of golf. While it did not replace baseball in the public psyche, the audience for golf grew, particularly as tournaments and special events like *Shell's Wonderful World of Golf* began to be televised. (The show was the creation of Fred Raphael, who did not play golf at the time!)

A sure sign that enough people in the United States were interested in the sport was that Hollywood made a movie about it—specifically, about Ben Hogan and his courageous recovery from the car crash that nearly killed him. *Follow the Sun* was released in 1951, starring Glenn Ford and Anne Baxter as Ben and Valerie Hogan, and it was well received by both critics and audiences. (Though very much a formula picture, it still holds up as entertainment.)

So the odds were not in favor of the British Ryder Cup teams. Every two years they were sent out to battle—and on American soil every four years—against the cream of a steadily improving U.S. crop. When Hogan said at the 1967 Ryder Cup that he was introducing "the best golfers in the world," he wasn't exaggerating. In this light, it may be more surprising that Great Britain was able to win one Match and tie another through 1983, a testament to the grit, resilience, and stiff-upper-lip attitude that had helped win a war.

In 1949, without Hogan or Nelson available to play, the U.S. team was indeed depleted, and the Brits were playing at home. The result was a close Match. The Americans won 7–5, and they did it by taking six of the eight singles matches on the second and final day.

"I remember that year the Americans brought their own steaks to have for dinner," Faulkner said, laughing. "They brought a steak for each of us on the team, too . . . but didn't give them to us until the last night, when the Match was over."

Besides the dramatic comeback of the United States after being down 3–1, the weekend was notable for a controversy involving the home team's clubs. Apparently Hogan had been miffed two years earlier in Portland when Henry Cotton, the British captain, had alleged that Hogan's clubs contained illegal grooves. The charge turned out to be unfounded, but Hogan was not happy that his integrity had been questioned.

The day before the 1949 Ryder Cup was to begin, Hogan made a similar allegation about the Brits' clubs. This time, after an inspection by Bernard Darwin, chairman of the Royal and Ancient Rules of Golf Committee, it was discovered that the clubs Hogan had questioned were indeed nonconforming. Jock Ballantine, the host professional at the Ganton Golf Club where the matches were being held, spent the night filing away the illegal grooves. Perhaps miffed themselves, the Brits jumped out to a good lead on the first day, but they couldn't withstand the U.S. counterattack the last day.

The Americans sailed home with the Ryder Cup, and given that they had outscored the British 18–6 in the two postwar Matches, it seemed like the cup would stay in the Colonies indefinitely. But at the time, who held the cup was of secondary importance—what truly mattered was that there was still a Ryder Cup to fight over.

All was right in the world of golf.

Chapter 4

"THE BEST GOLFERS IN THE WORLD"

While it was very good news that the Ryder Cup had survived as an event, there was little opportunity for great joy in Great Britain. The postwar period was a time when America made use of its many advantages and beat up on its opponents. When the 1950s dawned, the "golden age" for the United States in the Ryder Cup and in golf generally was in full swing.

The first Match of the decade was held at Pinehurst in North Carolina (site of the 1999 U.S. Open), which consistently ranks as one of the top ten courses in the country. It was an easy win for the Americans with Jimmy Demaret, making his last Ryder Cup appearance, pushing his Ryder Cup singles record to 6–0. The 1951 Match was the only time that Ryder Cup play was suspended so the teams could go watch a football game, with North Carolina beating Tennessee 27–0.

In a happy sidebar event for the Brits, the team's captain, Arthur Lacey, while at Pinehurst, met a wealthy woman from Pittsburgh, whom he eventually married. The neighborhood near the golf course became their winter home, where for years they entertained many golfing guests from around the country and the world.

At Wentworth in England in 1953, there was a close call for the United States, with the visitors eking out a 6½–5½ victory.

Peter Alliss and Bernard Hunt made impressive debuts for the British. Ben Hogan, though having an excellent year on the PGA Tour, wasn't part of the U.S. team.

Because his legs never completely recovered from the auto accident, Hogan was less able in his forties to play thirty-six holes at any one time, and during this period the Ryder Cup had thirty-six-hole matches. During the years of losing to the Americans, the one advantage for the British was that Hogan, considered one of the top two or three golfers of all time, played in just two Ryder Cups (1947 and '51) and had only a 3–0 record.

Things went back to form two years later, at the Thunderbird Golf and Country Club in Palm Springs, California—at the dawn of that area's emergence as a golf mecca—when the U.S. squad retained the cup with an 8–4 triumph. All of the Americans' points were racked up by Tommy Bolt, Jack Burke, Jr., Doug Ford, and Sam Snead. The British team of 1955 vowed to be ready next time by "going back to practice in the streets and on the beaches," according to Lord Brabazon of Tara, head of the PGA of Great Britain.

The British were not poor golfers by any means. They were, however, up against a surging wave of American talent and still recovering from the ordeal of World War II, without many of the material advantages the U.S. players enjoyed. More than a few of the British professionals were not full-time players but had to combine participating in pro tournaments with working as club and teaching pros.

"It was first class all the way for the Americans," recalled Max Faulkner, who was on five British Ryder Cup teams between 1947 and 1957. "By the 1950s the U.S. were putting on the course all full-time players, part of a regular tour, and they always had the best in transportation and accommodations. Some of our fellows had two or three jobs and tried to win the occasional tourney. It was a bit irritating, but we so enjoyed the competition."

And, alas, there was a talent gap. Even former British players concede that the Brits couldn't match up with the consistent and superior depth of the U.S. teams. Apparently this is why Great Britain did pretty well in the foursome and fourball matches, where the strong play of one player could compensate for a weak teammate, but routinely lost the majority of the final-day singles matches, when there weren't enough top-talent players to take on all the Americans.

"When you don't have the depth down to the twelfth man, as the Americans usually did, there is a difficult choice for the captain to make," said Brian Barnes, a strong player on six British Ryder Cup teams who is now a successful competitor on the Senior PGA Tour in the United States. "If you play your best as much as you can in fourball and foursomes, those fellows are bloody well fagged by the singles. If you try to rest them here and there, you risk that by the singles, victory is no longer an option."

This may be an overlooked reason why the Ryder Cup Matches of the 1980s and 1990s have been so competitive— the European teams, with their increasing depth of talent, can put the same number of quality players on the course as the U.S. teams.

"We just really had the best players in the world at that time," stated Jack Burke, Jr., who played on five U.S. teams (with a 7–1–0 record) and captained teams in 1957 and 1973. "With the British facing us only once every two years, they did not regularly compete with the best and thus get better themselves. So the situation didn't change much over a long period of time. Here we played each other, best against the best, then every two years we kicked butt."

However, Burke added, "I never took the British lightly and never felt that my matches were one-sided. I'll never forget I played a guy from Ireland and I saw his grip and I'm thinking, 'I can beat this guy.' Well, I shot 65 and he shot 65 that morning. Then in the afternoon I beat him by one stroke. That was a rough day, and pretty typical. You beat 'em, but not by much, and they never backed down."

"Believe me, we *never* went into a Ryder Cup Match taking it lightly, because if we had done that, I don't think we would have won," said Gene Littler, who played on seven U.S. teams from 1961 to 1975 and shone with a 14–5–8 record. "Everybody on both sides tried as hard as they could. Nobody wanted to be on a losing team."

History has shown that the British are nothing if not resilient, and they were a little more ready for the U.S. team in 1957, captained by Jack Burke, Jr. They hadn't won in twenty-four years, and enough was enough.

The Ryder Cup that year was held at the Lindrick Club in Sheffield (with young Jimmy Patino in the gallery). The location was chosen by Sir Stuart Goodwin, who had put up 10,000 pounds to underwrite the British team. (They *were* serious that year.) The British captain was Dai Rees, by this point the only holdover from the pre–World War II teams. The home team finally broke through on British soil, winning 7½–4½. It was an especially sweet moment for Rees, who had been waiting twenty years to finally taste victory.

There were three crucial factors in the British triumph. One was that the Americans agreed to use the smaller British ball (1.62 to 1.68), and this difference, though slight, threw the U.S. players off. Another was that the visitors seemed to take the second day of the matches for granted. The first day they had jumped out to a 3–1 lead, and they perhaps felt that they could phone in the final day. But the British roared back, winning the singles matches 6½–1½ (with the grizzled veteran Rees winning his match 7 and 6) to shock the United States.

The third factor? Some wily course preparation by the folks at home. "We players got the course ready, and we made it very English," Faulkner said. "We didn't water the greens for three days before the Ryder Cup, and we left the grass around the green an inch and a half long. In those days the Americans didn't know how to play a shot from there.

"I remember on practice day I was playing the sixth hole with Dai Rees and Ken Bousfield, and Jack Burke was backed in this grass, and he had one stab at it. He grabbed the club too tightly, and the ball just jumped in the air and went a foot forward. He did it again, and it jumped a foot forward. Then he picked the ball up and walked away. We saw before official play started that we had an advantage."

To give them their deserved due, the British also won because of teamwork and their never-say-die competitive spirit. Rees decided that since they hadn't had a good weekend thus far, he would sit Harry Weetman and Max Faulkner during the singles matches. Weetman complained to the press, then sulked. Faulkner decided to turn the situation to the team's advantage.

"I think a part of me knew that was my last Ryder Cup, and all I cared about was winning, whoever played," Faulkner said. "If I couldn't do it with a club in my hands, there were other ways."

Indeed. In addition to becoming an effusive cheerleader for his team during the singles matches, he became a fleet-of-foot messenger. In the absence of leader boards on the course, Faulkner ran from match to match to let his teammates know the other scores and to encourage them against the Yanks. His efforts and inspiration are credited with the unusually impressive singles performance by the Brits.

"It was the highlight for me, to finally break through," Faulkner said. "We were rather like heroes for a while. It was a great, great cap on my career."

Did the win at Lindrick represent a turn of fortune for the British in the Ryder Cup? Hardly. The Americans weren't about to let that happen again—and didn't until twenty-eight years later. Not even Dai Rees could have imagined such a long victory dry spell.

The American domination resumed in 1959 at the El Dorado Country Club in Palm Springs. Exposing the British to the dry heat of the desert added to the American advantage. The United States won easily, 8½–3½. To add insult to injury, a violent storm nearly downed the plane carrying the British squad from Los Angeles to Palm Springs.

Let's face it: After the 1957 win for Great Britain's team—which now has to be viewed more as an aberration than a turn of the tide—the Ryder Cup was not really much of a contest. The American golfers were getting better, and there were more of them to choose from; in Great Britain the talent pool was smaller.

It's reasonable to suppose that interest in the Ryder Cup would dwindle because of the one-sided outcomes. However, the event was about to get a jolt that made it the center of attention on the international golf scene.

Arnold Palmer has long been referred to as "the King," a legendary and dignified figure revered everywhere he goes. It is a role he has certainly earned. His sixty PGA Tour victories (ninety-one total wins worldwide, including seven majors and ten Senior PGA Tour wins) place him fourth on the career list behind Snead, Nicklaus, and Hogan, and he may well remain in the top five as long as golf is played. Though he will turn 70 two weeks before the 1999 Ryder Cup and has fought off cancer, Palmer still makes appearances in Senior PGA Tour tournaments and special events (like the Senior Skins Game), and the galleries are still thrilled when he shoots a good round.

But the Arnold Palmer who first appeared on the Ryder Cup scene in the early 1960s was quite different from the venerable elder statesman of today. He was a young, strong, and brash newcomer, a win-at-all-costs competitor who symbolized and solidified the American domination of the international golf scene. In addition, his magnetic presence significantly upped the interest in the Ryder Cup as an event on both sides of the Atlantic.

Palmer was at the head of a new group of American players who would prove invincible in the battles with Great Britain. In 1959 several mainstays of the U.S. team played their last Ryder Cups: Sam Snead (also the captain); Jack Burke, Jr.; and Cary Middlecoff. Two years later Palmer along with Billy Casper and Gene Littler joined Jerry Barber, Dow Finsterwald, Doug Ford, Mike Souchak, Art Wall, and others to form an unbeatable combination.

With Palmer's participation, the Ryder Cup's U.S. teams were that much stronger, a golf equivalent to piling on in football. It would seem that crowds in Great Britain would become less enthusiastic about the event, but instead the interest level soared because everyone was wild about Arnie.

The British shared the excitement of the American golf fans—Palmer was a charismatic, dynamic player ushering in a new era in golf. He not only won a lot but did so in dramatic fashion, a final-round charge that had "Arnie's Army" in the gallery following and cheering him at every hole. With his mannerisms, bravado, and wonderful smile, his fearlessness and brilliant play, he was just so much darned fun to watch. Thus, Palmer's participation in any event made it more special.

Moreover, Palmer helped revive interest in the British Open and solidify its stature as one of the four majors. In the United States, up to this point, not nearly as much attention was paid to the British Open as to the three other majors, all held in the United States, and from time to time the top American players even skipped the trip overseas.

"I never played in the British Open because I didn't want to spend the five hundred dollars to enter and spend three weeks on a boat back and forth," Burke said.

Unlike today's easy Concorde flights, in the 1950s the trip to England or Scotland every year for just one tournament was quite an ordeal, and it often left players unable to enter the American tourneys held before and/or after the British Open. When Hogan won the Masters, U.S. Open, and British Open in 1953, he wasn't able to get back in time to try to win the PGA Championship and complete the coveted Grand Slam.

But Palmer, who has always placed enormous value on the traditions and heritage of golf, embraced the British Open as a wonderful opportunity. When he won it in 1961, both British and American audiences were mesmerized. Palmer was nearing his peak. He was only 31 years old, yet he had won twenty-six tournaments through 1961 (including two Masters and a U.S. Open), an amazing eight of them the previous year.

Only three months after that first British Open victory, he would be back for his first Ryder Cup, at Royal Lytham and St. Annes. When he returned in '62 and won the British Open a second time, his image became even more firmly entrenched in the British psyche.

While Palmer's brash style and charismatic presence captivated the British and made the Ryder Cup a more popular event worldwide, that same style and supreme self-confidence caused him a few problems. They were not problems with performance— Palmer's career Ryder Cup record of 22–8–2 contains the most American wins, with Lanny Wadkins, Billy Casper, and Jack Nicklaus trailing behind. (At present, twenty-six years after Palmer's last appearance, no U.S. player is close to matching his twenty-two Ryder Cup victories.) But Arnie's bold style clashed with the older, more reserved Ryder Cup style.

This was most evident in the 1967 event, at the Champions Golf Club in Houston. Palmer won four times and had four second-places that year, picked up his fourth Vardon Trophy for lowest stroke average, and won $184,000—the most he ever earned in a single year on the PGA Tour. None of this, though, impressed the U.S. Ryder Cup captain, Ben Hogan.

Hogan and Palmer weren't very fond of each other to begin with. Perhaps Palmer didn't show enough deference, and Hogan probably still simmered from the 1960 U.S. Open when Palmer came from six shots back in the final round to deny Hogan his fifth National Championship. Hogan never referred to Palmer by name, just as "fella."

Palmer didn't seem to care, and after Hogan's gruff greeting on the Champions practice range, Arnie went out on Friday and, paired with Gardner Dickinson, won both of his first-day Ryder Cup Matches.

Was Hogan happy? Well, when he announced the pairings for Saturday morning, Palmer was on the bench, causing a stir among the crowd and questions from reporters. Hogan was apparently miffed that Palmer had given a British player a ride in his private airplane—the captain, the Bob Gibson of golf, didn't like consorting with the enemy—and for fun Palmer had buzzed the golf course.

That afternoon Palmer was back out of the doghouse. Perhaps as a dig on Hogan's part, he was paired with Julius Boros, who in 1963 had beaten Palmer in a playoff in the U.S. Open at The Country Club in Brookline (site of the 1999 Ryder Cup). Halfway through the match the Americans were down by four to George Will of Scotland and Hugh Boyle of Ireland, and it looked like Hogan might have intimidated the bold upstart.

But backing away from a challenge was not part of the Palmer style. Jack Burke, Jr., who had built the Champions Golf Club with Jimmy Demaret and was no slouch with a 7–1 Ryder Cup record (he had last played in 1959), confronted Palmer: "I told him, 'Well, I've heard about these famous charges. Let me see you get out of this one with one of 'em,'" Burke recalled. "Arnie's so used to challenging himself, he's surprised when he's challenged by someone else. So he said, 'You follow me.' I did, and I'm a son of a gun if he didn't pull that damn match out."

The challenge was enough to light the fire. Palmer birdied three of the next four holes, and he and Boros won the match 1-up. (Burke built Palmer a clock with the twelve letters of his name replacing the numbers, and Palmer still has it to this day.) By the time the U.S. team won 23½–8½, Palmer was 5–0 and his Ryder Cup record was 14–3–2. There was a new sheriff in town. Palmer would win eight more matches and was a two-time captain of the U.S. team.

We want to make sure that we don't overlook the enormous Ryder Cup contributions of Billy Casper, which can easily happen because throughout their golf careers the captivating personality of Palmer earned him more attention from fans and the media than the soft-spoken, down-home style of Casper.

Billy Casper is the U.S. version of Nick Faldo—the American leader in Ryder Cup points, with 23½. During his peak years, from the early 1960s to the mid-1970s, Casper represented the United States repeatedly on Ryder Cup teams, and in most matches he swept away the competition.

"Every two years it was the highlight of my career," Casper said. "I felt very fortunate to have played on eight consecutive teams. At the time that I made the team, you had to earn the points, there was no picking of players on the team, so you really had to earn what you got."

Billy Casper certainly did earn what he got. In his own somewhat quiet way, he made sure that the Ryder Cup stayed on American shores.

While the participation of the charismatic Palmer was good for the British because it heightened the Ryder Cup's visibility and brought more fans to cheer on the home team every four years, the attention lavished on him disguised for a while the fact that the U.S. domination had become cruelly routine. Not even various experimental changes in format seemed to help.

In 1961 at Royal Lytham and St. Annes (where the event for the first time was extended to three days), the United States won 14½–9½, with Palmer and Casper leading the way. Two years later at the East Lake Country Club in Atlanta, Georgia, with Palmer as player-captain, the United States crushed the visitors 23–9, with Casper collecting 4½ points. Palmer boasted that the 1963 U.S. Ryder Cup team would "beat the rest of the world combined," which was certainly rubbing the Brits' noses in it.

At Royal Birkdale in Southport in 1965, the tough Peter Alliss defeated Casper and Ken Venturi (who had won the U.S. Open the year before), but it wasn't nearly enough, as the Brits lost 19½–12½.

It looked like the domination would never end, and Hogan wasn't about to ease up on the British. During the gala dinner preceding the 1967 Match in Houston, the seemingly ageless British captain, Dai Rees, making his last appearance as a Ryder Cupper, introduced his players by giving a long and proud speech about each one. The audience was all set to burst into applause.

But when Hogan in turn stood up and asked for silence, he said his introduction would be much shorter. Gesturing to his team, Hogan said, "Ladies and gentleman, the best golfers in the world." Then he sat down.

The outcome proved him right. In the harsh heat of Houston, the Americans won 23½–8½, with Gardner Dickinson going 5–0.

As tactless as the introduction may have been, Hogan had spoken the absolute truth.

The 1969 Ryder Cup was especially notable for two reasons. It was the closest the United States came to a loss in twelve years, and it was an example of why the Matches are frequently cited as examples of true sportsmanship.

From start to finish, the Match was closely contested. Perhaps smarting from Hogan's remarks two years earlier and egged on by a raucous crowd, the British players were not the least bit in awe of the Americans. In fact, the Welshman Brian Huggett and the Scot Bernard Gallacher, during their fourball match on the second day, were shouting insults at their opponents, Dave Hill and Ken Still. "Best golfers, eh? Well, prove it *this* year!" was the gentlest remark.

On the last day at Royal Birkdale Golf Club in Southport, the United States and Great Britain were tied 15½–15½. More than half of the matches had been determined on the last hole, and fittingly, the outcome of the Ryder Cup would be decided in the last match. It pitted Tony Jacklin—who had won the British Open two months earlier, the first British player to do so in eighteen years—against Jack Nicklaus, who was making his first appearance in the Ryder Cup.

Earlier in the weekend Jacklin and Neil Coles had defeated Nicklaus and Dan Sikes. "That match is probably my favorite Ryder Cup memory," Coles told us. "The match was all-square on the seventeenth tee. I was first away with the second shot and got up on the par-5 seventeenth in two. All the three other members of the group missed the green, having failed to get there in two. I two-putted from a long distance to a back left pin to go 1-up. Tony made four at the last for us to win the match."

Jacklin had gone on to beat Nicklaus again, in singles, to put the Brits up by a point. After the other matches were completed, the teams were knotted at 15½. Jacklin was behind on the back nine, but—ever the warrior—he eagled the seventeenth to draw even with Nicklaus.

Nicklaus himself just missed eagling the par-5 eighteenth. After Jacklin missed his birdie putt, Nicklaus made his last putt to ensure at least a tie, meaning the Americans would retain the cup. However, given the U.S. record and that a Ryder Cup Match had never ended in a tie before, for U.S. fans and some of the players nothing less than outright victory would do.

Jacklin's ball was on the green three feet short of the hole. Given the pressure of the two days and of that match, this was definitely a missable putt. But Nicklaus picked up Jacklin's marker, conceding the putt and the tie.

"I don't think you would have missed that, Tony," Nicklaus said, "but under these circumstances I'd never give you the opportunity."

"The length of the putt has varied after almost thirty years," Jacklin told us. "It's been reported as long as four feet. But my recollection is twenty inches. Of course, I could have missed it; there are no guarantees in golf, especially in the crucible of the Ryder Cup, but I believe I would have made it. But Jack saw the big picture—two months before I had become the first British player in eighteen years to win the British Open—so there was very much a pro-British fervor at the Ryder Cup in England that year. Jack saw that that putt on the last hole in 1969 meant a heck of a lot more to the Ryder Cup than who won or lost that particular Match. It was a great moment."

Considering how fierce a competitor Nicklaus has always been, the British actually caught a break during the 1960s. Nicklaus had turned professional late in 1961, won the U.S. Open the following year, and during the decade had twenty-nine PGA Tour wins alongside the U.S. Open victory, a PGA Championship, and three Masters. But he wasn't on a U.S. Ryder Cup team until 1969.

During the 1960s the PGA had a rule that one had to be a "Class A" member of the organization before being eligible for the Ryder Cup, and one had to be a pro for five years to receive this designation. That took care of the '63 and '65 teams, and once Nicklaus became Class A in late '66, he had only nine months to earn enough points to make the team—not enough, it turned out, to exceed players who'd had the full two years. Nicklaus missed almost all of the Ryder Cup Matches in the 1960s.

"I can't really say I was frustrated," Nicklaus told us. "Those were the rules, so those were the rules."

The British had to be thankful for small blessings.

The American domination continued in the 1970s, though the British team received an injection of new, more aggressive players such as Bernard Gallacher, Brian Barnes, and Peter Oosterhuis.

"We felt a change in the air because a group of us were coming of age who were committed to giving the Yanks a very serious run and turning things around," said Barnes. "Of course, this didn't happen overnight, and it took more than the British and Irish could do. But we were determined to give as good as we got—we weren't afraid at all."

For the 1971 team the United States was also adding some fresh faces: Charles Coody, J. C. Snead, and Dave Stockton. With Lee Trevino still recovering from an appendectomy and Billy Casper hoping a broken toe would heal in time, maybe the British could steal this Match.

Not a chance. At the Old Warson Country Club in St. Louis, Nicklaus's five wins led the United States to an 18½–13½ victory. Jack obviously was making up for lost time.

In 1973 there were two changes: The Republic of Ireland joined Great Britain as a Ryder Cup participant, and for the first time the cup was contested in Scotland, at Muirfield. However, the outcome was the same, the United States winning 19–13, with Nicklaus and Trevino, who had both previously won British Opens at Muirfield, combining for 8½ points.

It didn't help that British team member Gallacher fell ill with food poisoning and had to be replaced at almost the last minute by Peter Butler. Butler did become the first player in Ryder Cup history to score a hole-in-one, but he and Barnes were beaten twice, by Nicklaus and Tom Weiskopf and then Palmer and J. C. Snead.

The American win was a great relief to the U.S. captain, Jack Burke, Jr. "I didn't think I was going to get that one either— looked like 0–2 to me," he recalled. "But I had Trevino and Nicklaus and Gay Brewer and some other great players, and we pulled away. No way was I about to put my hands on the Ryder Cup until the last match was over."

Nicklaus, coming off his fifth Masters and fourth PGA Championship, faltered in the 1975 Ryder Cup at the Laurel Valley Golf Club in Pennsylvania, losing to Brian Barnes in two singles matches. (Barnes caused a bit of a stir by wearing shorts and puffing on a pipe as he played.) Otherwise, though, the Americans romped, 21–11.

There was some consolation, especially for Barnes, that he had beaten the great Jack twice in the same day. "That was my finest Ryder Cup moment, without a doubt," he said. "I've always admired Jack enormously, and here I was playing for my country and defeating the greatest golfer of all time twice in the same day. My God, what do you do for an encore?"

As it turns out, Barnes almost didn't have the opportunity to beat Nicklaus twice. The morning match was a surprisingly easy 4 and 2 victory for Barnes. Well, Nicklaus did lose *sometimes,* so this loss to Barnes shouldn't have been that big a deal, and according to the players, during the match they stayed relaxed by focusing on fishing stories. Each player presumably would face other opponents in the afternoon. Here the plot thickens.

As Barnes tells it: "Palmer goes to Jack and says, 'That bloke Barnes is lording it up as though beating you was a walk in the park and he could do it again with his eyes closed.' Jack seethes. He can't let this go by.

"Now Arnie, he's doing this for the crowd, because it's the final day and the Americans have things in hand, and he wants the people who stick it out to have a good show. Well, his ploy works. Jack goes to the captain—who just happens to be Arnold

Palmer—and says, 'I've got to take on that bloody Barnes again,' or words to that effect. Well, just by chance, I guess, we *are* paired up again.

"Jack fixes me with a glare and says, 'You beat me once, but I'll be damned if you'll beat me twice.' My knees should've been shaking, but I figured, 'What the hell, let's just play,' and wouldn't you know, I win again. Jack's fit to be tied, but great sportsman he is, he puts his hand out. I was rather stunned, actually."

At Royal Lytham and St. Annes in 1977, another format change—a reduction in total matches to twenty—didn't faze the United States, which won 12½–7½.

However, 1977's Ryder Cup would have a profound impact on the future of the competition. Part of that impact was the first appearance of Nick Faldo, all of twenty years old (the youngest ever to play for Great Britain) on the British team. Faldo went 3–0 to begin his record-breaking career.

"I'm proud of the way I played in my debut," Faldo told us. "In my favor was the course, Royal Lytham—unfortunately, the last links venue—and I had a great partner in Peter Oosterhuis. And to be fair to Tiger Woods, there was a lot less pressure and hype in 1977."

The most profound change that occurred in 1977 came about as a result of a conversation Nicklaus had with the head of the PGA of Great Britain. It resulted in Ryder Cup eligibility being expanded beyond Great Britain to all of Europe.

The 1979 Ryder Cup at the Greenbrier in West Virginia was the first to include players from other European countries. The United States won running away again, 17–11. Larry Nelson starred, winning all five of his matches, four of them against a Spanish newcomer who also was brash, self-confident, handsome, strong, charismatic, and extremely talented. Seve Ballesteros would come to symbolize the changing face and personality of the U.S. opponent.

The second Ryder Cup crisis was coming to a head: For many golf fans and even some of the players, the every-other-year contests were losing their luster. While some individual matches were competitive, overall the results of the Matches—the Americans winning big—were dull and rather routine. As nice as it might be for American fans to see the U.S. teams loom so large both home and away, the Ryder Cup as an event had declined in excitement. Its future faced the biggest threat since the start of World War II.

The team that truly epitomizes the American domination was the one fielded in 1981 at the Walton Heath Golf Club in England. At this time the U.S. golf wave crested, and Hogan's appraisal of the U.S. team was never truer than it was that year. All the queen's horses couldn't have pulled out a victory against this imposing squad.

The captain was Dave Marr, and in his stable were Jack Nicklaus, Lee Trevino, Larry Nelson, Tom Watson, Tom Kite, Raymond Floyd, Hale Irwin, Johnny Miller, Ben Crenshaw, Bruce Lietzke, Jerry Pate, and Bill Rogers. (Perhaps hoping to recapture the magic of the height of American glory, Crenshaw chose Lietzke and Rogers to be assistant captains for the 1999 Match.) Marr must have felt like the managers of the Yankees filling out lineup cards in 1927, 1961, or 1998.

In total the players on the U.S. team had won thirty-six majors. It didn't help the home team's cause that in a controversial move Tony Jacklin, who had earned seventeen Ryder Cup points (the most by any British player up to that time), was not selected as a captain's pick after failing to qualify for the team, and Seve Ballesteros, who had won his first Masters the year before, was declared ineligible for not having participated enough on that year's European PGA Tour.

That Friday, September 18, 1981, started out well enough for Europe as the four morning foursomes were split. Things got even better that afternoon, when the United States won only 1½ out of 4 points in the fourball matches. As Saturday dawned, the home team had to feel pretty good about having faced the American might and being in the lead, 4½–3½.

Then came the deluge. The U.S. squad took three out of the morning's four foursomes. The afternoon was a disaster for the local boys, as they lost all four fourball matches.

On Sunday the good news was that the Europeans won four singles matches—the bad news was that they lost eight. The final score was 18½–9½. It wasn't the widest victory margin in Ryder Cup history, but the one-sided nature of the American domination can be seen in the fact that on Saturday and Sunday, the U.S. team won 15–5.

For Dave Marr, teaming Jack Nicklaus and Tom Watson had to be as thrilling as writing Ruth and Gehrig or Mantle and Maris on a lineup card. They teamed up to notch three victories—downing Nick Faldo and Peter Oosterhuis 4 and 3, Jose Maria Canizares and Des Smyth 3 and 2, and Bernhard Langer and Manuel Pinero 3 and 2. Nicklaus was 4–0 overall after winning his lone singles match 5 and 3.

The icing on the cake was the continued strong Ryder Cup play of Larry Nelson, who was also 4–0. "I remember that I did well, but that's not what has most stayed in my mind about the Ryder Cup," Nelson, a talented yet modest man now excelling on the Senior PGA Tour, told us. "I remember most being in the locker room after we won and feeling so proud of being part of a team, and I had done my part, as had others, in the team effort. It's an unusual feeling for a professional golfer to think of team first, but doing that is what means the most to me about the Ryder Cup."

An irony about the '81 U.S. runaway win was that a crucial change four years earlier in the event's rules was already having an effect. Never again would the Americans romp in the Ryder Cup—in fact, they would win only three of the next eight Matches through the "Trauma at Valderrama."

The combined might of Europe's talented new players was about to toss Hogan's statement on the trash heap of history.

Chapter 5

CONTINENTAL COMEBACK

No one could have predicted that the informal conversation Jack Nicklaus had with PGA officials in Great Britain in 1977 would lead to the most sweeping and positive change ever to affect the Ryder Cup. Happily, the resulting inclusion of European players not only allowed the Ryder Cup to survive the crisis of declining interest but paved the way for it to become the popular international event it is today and certainly will be tomorrow.

Ironically, perhaps more than any American, it was Nicklaus who paid the price for the influx of new players. Still, he doesn't regret pushing for the change. "When I'm asked what my favorite Ryder Cup moment is, it's funny but I don't think of something that happened on the course," Nicklaus said. "Making it more inclusive is my best Ryder Cup memory."

The conversation was prompted by the familiar outcome in the 1977 Match. That September the Ryder Cup was being contested at Royal Lytham and St. Annes in England, and once again, twenty years after their last loss and with only one tie in between, the U.S. team was in the process of winning easily.

Dow Finsterwald, four-time team member and owner of an admirable 9–3–1 Ryder Cup record, was the captain. His roster included players who were at or approaching their peak: Nicklaus, Raymond Floyd, Hale Irwin, Dave Stockton, Lanny Wadkins, and Tom Watson. That the final-day singles matches ended in a 5–5 tie was only a formality, because the United States had jumped out to a 7½–2½ lead after two days and would keep the Cup in the States with a 12½–7½ thrashing.

It wasn't that Great Britain and Ireland couldn't put a good team out on the historic course. Brian Barnes, Bernard Gallacher, Mark James, Eamonn Darcy, Peter Oosterhuis, and Tony Jacklin were all strong competitors, and the 20-year-old rookie Nick Faldo went 3–0 in the '77 Matches. Yet it was clear that something was missing. The U.S. teams were getting more powerful, and their opponents just weren't gaining ground.

During the weekend a past president of the PGA of America, Henry Poe, and Lord Derby, president of the PGA of Great Britain, had discussed how to improve the level of competition. However, the clincher came when Nicklaus approached Lord Derby at the Clifton Arms Hotel and argued for widening the selection process to include European players.

Lord Derby's response was "Jack, I think it's a good idea. Leave it with me."

No doubt a suggestion from a player with the prestige and track record of Jack Nicklaus demanded consideration. Why did Nicklaus make this suggestion? He has always been a strong competitor and a guardian of the integrity of golf. The Ryder Cup Matches had become predictable for fans and less challenging for the players, so making them true contests would be good for the game and, specifically, for the Ryder Cup as an international showcase, which it had become after half a century.

Having the suggestion come from the American side made changing the rules so drastically a more likely prospect, because it didn't seem like sour grapes on the part of the British and Irish. Officials on that side of the Atlantic were taking note of players from other European countries, such as Severiano Ballesteros (who would capture the British Open before the next Ryder Cup Match), who were winning tournaments not just locally but beyond their borders. Clearly, the time to take advantage of an expanded talent pool had come.

The British PGA took the idea to the descendants of Samuel Ryder, who approved it, and officially the selection procedure was widened so "that European members" of the British PGA European Tournament Division Order of Merit would "be entitled to play on the team."

Not every member of Ryder's family was completely sold. "I'm convinced that, had Sam Ryder been alive, he would have resisted this decision," declared his nephew, Thomas Anderson Davis. "However, this decision by the trustees detracts not one jot from the spirit in which the Cup was conceived, prepared, and presented."

This expansion was an enormous change. The talent pool that would oppose the U.S. team suddenly became the size of an entire continent. Players from every country in Europe were eligible to earn Ryder Cup points.

"The players elsewhere in Europe were very excited about this development," recalled Jose Maria Canizares, who played on four of the first five European Ryder Cup teams. "It added another goal for us to achieve. The schedule then in Europe was somewhat limited, and to have something added to the plate was greeted very highly."

The potential audience for the Ryder Cup Matches ballooned from tens of millions to hundreds of millions. With more people to support their countrymen's efforts, the visibility of the event soared. Everyone and every group associated with the Ryder Cup would benefit—except, of course, those marginal British and Irish golfers who would be replaced on the rosters by better European players.

The change in Ryder Cup rules couldn't have occurred at a better time. More than ever before, the Continent was producing players with the talent, skills, and determination to compete on the international stage. Players on the European Tour had to cope with different courses, climates, accommodations, crowds, and so on, meaning that as they gained experience, they also gained unprecedented resiliency and adaptability.

The decade following 1977 saw European players not only winning consistently but winning in the United States—and winning majors. Ballesteros won the Masters in '80 and '83, and Bernhard Langer of Germany won the Masters in '85 (and would win it again in '93).

"I supported the idea of introducing European players," Nick Faldo told us. "What we achieved in the 1980s, in contrast to the 1960s and 1970s, could not have been achieved without the likes of Seve, Langer, and Olazabal."

He continued: "Today there are some fine British players— Lee Westwood, Darren Clarke, and Colin Montgomerie, for example—but a purely 'British team' would still have very little chance of beating the United States. 'David versus Goliath' contests are intriguing, but less exciting. 'Europe versus U.S.A.' makes for a better Match, a real clash of continents."

The emergence of this fresh batch of talented players would indeed break the four-decade American stranglehold on the Ryder Cup.

The first European team was fielded in 1979 at the Greenbrier in White Sulphur Springs, West Virginia. Initially the new composition of the team didn't make much difference, with the U.S. squad—captained by Billy Casper and containing top guns like Hale Irwin, Tom Kite, Gil Morgan, Larry Nelson, Lee Trevino, Lanny Wadkins, and Fuzzy Zoeller—winning 17–11. And in fact the European team wasn't very different from the previous British and Irish teams, with the exception of Antonio Garrido and the 22-year-old Ballesteros.

"I didn't get a strong sense of the opposition being that much changed," recalled Casper, who holds the record for most points (23.5) by a U.S. player in Ryder Cup history. "But we never took them for granted, and I especially wasn't going to as captain. The overall score wasn't that close, but many matches went down to the wire. As it turned out, the scales were soon to tip the other way."

At Walton Heath in 1981, the European roster was a bit more inclusive, with Jose Maria Canizares, Manuel Pinero, and Bernhard Langer joining the team, though it was without Seve

Ballesteros and Tony Jacklin. However, it probably wouldn't have mattered who was in the home-team lineup that year, given the awesome artillery that the United States had.

The impact of the rules change wouldn't really be felt until 1983, when the U.S. team, captained by Jack Nicklaus of all people, received quite a shock.

After the 1981 debacle it was time to change captains of the European team. John Jacobs was shown the door. Jacklin was still simmering over not being placed on the '81 team (though this is a bit like not having been allowed on the *Titanic*), yet he sucked it up and agreed to be captain for the '83 Ryder Cup Match.

Jacklin was not just a hard-nosed competitor who knew what it took to win; he was a veteran Ryder Cupper. He had participated in seven Matches, including the 1969 team that had tied the Americans. On the surface, his 13–14–8 Ryder record may not appear illustrious, but thirteen victories and eight ties is a remarkable achievement when you consider that (with one exception) he played on teams that were routinely trounced. He had endured loss after loss undaunted, and after suffering for sixteen years, he was especially keen on winning in 1983.

Right off the bat, Jacklin was a more aggressive captain. In agreeing to lead the team, he demanded that the European team receive the same first-class treatment as that to which the U.S. teams were accustomed. This included flying to the United States on the Concorde, staying in first-class hotels, wearing fine uniforms, having their own caddies accompany them, and in other respects not being made to feel like Ryder Cup afterthoughts. If Europe was serious about winning the Ryder Cup, it had to make its team as much of a priority as the PGA of America made its team. Desperate to change an unhappy history and to keep Jacklin on board, the European Ryder Cup Committee agreed.

"The most significant thing to happen to the European teams in the 1980s was that Tony Jacklin was appointed captain," stated John Hopkins, a writer for *The London Times* who has covered every Ryder Cup since 1981. "He agreed to do it only on the understanding that everything would be upgraded and improved. He went out of his way to try and make sure that the players felt that they matched the Americans in every respect, not just the ability to play golf. That was a tremendous psychological boost.

"Suddenly money was made available, and all the things Jacklin wanted were made available," Hopkins continued. "This certainly made it easier for him to turn around and get the best out of his players—and, of course, he was getting better players."

According to Jacklin, his becoming captain, and the eventual turnaround of the Europeans' fortunes, dates back to 1979 because of the combination of including players from outside Great Britain and Ireland, substantially increasing the talent pool, and that Jacklin was unhappy with the way the team was run.

"It was second and third class all the way, and there were a couple of players who obviously didn't want to be there," he recalled. "So at best we made sort of a ragtag presentation, and predictably got our butts kicked again."

Jacklin was unhappy over the biennial defeats and that nothing appeared to be changing, and then furious in 1981 when he wasn't picked to be on the team at all. "Of all people, Mark James got chosen in my stead," Jacklin said. "That was my reward for trying to make things right in 1979, and all my previous efforts. For fourteen years I'd given my heart and soul to the thing, and this is what I got. I felt I'd been betrayed, and they could stick the Ryder Cup in their ears."

Coupled with that, the Ryder Cup Committee in Europe decided that Severiano Ballesteros was not eligible to be on the Ryder Cup team. Then, adding insult to injury, the committee suggested that Jacklin get to attend the 1981 Ryder Cup as an official.

"The decision about Seve, who was arguably the best player in the world at the time, was sheer insanity," Jacklin said. "He was royally pissed off and threw his hands up and walked away—completely understandable. The man deserved better and was treated awfully. I was pissed off about the way I was treated. So in 1981 we both walked off, ignored Walton Heath, and went about our own business."

For Tony Jacklin, participation in the Ryder Cup was no more than a memory. He had more tournaments around the world to win and personal interests to pursue, so like Cincinnatus he tended to his farm—until the call came, and it was time to rescue Rome.

"In April 1983 I was playing in a tournament in Leeds and Ken Schofield came up to me and said he'd talked to the lads and they wanted me as captain," Jacklin said. "Well, you could've knocked me over with a feather. How now, so *I'm* supposed to turn things round?

"I thought about it for a long while and realized we were never going to win the way we were going about it, disorganized and believing we were inferior. We were 2-down before we ever hit a ball by the way we approached the thing. I also realized the Ryder Cup is going to be around a lot longer than I am, and there are things to be set right.

"Fine," Jacklin continued, "I'm still mad as hell, I didn't care what I said, so next day I told them here's what I want: Concorde, cashmere, caddies, first-class accommodations, three captain's picks, and such and such. Ken said they'd have to think about it. Then he came back, they had said yes, I asked for more, they kept saying yes. Clearly, the attitude had changed and *everyone* over here was tired of losing. We were just not going to take it anymore."

Compiling the 1983 European team in a very short amount of time, Jacklin saw he had a strong nucleus in Faldo, Langer, Woosnam, Lyle, Canizares, Torrance, and a couple of others. But there was a major ingredient missing: Ballesteros, who by 1983 had become the most formidable player in the world. The captain knew it might be a waste of time to play without him.

"I went to Lord Derby and said, 'What about Seve?'" Jacklin said. "He replied, 'Since you're the captain, he's your problem now.'"

Jacklin hunted up Seve at the Prince of Wales Tournament at Royal Birkdale and took him to breakfast, which turned into a two-hour-plus meeting. "His eggs got cold," Jacklin recalled. "I was mad, but he was beyond anger. He was laughing at the whole thing, and it suddenly flashed to me that if we were ever going to have parity or better in the Ryder Cup, we've got to have the best of the best, world-class players, on board all at the same time—Seve, Nick Faldo, Ian Woosnam, Bernhard Langer, and the rest of that core group. If we weren't going to do that, then why bother? Let's *win*. And after enough persuasion, Seve agreed."

Aside from Jacklin's leadership, the European team that arrived at the PGA National Golf Club in Palm Beach Gardens, Florida, in 1983 was probably the strongest talentwise since before World War II. Ballesteros and Nick Faldo were both 26 and were starting to dominate tournaments (Seve had won his second Masters that April), and Faldo was on his fourth Ryder Cup team. Veterans Canizares, Bernard Gallacher, and Sandy Lyle (he would win a British Open in '85 and a Masters in '88) were back. Also on board were Langer, Sam Torrance of Scotland, and Ian Woosnam of Wales. The visitors had muscles to flex.

Not that the Americans were about to roll over. After all, the U.S. team had lost only one Match in half a century and had never lost in the States, so maybe it didn't matter all that much who showed up to oppose them. Among the battleships Nicklaus could choose from were Ben Crenshaw, Raymond Floyd, Tom Kite, Craig Stadler, Curtis Strange, Lanny Wadkins, and Tom Watson—not too shabby.

Still, it was almost not enough. On Friday, October 14, 1983, the Europeans clawed their way to a 4½–3½ lead. Two high-profile contests were Crenshaw and Watson defeating Gallacher and Lyle 5 and 4, then Faldo and Langer besting Wadkins and Stadler 4 and 2 during the morning foursomes. The following day the Americans made a comeback, but not a huge one, squeaking by 4½–3½ to knot the Match at 8–8.

Not having a lead going into Sunday was an unusual position for the United States, so clearly this Ryder Cup was not like the ones from years past. As in 1969 but this time without clubs in their hands, Nicklaus and Jacklin were going toe to toe, and the Match would go down to the wire.

That night Nicklaus growled to his players, "I do *not* want to be remembered as the first captain of an American team to lose on American soil." No one in the room needed more motivation than an angry Bear.

The singles matches on Sunday were an epic struggle, each team firing broadsides. Fuzzy Zoeller halved with Ballesteros—it could have been a U.S. win, but Seve made one of the greatest shots in Ryder Cup history, a bunker shot from 240 yards out to the green on the eighteenth hole to salvage the tie. Europe forged ahead, with Faldo beating Jay Haas 2 and 1 and Gil Morgan losing to Langer 2-up.

Then it was the Americans' turn: Bob Gilder defeated Gordon Brand, Sr., 2-up; Crenshaw downed Lyle 3 and 1; and Calvin Peete (until Tiger Woods, he and Lee Elder, in '79, were the only two African-Americans to play on a U.S. Ryder Cup team) won over Brian Waites 1-up.

It went back and forth the rest of the afternoon, with Paul Way beating Strange, Kite and Torrance halving, Stadler over Woosnam, Ken Brown defeating Floyd, and Watson downing Gallacher.

The deciding match was Jose Maria Canizares and Lanny Wadkins. As they teed off at the eighteenth, the Spaniard was up by one. Later in the hole, Wadkins made a shot that is also considered one of the best in Ryder Cup history, a sixty-yard pitching wedge into the wind that landed a foot from the pin. He birdied, Canizares parred, they halved the match, and the United States won 14½–13½.

While the United States had needed only 14 points to tie the Match and retain the cup, a tie on their home turf would have surely felt like a loss.

Jack Nicklaus was so relieved to escape with a win against the suddenly more dogged European team that he knelt and kissed Wadkins's divot mark. The Europeans went home feeling disappointed but far from defeated.

"Right after the Match Seve and Faldo went to the other players and encouraged them not to be down," Hopkins said. "They were already thinking about 1985, and what had just happened showed they had the stuff to win. With Seve, Faldo, and Jacklin, you had a group that simply would not lose anymore."

"We were very disappointed that we didn't win in 1983 at West Palm Beach," Jacklin said. "We were so close, then Lanny [Wadkins] hit that stunning shot on the last hole, and I can remember Jack [Nicklaus] kissing that divot like it was yesterday. What was kind of irritating and funny at the same time is that the British press was used to us losing, so on Sunday they all took off to Disney World. But they must've gotten word that we had a real chance, because they all came rushing back, and during the post-Match press conference we were facing these fellows in suits holding pens and notebooks wearing Mickey Mouse and Goofy hats, T-shirts, and bags over their shoulders."

"Coming so close was the extra bit of motivation we needed," Canizares said. "We realized we could take it to the next level and win. For so long the Ryder Cup was dominated, it was almost viewed as a losing cause. And then, when we knocked on the door, we realized the goal was in reach. It especially helped the younger and lesser-known players in that actually slaying the giant, if you will, meant immediate global recognition. We all felt that if we came so close this time, we could win next time."

The tide was indeed turning. Nicklaus knew it. "We will not be the favorites when we go to the Belfry in two years," he said. "This score was no fluke."

As usual, Jack was right.

The Americans could reasonably expect to get things back on track the next time around. For the 1985 Ryder Cup, they fielded another superstrong team: Floyd, Kite, Peete, Stadler, Strange, Wadkins, and Zoeller, joined by Andy North (who had won his second U.S. Open that year), Hal Sutton, Peter Jacobsen, Mark O'Meara, and Hubert Green (winner of the PGA Championship the month before). The captain was proven winner Lee Trevino.

With just a few exceptions, the European team was the same as the one two years earlier, though perhaps stronger, with Bernhard Langer having won the Masters and Sandy Lyle having won the British Open earlier in the year. Jacklin, again at the helm, reminded them of how close they had come in '83. This time, though, the team was playing at the Belfry in England, the home course of the British PGA, codesigned by former Ryder Cupper Peter Alliss. A large crowd, sensing that this could be the first time since 1957 that the Ryder Cup stayed on this side of the Atlantic, turned out and cheered lustily.

It was probably time for a better showing anyway, but the European team was about to fully realize the talent pool and the passion of their golfers. Yes, there were strong contributions from Langer and Costantino Rocca, but much of this heightened ability and will to win came from Spain.

Called the "Spanish Armada" (later, this would refer specifically to the pairing of Ballesteros and Olazabal), Spain was represented during Europe's surge by six players: Seve Ballesteros, Antonio Garrido (whose son was on the '97 team), Manuel Pinero, Jose Maria Canizares, Jose Rivero, and Jose Maria Olazabal. Combined, they won ninety-five times on the European Tour, and in the Ryder Cup Matches they combined for 51.5 points.

The skills, experiences, personalities, and idiosyncrasies of the Spanish golfers, who fully supported each other and had a mutual desire to defeat the Americans, was a new obstacle for the U.S. players. No more of that British reserve and "Well done, old boy." This Spanish Armada was not going to sink. As it turned out, they would help in a big way to bring the Ryder Cup back across the Atlantic.

It didn't start out quite that way in the 1985 Match, though. With Peete and Kite, Wadkins and Floyd, Stadler and Sutton, and Floyd and Wadkins teaming up for wins, and Stadler and Sutton halving their second match, the Americans ended the first day with a 4½–3½ lead. So much for being the home team.

Then came a truly Continental comeback on Saturday, September 14. The duos of Sam Torrance and Howard Clark,

Paul Way and Ian Woosnam, Jose Maria Canizares and Jose Rivero, Seve Ballesteros and Manuel Pinero, and Bernhard Langer and Ken Brown won their matches, and Langer and Sandy Lyle halved theirs with Stadler and Strange.

In one of the most crucial missteps in Ryder Cup history, Craig Stadler missed a fourteen-inch putt that would have resulted in the United States winning the match and perhaps slowing down the European momentum. He had carelessly taken the short putt for granted and given the ball a casual swipe, sending it trickling past the hole. There was a stunned silence, then the crowd roared.

"I'm convinced it was the turning point," Jacklin said. "Our team seemed to take it as meaning the Americans weren't supermen after all, that they were as susceptible to pressure as we were—in other words, human. It's a cruel game."

"Every one of us has missed a putt of that length, more than once," said Curtis Strange, who was paired with Stadler in that match. "But you do it in the Ryder Cup, and it stays with you forever."

With only the duos of O'Meara and Wadkins and Strange and Jacobsen winning matches for the United States, the European team notched 5½ points on Saturday. Going into the final day, the home team was ahead 9–7.

It was not unheard of for the Americans to face Sunday holding the short end of the club. In both the '73 and '83 Matches, the two teams had been tied entering Sunday, and defeat was possible. But the U.S. players had always been strong in singles, so unless they faced too large a deficit to overcome—and 9–7 wasn't it— they could be confident about keeping the cup in the States.

Such thoughts apparently didn't impress Jacklin's troops. For the first time since 1929, the Americans were given a thorough drubbing on the final day—and this with Ballesteros only halving his match with Tom Kite and Faldo losing his to Hubert Green.

Convincing wins by Pinero, Way, Lyle, Langer, Torrance, Clark, and Canizares wrested the Ryder Cup from the twenty-eight-year American grasp in a 16½–11½ triumph. Curtis Strange wouldn't give in; he tried to stop the stampede by winning his singles match—but it was too little, too late.

"I was very much aware during my match [with Fuzzy Zoeller] what was happening, that we were about to win the Ryder Cup," Canizares recalled. "I saw the scoreboard, I was talking to Tony [Jacklin], yet I didn't want to be distracted. The Americans were talented and very dangerous, and I didn't want to do anything that would allow the momentum to shift. I just knew I had to get it done, and I did. And we did—finally."

It was a very long ride home for the U.S. squad. Every member had lost tournaments in frustrating, even crushing ways, but this was very different. As a team, playing for their country, and with a legacy of only three losses in fifty-six years, they had lost.

For the Europeans, on the other side, the outcome was pure joy. After Sam Torrance had made an eighteen-foot birdie putt on the eighteenth to clinch his singles match, he raised his arms and burst into tears. The entire team leaped and screamed in jubilation along with the partisan and especially proud crowd.

The grin on Tony Jacklin's face as he held the trophy aloft was almost as big as the Ryder Cup itself. His players were delirious with joy, hugging, burying their heads in each other's shoulders, swinging their wives around, raising clenched fists to the swarming spectators. Team Europe had finally come into its own.

Well, the United States had lost before and then immediately snapped back into shape. The '85 outcome would, presumably, be a different story two years later, when the Europeans had to come to the Muirfield Village Golf Club in Ohio, a course built by Jack Nicklaus and where Nicklaus would be captain of the home team. Among the players he would pencil in were Mark Calcavecchia, Ben Crenshaw, Tom Kite, Larry Nelson, U.S. Open winner Scott Simpson, Payne Stewart, Curtis Strange, and Lanny Wadkins. Surely the visitors would be devoured in the Golden Bear's den.

But the close call in 1983 and the European victory in 1985 really had signaled a change. In addition to Tony Jacklin having instilled a steely resolve in the former patsies, the caliber of the European players had kept creeping upward, and a solid nucleus had formed that would contribute to the United States winning only two Ryder Cup Matches from 1985 through 1997.

While some of the supporting cast would change during the next decade, the core of the European team that jetted across the Atlantic in 1987 would remain intact. With Palmer, Nicklaus, Trevino, Irwin, Miller, Watson, and other American greats in the second half of their PGA Tour careers, these players were the ones winning consistently on several continents:

- *Seve Ballesteros of Spain:* He is the winner of seventy-two tournaments worldwide, including British Opens in '79, '84, and '88 and the Masters in '80 and '83. During the 1980s he was the most feared competitor in the sport.
- *Nick Faldo of England:* He has thirty-three international victories, including British Opens in '87, '90, and '92 and the Masters in '89, '90, and '96. (The last is the most memorable, with a crushing comeback win over Greg Norman.) He had been the first spark in the dark days of the 1970s that turned into the European flame of the 1980s and 1990s.
- *Bernhard Langer of Germany:* He is one of the most consistent players in the world (he won at least a tourney a year in 1980–95) and is capable of brilliance. He has fifty-one worldwide wins and two green jackets from winning at Augusta in '85 and '93. A steady, respected teammate.
- *Jose Maria Olazabal of Spain:* Only 21 in 1987, his talent and youth and Ballesteros's talent and experience would combine for a lot of wins. He won the Masters in '94.
- *Sam Torrance of Scotland:* This very popular veteran player would get especially pumped for the Ryder Cup. He is the winner of more than two dozen international events.
- *Ian Woosnam of Wales:* He has forty-one wins around the world, including the Masters in '91, and he led the European

PGA Tour in money in '87 and '90. His singles record is not great, but he is very strong as a teammate in foursomes and fourball.

This group forged a solid center of resilient players who were challenging and to some extent dismantling American supremacy in golf. Winning regularly at the Masters showed that these Europeans could go anywhere and beat the best. Even better for Europe, as it turned out, the nucleus expanded over the years to include Costantino Rocca of Italy, Mark James of England, and Colin Montgomerie of Scotland.

"You have to remember too that this was a time of significant change in international golf," said John Hopkins. "Many of the top European players played regularly around the world and especially in the United States. Some of them, like Per-Ulrik Johansson and Colin Montgomerie, had even gone to university there. They know what America's like, and the travel and being there is not a big deal anymore."

So the team that arrived in Ohio in September 1987 was not full of lambs heading for slaughter. However, it hardly seemed possible that a Nicklaus-led team could be defeated on his home course, or that the United States would lose two Ryder Cup Matches in a row.

But that is what happened. And on the very first day, the Europeans delivered what would prove to be the knockout blow.

Of the eight matches played that Friday, the Americans won only two. Faldo and Woosnam combined to win two matches, as did Ballesteros and Olazabal, and Lyle and Langer and even Gordon Brand, Jr., and Jose Rivero were victorious. There was no powerful U.S. comeback on Saturday. Though the score was closer, 4½–3½ Europe, as Sunday dawned the visitors were well ahead 10½–5½. Lyle and Langer and Ballesteros and Olazabal were again unbeatable.

The United States did rally on Sunday, but it couldn't overcome such a huge lead. In the singles matches Andy Bean, Calcavecchia, Stewart, Simpson, Kite, and Wadkins won, and

Larry Mize, Nelson, and Sutton halved, but the 7½ points didn't do it. With Ballesteros going 4–1 and Faldo 3½–1, Europe held on 15–13. For the first time, the United States had lost a Ryder Cup Match in the United States. (Ironically, Faldo had taken up golf at 14 after watching Jack Nicklaus win the British Open at the original Muirfield.)

"Winning in 1985 was enormous," Jacklin said. "Then it was exceeded. There's nothing like the first time for anything, and in 1987 we won for the first time on American soil, and nothing can top that. It was *the* sweetest moment of all."

"Captaining a U.S. team to its first loss at home at Muirfield Village in 1987 has to be my Ryder Cup low," Nicklaus reflected. "Looking back, though, I'm glad I was in that position, because I wouldn't have wanted anyone else to go through all the criticism and anger and second-guessing that came after that Match."

Though the news was not happy for the American audience, it was the best outcome for the Ryder Cup. Certainly Nicklaus's team losing at home—he *did* become the first American captain with this distinction—made headlines around the world, significantly raising the Cup's profile. The biennial event was much more interesting and exciting now that the outcome of the Matches was no longer predictable.

"I think the change in '79 is what has made the Ryder Cup what it is today," Nicklaus said. "If we hadn't made that change, the Ryder Cup would be the same event that we used to have, which was dominated by the U.S. and not a very good competition."

But having to "bear" the brunt of the change in 1987? "It sure was disappointing," Nicklaus replied. "It was inevitable that a European win in the United States would happen—but I would have preferred it be another time."

"While I understood what Jack was going through, the painful experience, I can't think of anyone else who has shoulders broad enough to bear the burden," said rival captain Tony Jacklin. "He's such a strong man, mentally as well as physically, that if someone had to cope with such a loss, it's best it's him, that he takes it for

America, because he will always come back, he is such a proud man and fierce competitor."

Also, with Europe having won the Ryder Cup twice in a row, it was clear to all that this event was now a real competition and that anything could happen. Never again could U.S. teams and sports fans take the Matches for granted.

The massacre at Muirfield served as an earthshaking wake-up call for the United States. Unlike the loss in 1957 and the tie in 1969, which were viewed as aberrations, losing two Matches in a row and losing at home for the first time ever meant that the tradition of American domination was in very serious jeopardy, if not over.

For the United States, the 1989 team veered off in a new and perhaps dangerous direction. Previously the majority of team members had experienced Ryder Cup victories and at crunch time could hearken back to those wins as motivation, a source of pride, and a way to intimidate opponents. But that chain had now been broken. With only four exceptions (Kite, Strange, Wadkins, and Watson), the U.S. team that headed to the Belfry in '89 was composed of players who were untested in Ryder Cup competition or who had experienced only defeat.

Clearly, the Americans had to regroup. Raymond Floyd was appointed captain. Making the team on points were Paul Azinger, Chip Beck, Mark Calcavecchia (who had just won the British Open), Fred Couples, Ken Green, Tom Kite, Mark McCumber, Mark O'Meara, Payne Stewart (winner of the PGA Championship the month before), and Curtis Strange. Floyd, looking for leadership and a strong track record, selected Lanny Wadkins and Tom Watson to be on the team.

Jacklin was back as the European captain. At the time he had an astonishing record against the United States—two wins and one very close loss. Playing at home and with Ballesteros, Canizares, Faldo, James, Langer, Olazabal, Torrance, and Woosnam on board, there would be less than a warm reception for the visitors.

This turned out to be true. American players and fans were still smarting over the boisterous, beer-filled celebration at Muirfield in '87. A record crowd (for a European Match) showed up at the Belfry and let the U.S. squad know what they thought of the happier turn of events in the Ryder Cup.

Adding to the festive and partisan atmosphere were the more than two hundred tents and similar structures, covering 350,000 square feet, that had been erected by the organizers and sponsors, the largest such creation for any sport in Great Britain. Again, while the two losses were bad news for the U.S. team, elsewhere they had resulted in unprecedented popularity for the Ryder Cup. For the first time a golf tournament in Europe was sold out.

Feeling as if the deck were stacked against them, Floyd sought to bolster his troops by borrowing Ben Hogan's line. At the pre-competition gala he described the U.S. team as "the twelve greatest players in the world." This didn't go over all that well—Nick Faldo offered that Jacklin "should get up and introduce Seve as the thirteenth best player in the world"—and the home team set out to prove him wrong.

The results were mixed. The Americans didn't lose. But once again the Ryder Cup was Europe's to own.

It was a seesaw battle at the Belfry. On Friday Europe came out ahead 5–3, with the home team winning all four afternoon fourball matches. On Saturday the teams played to a standstill, 4–4, mostly thanks to the duo of Paul Azinger and Chip Beck, who won their two matches, defeating Gordon Brand, Jr., and Sam Torrance in the morning and then the formidable Nick Faldo and Ian Woosnam in the afternoon.

But a tie on Saturday wasn't enough—the United States was down 9–7 going into the last day.

Beck again came up big, beating Bernhard Langer in their singles match. Then Tom Kite beat Howard Clark and Paul Azinger banished Seve Ballesteros in a very tense, bitter match that to this day leaves the two players barely speaking to each other because of the rules disputes between them during eighteen holes.

Then it was Europe's turn. Wins by Mark James; Jose Maria Olazabal; Ronan Rafferty; Christy O'Connor, Jr. (he had last played on the Ryder Cup team in 1975, two years after his uncle's final appearance); and Jose Maria Canizares put Europe back in front and appeared to give the European team the momentum to turn the Match into a rout.

It was time for the United States to suck it up and either salvage a tie or go down swinging. Ryder Cup rookie Mark McCumber helped the cause by downing Brand 1-up. Then the veterans took over. Tom Watson beat Sam Torrance 3 and 1. Lanny Wadkins put it to Nick Faldo 1-up.

Ultimately, Curtis Strange saved the day for his team. Down to Ian Woosnam, Strange showed his mettle by birdieing the fifteenth, sixteenth, and seventeenth holes, then hit a 2-iron to eight feet of the hole on 18 to finish off Woosie 2-up. The U.S. team captured the singles matches 7–5 and managed a tie, 14–14. The crowd, though disappointed after thinking a third victory in a row was imminent, cheered the American effort.

The bad news, of course, was that the Ryder Cup stayed with the previous winner. Jacklin could close out his career as captain by losing only one of four Matches to the United States. The Americans had not won since 1983 and hadn't dominated since 1981. This was *really* serious.

The U.S. team's increasing desire to regain the Ryder Cup, the fact that the Match would be played at home, and recent world events made the 1991 competition perhaps the fiercest in the event's history. The Ryder Cup Match on Kiawah Island, South Carolina, wasn't dubbed the "War at the Shore" for nothing.

Bernard Gallacher, a very tough player who had been on eight Ryder Cup teams, was chosen as the European captain. Not only was the veteran European nucleus back (with Gallacher wisely making Faldo and Olazabal captain's picks), but that core was being strengthened with the addition of Colin Montgomerie. At 28 he was just about to enter his peak years.

For the Yanks, the captain was Dave Stockton, who had had a strong PGA Tour record, had been a member of the Ryder Cup team two times (with a 3–1–1 record), and was soon to embark on a lucrative Senior PGA Tour career. Stockton had on his side Azinger, Calcavecchia, Couples, Irwin, Wayne Levi, O'Meara, Steve Pate, Corey Pavin, Stewart, and Wadkins. To add experience and a recent Ryder Cup winner, Stockton selected Raymond Floyd and Chip Beck to join the team.

The '91 Ryder Cup was played only a few months after the conclusion of the Persian Gulf War, which, unlike many other military conflicts since World War II, was a clear-cut American victory. Patriotic emotions connected to Operation Desert Storm were still running high and spilled over to the Ryder Cup. Fans were boisterous, they waved American flags and wore red, white, and blue clothing, and they aggressively demanded that the U.S. team recapture the Cup. A few players even wore camouflage jackets and hats.

The atmosphere and sentiment clearly meant it was time for the Americans to reassert themselves on the golf course and begin a new era of domination.

Whatever the political leanings of the U.S. players and their feelings about the Gulf War, it was impossible for them to be immune to the jingoistic and belligerent urgings of the crowd. The European team felt that they had entered a hostile environment and that the crowd was overlooking the fact that several European countries had been U.S. allies in the recent war. The focus on the spectators was more that the Americans were seen as underdogs and the opposing team was both cocky and not American.

The atmosphere became further charged when, at the gala dinner the night before the Match officially began, a video on the Ryder Cup Matches was shown—and there was hardly a mention of a non–U.S. player. For the British and the rest of the Europeans, being dismissed like that was a pretty nasty welcome.

"They [the Americans] were there to do or die," Faldo said. "They had to win at all costs. They were so hyped up [that] they couldn't care less if we left there with a bad taste in our mouths— and a lot of us did. When they showed that video, our new boys looked at us with eyes as big as saucers as if to say, 'What do we do now?' We were just sort of spitting blood."

As exciting a Match as the '91 event was, it was also a low point in Ryder Cup history. Winning, while important, had always been within the context of fair play, good sportsmanship, and mutual regard. In the "War at the Shore," however, the atmosphere was one of defeating the invaders and sending them home beaten and bowed. The tension before the very first drive on Friday was thicker than the hot, humid South Carolina air.

The U.S. team started out strong, though far from dominating. After the dynamic duo of Ballesteros and Olazabal downed Azinger and Beck, the teams of Wadkins and Irwin, Couples and Floyd, and Stewart and Calcavecchia roared back with wins.

As a member of the board of directors of the PGA of America, Bob Joyce, former head pro at the Southampton (Long Island) Golf Club, was an on-course observer during the 1991 Ryder Cup Match. In every Match there are two referees and two observers— one from the U.S. PGA and one from the European PGA—who accompany the players. The referees are there to interpret the rules; the observers watch for where each ball lands and if there are any circumstances, such as an unplayable lie, that bring a rule into play. At Kiawah Island, Joyce's partner was none other than Jimmy Patino, and that first day they were assigned to the match that pitted Paul Azinger and Chip Beck against Seve Ballesteros and Jose Maria Olazabal.

"There was already no love lost between Paul and Seve after Paul beat him in that bitter singles match at the Belfry in 1989," Joyce recalled. "So here you have two super-intense competitors who don't like each other, the whole 'War at the Shore' mentality surrounding the event, and the very first match of the Match. I have never seen two guys more agitated and committed to winning as on that day."

Aside from not conceding putts and refusing to speak to each other, Azinger switched to a different ball during the match. However, it was not discovered until two holes later, and Ballesteros was fit to be tied when told the rules dictate that a protest must be lodged within one hole of the alleged infraction. As 10,000 people watched, for twenty minutes on the tenth hole Seve argued his case with steam coming out of his ears.

"That set the tone for the whole weekend: Don't give an inch, and winning is all that matters," Joyce said. "It turned out that Seve and Olazabal won that match, and I have never seen a competitor more emotional than Azinger. He was just devastated by losing to Seve."

In the Friday afternoon fourball matches, Couples and Floyd won again (over Faldo and Woosnam), but so did Ballesteros and Olazabal. Combined with a win by Steven Richardson and Mark James (a surprising 5 and 4 trouncing over Pavin and Calcavecchia) and a halve by Torrance and David Feherty, the Europeans ended the day only slightly behind, 4½ to 3½.

The second day was almost a repeat of the first, though with a European twist. On Saturday morning the Americans shot out of the box. Azinger and O'Meara dusted David Gilford and Nick Faldo 7 and 6, Wadkins and Irwin put it to Feherty and Torrance 4 and 2, and Stewart and Calcavecchia got by James and Richardson 1-up. All that prevented a foursome sweep was Ballesteros and Olazabal winning the clash of the titans, beating Couples and Floyd 3 and 2.

Then it was the visitors' turn to launch a counterattack. With a halve against Ballesteros and Olazabal, only Stewart and Couples scored for the United States in the Saturday afternoon fourball matches. Victories by Woosnam and Paul Broadhurst, Langer and Montgomerie, and James and Richardson had earned the Europeans a tie, 8–8, by the end of the second day of competition. The Iraqis had been a lot easier to defeat.

That Sunday saw a rare occurrence in Ryder Cup history, putting a player in an envelope. Not literally—this phrase means that if a player is unable to perform due to injury, the captain of the other team places the name of one of his players in an envelope. If the player indeed can't play, the player in the envelope has to sit out too, and each team receives half a point.

In this instance Steve Pate had received some painful cuts and bruises in a car accident on his way to the gala dinner on Thursday night, and by Sunday he hadn't recovered enough to play his singles match. Gallacher put David Gilford in the envelope, which had to be embarrassing as well as frustrating. So before the first ball was struck on the final day, the score was 8½ to 8½.

The situation was frustrating too for Dave Stockton. Having Pate and Gilford sit out hurt his team more than Gallacher's. Not only was Gilford 0–2 in the Match, but the awarding of half a point to Europe put the visitors in a better position. As owners of the Ryder Cup, Europe needed only a tie to keep it. Now with 8½ points, the European team needed just 5½ points out of the eleven last-day matches to tie and retain the cup again.

Halfway through Sunday, things looked grim for the United States. Feherty beat Stewart 2 and 1, Faldo defeated Floyd 2-up, Montgomerie and Calcavecchia halved, and the pumped-up Ballesteros went 3 and 2 over Wayne Levi. The score was 12–9. Europe needed only 2 points in the remaining seven matches to jet home with the Ryder Cup. All the shouting and flag-waving might not make any difference at all.

Wounded and with their backs to the wall, the Americans stormed back. Pavin downed Richardson 2 and 1. Olazabal finally lost, to Azinger 2-up. Beck battled Woosnam and emerged with a 3 and 1 win. There was a setback when Broadhurst beat O'Meara 3 and 1, but Couples conquered Torrance 3 and 2, and that was also the score as Wadkins won over James.

It was 14–13 United States, and the 1993 Ryder Cup would be decided by the outcome of the last match between steel-nerved veterans Hale Irwin and Bernhard Langer. A halve by the United States would return the cup to the States—a win by Langer would keep it on the other side of the Atlantic.

The match turned out to be an epic struggle. Neither man gave an inch. As gutsy a grinder as Irwin is, one has to admire Langer's courage: The Ryder Cup was on the line, it was the last match of the weekend, the climate was exhausting for a European player, the crowd was hostile, and the entire golf world was watching. Hole after hole they went at it, and predictably it all came down to the eighteenth.

It wasn't one of Irwin's best moments. His approach shot took off and norked a spectator, his chip won't be seen on any future highlight videos, and his par putt was off by a foot. The pressure could get to anyone. Langer conceded Irwin's bogey putt. Now all he had to do was par to win the match and secure a tie for the Ryder Cup.

But Langer was not a machine. Despite his years of success and Ryder Cup experience, the eighteenth hole on September 29, 1991, on Kiawah Island was probably the biggest challenge of his career. He was left with a forty-five-foot putt for birdie. The ball slid six feet past the hole. A six-footer for par and the Ryder Cup, that's all. Langer lined it up, stood over the ball, got set, swung smoothly— and just missed. The Ryder Cup sailed back to the States.

It was a bitter pill for the European team to swallow, especially when being subjected to the whooping, hollering, and celebrating of the raucous fans. Honorably, and out of respect for Langer, players on both sides tried to console the forlorn German.

"Nobody in the world could have made that putt. Nobody," declared Ballesteros. Irwin added: "I would never, ever, *ever* wish that last hole on anyone."

Okay, maybe this victory would be seen as an aberration like the U.S. losses prior to 1983. Next time, it was back at the Belfry. Europe may have let the door open a crack, but they weren't about to let the Americans barge through.

But they did. In September 1993 the U.S. team arrived at the Belfry at Sutton Coldfield, England, and proceeded to win, 15–13. Another close match, yes, once again decided on a six-foot putt on the eighteenth green—Davis Love III, in his first Ryder Cup, defeating Costantino Rocca—but the bottom line was the same.

Gallacher, now 0–8–1 as a Ryder Cup player and captain, was at the European helm again, and the U.S. squad was led by Tom

Watson, who had a gritty 10–4–1 record as a player. Both captains were largely successful in achieving a mutual goal: returning civility, sportsmanship, and fair play to the Ryder Cup.

This might have been a bit more difficult for Gallacher, with players like Ballesteros declaring, "It's going to be *our* turn." It didn't help either that Watson blundered by refusing to sign autographs for Sam Torrance and others from the European team during the gala dinner. But for the most part the "Battle at the Belfry" was rather benign compared to the "War at the Shore." The goal was to keep the combat on the course and use the players' skills and the captains' strategies as the only weapons.

"I have to reduce this 'War at the Shore' mentality created in the last couple of Ryder Cups," Watson said at the time. "The event is bigger than that."

For the home team, joining the somewhat expanded nucleus of Ballesteros, Faldo, James, Langer, Montgomerie, Olazabal, Rocca, Torrance, and Woosnam were Peter Baker, Joakim Haeggman, and Barry Lane. Rocca, by the way, who hailed from Italy, had very literally earned his way onto the Ryder Cup team. He had been a laborer in a box factory while perfecting the golf skills that, complemented by his strong determination to excel, got him on the European Tour and eventually the Ryder Cup team.

Watson may quite possibly have had the strongest U.S. team since the '81 Ryder Cup. Returning was Azinger, fresh off his PGA Championship, Beck the battler, Couples (3–1 in '91), Floyd (who had also been 3–1), Love, Pavin, Stewart, and Wadkins. The squad was fleshed out by John Cook; Jim Gallagher, Jr.; Lee Janzen (winner of his first U.S. Open that year); and the veteran Tom Kite, who with four wins (including the U.S. Open) in '92 and '93 was adding to his record-breaking earnings total.

The early advantage went to the home team. By the end of Friday, Europe was up 4½–3½ thanks to wins by Woosnam and Langer, Faldo and Montgomerie, and the duo that was continuing the legacy of the "Spanish Armada," Ballesteros and Olazabal, as well as a tie in the match between Faldo and Montgomerie and

Azinger and Couples. On the U.S. side, the nearly unbeatable Wadkins and Pavin had combined for two victories, with Kite and Love picking up the other one.

The American position was more tenuous by the end of the second day, but things could have been worse considering how Saturday started off. In the morning foursomes there were wins by Faldo and Montgomerie, Woosnam and Langer, and of course the "Spanish Armada." Only a 3 and 2 decision by Floyd and Stewart staved off a sweep.

The United States reversed the results in the afternoon fourball matches, thanks to wins by Cook and Beck, Pavin and Gallagher, and Floyd and Stewart once more. The lone European triumph came courtesy of a 6 and 5 crushing of Azinger and Couples by Woosnam and Baker.

"That was the critical match of the whole week," Watson said, referring to the Cook and Beck win. "Neither of those guys had played yet, then they bounced off the bench to take on Faldo and Montgomerie. They showed real true grit."

That night, for the second Ryder Cup in a row, a player had to go in the envelope. Torrance came up with an infected toe, and given the possibility that he might not be able to play in the next day's singles, Watson had to select a player to sit out. Wadkins saved the captain from making an agonizing decision.

Though he was a veteran Ryder Cup warrior, Wadkins knew that by volunteering to go in the envelope (hoping, of course, that Torrance would recover by the A.M.), he was taking one for the team and lightening the load on Watson's shoulders—two things that might give the U.S. squad a psychological and/or emotional lift on the visiting team's final day. And as it turned out, Torrance was unable to compete. The American player who needed only two more wins to tie Arnold Palmer's record of twenty-two Ryder Cup wins—and who, at 43, could well be participating in his last Ryder Cup—was forced to watch Watson's team from behind the ropes.

"Lanny took me aside and said, 'Tom, I want you to put my name in the envelope,'" recalled Watson, who still views this act on

Wadkins's part as one of the noblest he has ever seen in golf. "I said, 'I'm not going to do that. You're one of the best competitors here.'

"He said, 'No, Tom, you have to because I was chosen—you chose me as one of the two players to join the team, I didn't qualify for the team. I don't want to knock somebody out who qualified for the team and has the opportunity to play.' Well, it was tough logic, but it was true, and I had to go along. When I think about winning the Ryder Cup in '93, I think about how much Lanny's unselfish act contributed. It was for team and country."

With tears in his eyes, Watson accepted his longtime colleague's offer to go in the envelope.

That same night came another example of Ryder Cup fair play and generosity of spirit. It was learned that Peter Baker's eleven-month-old daughter had been rushed to the hospital, and the initial diagnosis was spinal meningitis. The rules allowed that if a second player is not available, the other team can declare a forfeit and be awarded a full point.

Clearly, for the Americans, who badly needed a point, this was a wide-open door. But they refused to step through it. Raymond Floyd declared that if Peter Baker couldn't play, he would sit out, for another halved match. The team sent this news to Gallacher along with their best wishes for Baker's daughter. They learned in the morning that the baby had only an ear infection, and Baker was back to play. (As it turned out, the United States was lucky that Floyd didn't have to sit out.)

At first the unselfish act of Wadkins and Floyd didn't appear to have inspired their teammates. With the halved unplayed match, the score was 9–7 Europe as Sunday started off. While Beck was beating Barry Lane, Montgomerie, Baker, and Haeggman were taking care of Janzen, Pavin, and Cook, and the match between Couples and Woosnam ended in a tie. This was not very good at all—with the score at 12½–9½, Europe needed to take only two of the remaining six matches to keep the cup on the Continent. Perhaps the American win in '91 was an aberration.

With a Palmer-like hitch of the pants, the American players stepped up and hit better shots. Payne Stewart sent Mark James packing 3 and 2. With a 1-up win, Davis Love III made Costantino Rocca think fondly of the factory. Afterward Love said of the tension during the match, "I almost threw up on myself. I could not breathe. There was no saliva in my mouth."

In a huge upset Jim Gallagher, Jr., showed that Seve Ballesteros was not invincible, outdueling him 3 and 2. And who says the Ryder Cup is only for players in their prime? Captain's pick Raymond Floyd, at 51, showed Jose Maria Olazabal some new tricks in defeating him 2-up. Floyd made three birdies down the stretch, and when Olazabal put his ball in the water at 18, he conceded what turned out to be the pivotal match to the American veteran.

"Of all the matches I played, that one with Olazabal was probably the best moment for me," recalled Floyd, now a very successful Senior PGA Tour player. "The Ryder Cup was on the line, you've got your most experienced players out there, and Tom [Watson] had placed me in a very meaningful slot to take on one of the better players in the world. It was going to come down to whoever played best toward the end would win. I'm sure the Ryder Cup experience I had helped me not to falter at that crucial moment."

With a 5 and 4 licking, Bernhard Langer fell to Tom Kite. By the time Paul Azinger—who courageously carried on despite the painful symptoms that would lead to a diagnosis of cancer two months later—halved with Nick Faldo, it was already over. The Ryder Cup would be staying in the Colonies, thanks to the 15–13 victory.

As Watson held the cup aloft, he declared, "This is the finest experience I have had in the game of golf"—this, from a great player who had won five British Opens, two Masters, and a U.S. Open.

The Ryder Cup was faced with a good news–bad news situation. On the plus side, the competition was keener than ever, with the previous five Matches decided by a total of only 11 points. Never before in the event's history had there been a decade with so many close calls. By this time no player, captain, PGA official, or fan took any aspect of the Ryder Cup lightly. This was serious business, and the stakes were getting higher.

Even better, the audience among golf fans and sports fans in general was growing rapidly, fueled by the more intense competition, the high-profile players on both sides, and the soaring interest of television executives in providing more extensive coverage.

However, on the downside were the back-to-back wins by the United States, the most recent one in England. Was the Ryder Cup reverting to the ways of the past? Was the emergence of European golfers in the 1980s and their Continental comeback over? Would the United States reassert itself as the top producer of top-level players? Given that the European team would face the United States in the States and could lose three Matches in a row, was the Ryder Cup's popularity curve poised to take a downward dip?

Many of these concerns had few teeth to them. Though a tad nervous about the Ryder Cup becoming a repetition of past one-sided domination, TV companies were eager to keep expanding coverage. The audience still seemed to be growing. None of the players were taking the Ryder Cup for granted, the effort to make the team was stronger than ever, and being a member continued to be a great honor. However, even with the Matches tightly competitive, the same outcome every two years would eventually have an impact.

Gallacher had taken his lumps for two losses in a row (not to mention being 0–9–1 as a player and captain), but he was back at the helm for the 1995 Ryder Cup at Oak Hill in Rochester, New York. The weather was first rainy and then chilly, more suitable for England or Scotland. A divine message of support for the visitors? A better sign was the quality of players on the European team—the solid veteran core was back (except for the injured Olazabal), accompanied this time by Howard Clark, David Gilford, Per-Ulrik Johansson, and Philip Walton.

There couldn't have been a better choice for U.S. captain than Lanny Wadkins. His excellent Ryder Cup record, his aggressive leadership on the links, and the team-spirit act of going into the envelope in '93—well, it was payback time, *and* he was perfect captain material.

For Wadkins's squad Fred Couples, Davis Love III, and Corey Pavin were back, but otherwise the U.S. contingent was made up of players who were either new to Ryder Cup competition or hadn't made the team in four or more years: Ben Crenshaw, Brad Faxon, Jay Haas, Peter Jacobsen, Tom Lehman, Jeff Maggert, Phil Mickelson, Loren Roberts, and Curtis Strange. Such inconsistency was unusual for an American team.

Initially it looked like the United States was set to go three in a row. Victories by Pavin and Lehman, Love and Maggert, Maggert and Roberts, Couples and Love, and Mickelson and Pavin in the morning foursomes and afternoon fourballs ended the miserably soggy upstate New York day with a 5–3 home-team lead. The afternoon matches would have been an American sweep if not for Gilford and Ballesteros, the latter summoning up the last few ounces of his remaining game and beating Faxon and Jacobsen 4 and 3.

On Saturday the two teams fought to a standstill, which was not helpful enough to Europe, though the U.S. momentum was neutralized. The combos of Faldo and Montgomerie, Rocca and Torrance (a 6 and 5 blowout, and their second win in two days), Gilford and Langer, and Rocca and Woosnam scored for the visitors. On the U.S. side, points were racked up by Jacobsen and Roberts, Couples and Faxon, Haas and Mickelson, and Pavin and Roberts.

Wadkins and his squad felt pretty good about their chances on Sunday. With the tally 9–7, the U.S. team needed only 5 points out of the twelve singles matches to keep the Cup. Europe faced the daunting task of collecting 7½ points. With the traditional singles superiority of the Yanks, Wadkins could have said, "Put the champagne on ice, boys."

Not so fast. Sure, it looked even more like a done deal when Lehman blasted Ballesteros 4 and 3, when Couples halved with Woosnam—a big halve by Woosie because it prevented the bleeding from becoming a hemorrhage—and when Love rejected Rocca 3 and 2. Time to turn out the lights?

Don't touch that switch. Gallacher and his troops staged a remarkable rally that stunned the home team and the shivering partisan crowd. (The same rally would almost be repeated by the other team at Valderrama two years later.)

Clark conquered Jacobsen, James mauled Maggert 4 and 3, the surprising Gilford fought off Faxon, Montgomerie downed Crenshaw, Faldo stuck it to Strange, and Torrance got by Roberts. The decisive match was Haas against the virtually unknown Walton, who won on the last hole to give his team the precious 7½ points and 14½ overall.

By the time Pavin (who was 4–0 on the weekend) and Mickelson (who was 3–0) staged a comeback on their own by defeating Langer and Johansson, it was too little, too late. What made the finish especially agonizing for the U.S. team is that all that was needed down the stretch was for Strange, Roberts, Faxon, or Haas just to tie to retain the Ryder Cup. Haas gave it his best—down 3 with three holes to play, he won the sixteenth and seventeenth, but he came up just short on the eighteenth. Roberts had been 3–0 on the weekend but ran into a hot Sam Torrance.

Strange, unfortunately, took the brunt of the criticism, and some of it was pretty vicious. He hadn't won a tournament since his U.S. Open victory in 1989 and he was a captain's pick (for which Wadkins was roundly criticized), but he was 0–3 in the Match, and in his final duel with Faldo he stumbled the last few holes.

"I wanted to win very badly, and I sure wish I had," said Strange, looking back at the Match three years later. "I was totally unprepared for the reaction to that outcome."

The Ryder Cup coverage in the October 2, 1995, issue of *Sports Illustrated* was titled "Wrong Man, Wrong Time," and the lead summary was, "The stunning collapse of Curtis Strange and his U.S. mates handed the Ryder Cup back to an unheralded team from Europe." Ouch!

In the text of the article was this nugget: "When Strange got to the hardest miles—the last three holes against Europe's finest, Faldo, with the Cup on the line—he staged his own Heimlich festival, making three straight bogeys when one measly par would've been enough. It was Bill Buckner letting three straight balls go through his legs. It was Jackie Smith dropping three straight in the end zone. It was unthinkable, not possible. And yet it happened." Talk about kicking a guy when he's down!

But Strange, showing the strength of his character, stood tall and accepted the brickbats: "I probably deserve what I'm going to get now," he said that sorrowful Sunday. "No matter how bad you beat me up, it's not going to hurt as much as what I'm going to do to myself."

The best way for the Americans to recover from the devastating loss at Oak Hill—only the second time the United States had lost at home, but the second time in eight years—was to steam overseas and retake the Ryder Cup at Valderrama. Of course, as we know, this didn't happen. And because of that, the stakes for both teams are now higher than ever.

"There's a lot of people who have fallen in love with these Matches since '83," commented Johnny Miller. "They've been so tight. It's just great theater."

Not only has Europe gone 4–2–1 from 1985 through 1997, but it has won two in a row. A win at The Country Club in Brookline would be an unprecedented three in a row. (And a tie would make the 1990s as woeful for the U.S. as the 1980s.) It would be particularly humiliating for the U.S. team to lose for the third time in a row in front of their hometown fans—and only about fifty Tiger Woods tee shots from the site in Worcester where the Ryder Cup and the U.S. domination began.

The competition, the courage, the fair play, the agony, and the ecstasy all make up the Ryder Cup. Perhaps, though, more than anything else, the attention of the world and the increasing revenue have made the Ryder Cup, as it was labeled by British golf writer Peter Dobereiner, the "fifth major" and quite possibly a bigger event than the four major tournaments combined.

"I don't know that it was ever a totally relaxing event," Arnold Palmer told us. "The pressure was always on to win, whether it was the 1950s, 1960s, 1970s, or the 1990s. I don't think the outcome in the early days was indicative of how difficult the Matches were and how hard everybody worked to play well and win.

"But certainly the competition in the 1980s and 1990s has been more level than it ever was before. The U.S. usually had a little edge in the early days. Now that the edge has diminished to where the Matches are head to head, I don't think anybody really minds the pressure or that they all feel it—I think that is what makes the Ryder Cup Matches as great as they are."

Chapter 6

THE MAKING OF
A MAJOR EVENT

According to Gene Sarazen, the team members knew that the Ryder Cup was special because it set up a structure in which the intense rivalry that already existed between the United States and Great Britain could be played out. What no one, including Samuel Ryder and his family, could have envisioned is how large the Matches would grow as an international event.

While some people may be more familiar with the PGA Championship held every August, for the PGA of America the Ryder Cup is the crown jewel. The prestige of the seventy-two-year-old series and the revenue it generates make it *the* event for this enduring golf organization.

The Professional Golfers' Association of America, which now has 23,000 members, began in January 1916. Rodman Wanamaker, the department store czar, hosted a lunch in Manhattan to discuss forming an organization that would generate more interest in golf and be a mentor to golf professionals. With those in attendance agreeing, James Hepburn, formerly the secretary for the PGA of Great Britain, was appointed chairman of a committee to explore an organization.

Three months later, on April 10, eighty-two charter members approved the formation of the Professional Golfers' Association of America, headquartered in New York City. In October the first

PGA Championship was held, at the Siwanoy Country Club in Bronxville, just north of New York City. Wanamaker offered a purse of just over $2,500, and a trophy bearing his name (as it still does today) was awarded to Jim Barnes, who won the championship 1-up. (Through 1957, the PGA Championship was a match-play event.)

The organization began publishing a magazine, *The Professional Golfer of America* (now called *PGA Magazine),* in 1920, and it is the oldest continuously published golf magazine in the United States. Seven years later the first Ryder Cup Match was played, in Worcester, Massachusetts, under the auspices of the PGA of America and the PGA of Great Britain.

A spin-off of the PGA Championship, the PGA Seniors Championship, was first contested in 1937 at Augusta National in Georgia, the home course of the tournament that Bobby Jones cofounded, the Masters. After twelve tourneys, the championship was moved to Florida. In 1956, reflecting Florida's growth as a golf mecca, the PGA of America moved its headquarters there, to Dunedin. Only five years later the offices were moved again, six miles south to Baywood, Florida. Then in 1965 the headquarters took up ten thousand square feet of space at their Fort Worth location.

In 1968 a schism occurred within the organization. The touring professionals wanted more control of their livelihood, and despite strong efforts to keep the PGA of America intact, there was a split, and the Tournament Players Division was formed. It is now known as the PGA Tour, headquartered in Ponte Vedre, Florida, with Tim Finchem as the commissioner.

Most touring professionals are members of both organizations. The PGA of America and the PGA Tour work closely together, though there are also rivalries between the two groups and occasional downright disagreements, such as over the existence of the Presidents Cup.

Ironically, the PGA Tour is facing its own schism, for a familiar reason. In September 1998 more than fifty pros gathered to form the Tour Players Association. They contend that not enough information about the management of the PGA Tour is being shared with the players and that players are kept in the dark about finances. These rebels would like more direct control of the tournaments and the money. PGA Tour officials contend there is plenty of access and that professional golf doesn't need another organization. As this is being written, the two sides have been unable to bury the hatchet.

The PGA of America is now housed in Palm Beach Gardens, next to PGA National, a 2,300-acre golf course and resort development. The organization now has almost 150 employees. The current president, the PGA of America's thirty-first, is Will Mann, who hails from Graham, North Carolina. Jim Awtrey is the chief executive officer stationed at the headquarters.

As the premier organization of pro golfers, the PGA of America conducts tournaments (thirty in all), provides standards and a support system for club professionals around the country, owns golf courses—and oversees the U.S. Ryder Cup teams every two years and the arrangements for the event on home turf every four years. The PGA Tour does just what its name indicates, representing the players on the professional circuit, and among other events, it sponsors the Players Championship every March.

Though it is the governing body, the PGA of America does not select who plays on the U.S. Ryder Cup team. This is now done with the points system explained in Chapter 2. However, the PGA does choose the captain, usually within a couple of months of the last Ryder Cup. This selection is the most direct influence that the PGA of America has on the actual composition and effectiveness of the U.S. team, because it attempts to pick people who would perform well in the captain's role, and the chosen captain gets to appoint two players to the team.

The PGA of America's other role is organizing the Ryder Cup *event,* especially when it is held in the United States.

On the other side of the Atlantic, the setup is a bit different. Originally the PGA of Great Britain, following the rules set forth by Samuel Ryder, oversaw the Ryder Cup as far as the team and the home courses were concerned. This wasn't practical, however, once the Ryder Cup eligibility was extended to all of Europe, which occurred only a few years after a PGA European Tour was formed.

This tour has also done rather well, going from a total of 700,000 pounds in prize money in the mid-1970s to more than 23 million pounds today. There is also a PGA European Seniors Tour that has over a dozen tournaments and attracts some interest. Most likely, though, if that tour is to be truly successful, it must wait a decade or so to see if well-known players now in their forties—Nick Faldo, Seve Ballesteros, Sam Torrance, Ian Woosnam, Bernhard Langer, Mark James, and so on—decide to participate.

Nowadays there is a separate entity called the Ryder Cup Joint Venture, which is a partnership between the PGA of Great Britain and the PGA European Tour. The European Ryder Cup Committee has direct supervision over the team and is the group that selects the captain.

While the PGA of America headquarters can be a busy place in the months leading up to a Ryder Cup, nowhere is the effort more focused than at the host course. For Jimmy Patino, having the 1997 Ryder Cup held at Valderrama was the result of over two decades of striving, planning, preparing, and expanding, which finally culminated in a huge burst of activity.

Hosting the Ryder Cup has been six years in the making for officials at The Country Club in Brookline, Massachusetts. Planning and preparation began soon after it was announced as the 1999 site in 1993. The officials are well aware that the Match they are to host will be the biggest one in the history of golf.

A strong indication of the magnitude of the '99 event is that as early as the last Ryder Cup Match in Spain, the PGA of America and The Country Club broke previous U.S. home-site records by selling fifty-nine corporate tents—two full years before hosting the event! The club and the PGA will split the $15.2 million in revenue that the tents have brought in. And this is just the proverbial tip of the iceberg.

"We're fully aware that the 1999 Match will be the biggest one in Ryder Cup history," said Brendan Walsh, head golf professional at The Country Club, during an interview exactly one year to the day before the '99 Match begins. "One sign of that is everyone here is very excited, it is a constant topic of conversation, and every time we turn around, Ben Crenshaw, Rees Jones, Tom Roy, and others connected to the Ryder Cup are here to prepare for next year. We don't know *exactly* what to expect, with the club never having hosted a Ryder Cup before, but we do expect it to be very big."

And big for the area in the radius of a John Daly drive from the host course. We can't overlook the fact that the presence of a Ryder Cup Match is a dynamic economic boost for the surroundings.

In England, for example, having the Ryder Cup at the Belfry has almost become its own industry. Each wing of the hotel there is named after a previous Ryder Cup captain. If you want to play the course at the Belfry that hosts the competition, it will cost you over fifty pounds. Want to play on the course at the Belfry that isn't used for the Ryder Cup? That's only twenty pounds. (Expect prices to go up for 2001.)

"The Ryder Cup is *the* event in golf today," states Raymond Floyd. "Every two years you have the congregation of most of the best players in the world who have gathered for a very simple purpose: for one side to outplay the other. It really goes to the very basics of sports."

Describing how an event is organized and what goes into it doesn't necessarily account for why it can be an enormous success. To explain why the Ryder Cup has become one of the world's greatest sports events, not only exceeding golf's four majors but rivaling the Olympics and the World Cup for the attention of an international audience, we have to look at several other factors as well.

Consider the way golf has taken off worldwide, especially in the 1980s and 1990s. Up to the 1960s not a lot of attention was given to golf outside the United States and Great Britain. There were, of course, programs and aspiring players in other countries, but with few exceptions we rarely saw or heard anything about them. If you weren't a player from the United States or Great Britain, you didn't really exist.

Well, that sure has changed. For the last thirty-plus years, an increasing number of talented players have emerged from other parts of the planet. Gary Player of South Africa, Isao Aoki of Japan, Bob Charles of New Zealand, Jose Maria Canizares of Spain, T. C. Chen of Taiwan, and Peter Thomson of Australia, among others, were the first players to demonstrate the global spread of golf.

In the 1980s and 1990s the floodgates opened. Over the past fifteen years other countries have produced:

ARGENTINA: Eduardo Romero
AUSTRALIA: Robert Allenby, Stuart Appleby, Ian Baker-Finch, Steve Elkington, Wayne Grady, Bradley Hughes, Peter Lonard, Greg Norman, Craig Parry
CANADA: Dave Barr, Glen Hnatiuk, Richard Zokol
DENMARK: Thomas Bjorn
FIJI: Vijay Singh
GERMANY: Bernhard Langer
ITALY: Costantino Rocca
JAPAN: Kazuhiko Hosokawa, Yoshinori Kaneko, Shigeki Maruyama, Hajime Meshiai, Tateo "Jet" Ozaki, Naomichi "Joe" Ozaki, Masashi "Jumbo" Ozaki, Hisayuki Sasaki
NAMIBIA: Trevor Dodds
NEW ZEALAND: Frank Nobilo, Phil Tataurangi, Greg Turner, Grant Waite
PARAGUAY: Carlos Franco
PHILIPPINES: Frankie Minoza
SOUTH AFRICA: Ernie Els, David Frost, Retief Goosen

SPAIN: Severiano Ballesteros, Jose Maria Olazabal, Ignacio Garrido, Manuel Pinero
SWEDEN: Gabriel Hjertstedt, Per-Ulrik Johansson, Jesper Parnevik, Anders Forbrand
TRINIDAD: Stephen Ames
VENEZUELA: Vicente Fernandez
ZIMBABWE: Mark McNulty, Nick Price, Denis Watson

Also, thanks to Charlie Sifford, Ted Rhodes, Lee Elder, Calvin Peete, Jim Dent, Jim Thorpe, and more recently Walt Morgan, Bobby Stroble, and Tiger Woods, audiences have seen African-Americans play and win around the world, further opening the multicultural door. While many valid concerns remain about how sincerely country clubs welcome people of color, the fact is that golf, more than the other major sports played in the United States, has added a diverse group of international ingredients for a truly global flavor.

Yes, other events in golf match up players from different countries, such as the Walker Cup and the Solheim Cup. But first and foremost is the Ryder Cup—and to be quite blunt about it, no other international event has consistently featured for so long the highest level of competition on a golf course (though one could argue that the British Open qualifies). The legacy of the Ryder Cup is still that of the best playing the best.

So combine the strongest international competition available with the soaring interest in golf as a sport, and you arrive at the reason the Ryder Cup is such a big event. While the popularity of the other major sports—football, basketball, baseball, hockey, tennis, and soccer—ebbs and flows, golf appears to be the only one that sustains an upward trajectory.

In 1997, according to a survey by the National Golf Foundation, three million people in the United States tried golf for the first time, compared with fewer than two million the previous year. That same year, the number of rounds played in the United States jumped by 14.6 percent to more than 547 million.

To flesh out the context of these figures: Generally, for the previous decade, the total number of golfers in the United States stayed at around 25 million. Even though there had been increases during those years, they were more modest and the number of new golfers pretty much replaced those who had died or stopped playing. However, in 1997 the total number leaped by seven percent, to 26.5 million golfers. With preliminary figures for 1998 not indicating a reversal, it is clear that more people are interested in taking up golf and continuing to play the game than ever before.

What are the reasons for such gains? Inevitably there is the Tiger Woods factor. His dramatic entry as a professional, his win at the Masters in 1997, his being named Player of the Year that year, and his place near or at the top of the world rankings and money list since has gotten a lot of folks, especially youngsters, excited about the sport. Of those who played golf in 1997, 2.4 million were between the ages of 12 and 17, an increase of 600,000 over 1996 and almost double what it was ten years earlier. The admirable First Tee program of the PGA of America and World Golf Foundation is expected to attract more and more young people to the game.

Other reasons are the consistent good health of the economy, golf-equipment manufacturers' push to advertise on TV and in print, and the recent boom in golf course construction. Close to five hundred courses are opening every year—and that kind of access is most alluring to both novice and veteran players.

There may be one other reason worth pointing out: the celebrity factor. How many times in the past few years have you opened a magazine or changed a channel and seen an instantly recognizable person playing golf or promoting a golf product? Bill Gates, Alice Cooper, Michael Jordan, Celine Dion, and others portray golf as both fun and cool. It doesn't hurt that President Clinton, whether you like him or not, is shown teeing off whenever he's on vacation.

There are also an increasing number of tournaments that feature the famous. On the PGA Tour two of the better-known events are the Bob Hope Chrysler Classic and the AT&T Pebble Beach Pro-Am. Their rosters are filled with celebs like Jack Lemmon, Clint Eastwood, Joe Pesci, Bill Murray, and a former president or two.

On the Senior PGA Tour, the NFL Golf Classic offers spectators and viewers tournaments featuring top professional football players. Newly created events like the Isuzu Celebrity Championship cater specifically to the "Q rating" of the famous participants. In the entertainment world partying until the wee hours at a nightclub is out—playing golf with fellow celebs on a sunlit course in Palm Springs or Las Vegas is in.

During the 1990s a Ryder Cup Match has become the place to see and be seen. At Valderrama were Prince Andrew, George and Barbara Bush, Michael Jordan, Kevin Costner, Sean Connery, baseball star George Brett, Mike Mills of R.E.M., and plenty of other famous folk. It's certainly expected that in Boston this September there will be as many stars behind the ropes as behind the clouds.

Let's face it, though: No matter how many celebrities love golf, in this day and age what makes the biggest difference to the visibility and importance of an event is the extent of broadcast coverage. Without television, radio, and the Internet, a sporting event is like a tree falling deep in the forest—it happened, but no one is aware of it, and certainly no one cares. The Olympics and the World Cup have always been big events anyway, but broadcasting these events to a worldwide audience, especially by television, has made the audience grow exponentially in popularity.

So too with the Ryder Cup. It was a very important sports event well before TV took notice, and it would continue if TV disappeared tomorrow. But the 1997 Match at Valderrama was available to 700 million viewers and listeners worldwide. Because of that the Ryder Cup is one of the top three international sports events, and for the powerful (and lucrative) U.S. market, it is among the most beloved because it's the one global sports event that, until recently, America has often won.

A special point should be made about how particularly well suited golf is for television, and in some ways it can be more enjoyable for the viewer than the spectator. Let's take a baseball game: Sitting in the stands, you see the entire field and everyone on it. When the ball is in play, you can glance around to see all who are involved in the action. The entire contest is available to you from where you sit. Watching a baseball game on TV is somewhat limiting because you see only what the camera shows you, just one aspect of the total action.

Similarly, a spectator at a golf course can watch only one part of the tournament at a time, usually players teeing off or on the green putting. While golf tournaments have a very special atmosphere and we would never suggest staying home rather than attending one, the fact is that at any one time a spectator is seeing only a portion of the action and only two or three players.

But with cameras positioned around the golf course, and the director cutting from one piece of action to another, a TV viewer in a way is speeding from one hole to another with no delays in the action (except for commercial breaks, of course). In a half-hour span you can see a dozen or more players and watch them driving, chipping, pitching, putting, and so on. Of the major sports, golf may well be the most TV-friendly.

This quality of the sport and the fact that the Ryder Cup is the sport's most prestigious event make it obvious that once the event and TV finally found each other, both would grow enormously. A *Sports Illustrated* article previewing the 1995 Ryder Cup at Oak Hill offered, "The apotheosis of this [golf] craze arrives Friday, when a generation gone green plants itself in front of the television for twenty-three hours. The occasion is formally called the Ryder Cup, a storied bit of transatlantic golfing rivalry that was previously of interest only to fanatics. Evidently, there are now enough of us to justify the kind of coverage that the networks have trouble extending to political conventions."

Gone are the days when PGA officials and players had to beg the TV networks to beam the Ryder Cup into bars and living rooms. Only twelve years ago Jack Nicklaus, wanting to make sure people could see the Ryder Cup Match at Muirfield Village, had his own production company buy five hours of broadcast time on ABC. (Jack may have regretted this after the team he captained became the first to lose at home, but knowing Nicklaus, he cared more about getting the Ryder Cup out there for folks than himself.)

"We had a tiger by the tail and we didn't know it," lamented Jack Whitaker, a much-honored golf broadcaster and longtime employee of ABC. "The decision was made that if the Ryder Cup was going to be locked in to being played in late September, our higher priority for that time of year was to broadcast college football. Now, I'm not knocking college football at all, it is big business, but I'm not the only one who wishes ABC could've found a way to accommodate the Ryder Cup. In golf there's just nothing else like it."

In 1989 a cable network, USA, took a chance and paid the PGA of America $200,000 for rights to broadcast (using only four cameras) six and a half hours of the Ryder Cup from the Belfry, and viewers saw the United States and Great Britain play to a tie.

After seeing how viewers responded—ratings in 1989 were much higher than the typical sports event carried by a cable network—NBC got into the game by broadcasting some of the "War at the Shore" two years later. The agony of Bernhard Langer's missed putt and the euphoria of Mark Calcavecchia and other American players leaping into the ocean was captured forever, and a new sports media star was born. (The USA network has retained first-round coverage rights through 2005, with NBC having the other two days.)

"We were in the right place at the right time," said Tom Roy, a veteran golf producer at NBC Sports who coordinates Ryder Cup coverage. "The Americans taking the cup back after eight years, in South Carolina, the whole atmosphere—it was just exciting theater, and we covered as much of it as we could. We knew right then and there, we had an event that from an audience perspective was only going to get bigger. And it's gotten very big."

During the mid-1990s the price of TV rights went up considerably, with NBC paying $4.5 million to show the action from Valderrama, and the USA cable network kicking in $1 million for one day of coverage. And neither network lost a penny, with presenting sponsors eager to sign on. When all the ad money is counted up, it totaled in excess of $10 million.

According to a spokesman for Karsten Manufacturing, a maker of golf equipment, "From an ad-buying standpoint, the Ryder Cup ranks right up there with the majors. And after the majors, it becomes the focal point of the golf season."

Tom Roy explained, "It's all about capturing the emotion of the Match. That's the source of its growth—it's what people want to see." (It's pretty cool, too, the way the players scoop balls off the green after missed putts, something you don't see in stroke play.)

For the Valderrama event, NBC used eighteen cameras, including five handheld units. A total of twenty hours of action were aired. To provide special insight, USA hired Peter Oosterhuis and NBC corralled Tony Jacklin. Saturday's telecast scored a 4.3 Nielsen rating, a good-size jump from the 3.7 for Saturday in '95. With ratings expected to go through the roof in 1999 as America fights to finally get the cup back, with an older and wiser Tiger Woods leading the way, it's no wonder that NBC coughed up $10 million per event for Ryder Cup rights through 2005.

NBC intends to realize the most from its investment, providing perhaps as much as twenty hours of coverage from Brookline. Even though, as Roy pointed out, there will be a limit on commercial breaks so as not to intrude on the action, that still is a lot of time to sell.

With the USA network planning ten hours the first day, there could be thirty total hours of TV time devoted to the Ryder Cup. That's about as much airtime as a seven-game World Series or NBA final. Even the Super Bowl shows can't pack that much sports into one weekend.

On the other side of the pond, television broadcasts are handled by European Tour Productions (ETP), a collaboration between the

European Tour and Trans World International. It began planning for the Ryder Cup at Valderrama as soon as the last putt dropped at the Belfry in 1993, and it is already at work on televising from the Belfry again in 2001.

NBC won't be far behind. "Within two weeks of the Ryder Cup at Brookline, we'll start preparing for the next Match," Roy said. At Oak Hill in 1995, NBC alone brought in 125 miles of television cable. This was in addition to the 4,000 feet of cable strung along twenty-five utility poles brought in by Rochester Gas and Electric, the telephone cables buried under grass, the five miles of chain-link fencing, and the fifteen miles of rope and 3,000 steel stakes used to cordon off tees, fairways, and greens.

At Valderrama ETP deployed forty cameras around the course, including 34 up on platforms, and the main compound next to the twelfth fairway required 70 kilometers of camera cable. With 200 people on board, ETP offered 25 hours of coverage to Europe during the 1997 event. This was all in addition to extensive coverage provided by BBC television and radio.

A Ryder Cup Match is a particularly attractive TV event because of its match-play format and the fact that there are never more than four matches being played at one time.

"When you're covering a typical stroke-play event, we concentrate on the people on the leader board and also whatever handful of stories you may have, such as a Casey Martin, Matt Kuchar, Tiger Woods, or somebody challenging a course record," said Tom Roy. "But in the Ryder Cup every single match is critical, so we have to worry about every match. You can't just blow off a few players—they all matter."

One way to conserve resources is to give most of the camera time to the last few holes of matches, but this isn't easy. According to Roy, directors can't simply place their cameras on the sixteenth, seventeenth, and eighteenth holes, because in match play some matches don't get that far. If Mark O'Meara is beating up on Colin Montgomerie and wins 5 and 4, that match never got past the fourteenth hole.

Despite these and other obstacles, NBC believes that covering a Ryder Cup is well worth the huge investment. "For every Match the audience gets bigger," Roy said. "The Ryder Cup gets so much play now that it seems everyone knows about it, and I'm including people who aren't golfers. It has become an across-the-board, must-see media event."

Ratings have also made the investment by TV networks worthwhile. The Saturday matches at Oak Hill in 1995, for example, were watched by 4.5 million U.S. viewers, the biggest TV audience ever for a Ryder Cup and a 109 percent increase over the previous U.S. Match, on Kiawah Island in 1991. There was only a slight decline in '97, which is remarkable considering the significant time difference between the United States and Spain. It is not unreasonable to expect that the Ryder Cup Match from Brookline will see the American TV audience doubling again.

While television remains the most popular resource for golf fans, there is more to broadcasting the Ryder Cup and reaching those 700 million people around the world than just TV. Many of the major daily newspapers (especially in Boston and New York) devote special sections to the Ryder Cup, usually published the Sunday before it begins. *Sports Illustrated* and other major general-interest sports publications give the Ryder Cup big before-and-after spreads.

Excellent golf publications like *Golfweek, Golf Digest, Golf Magazine, Golf Journal,* and regional magazines like *The Massachusetts Golfer* will start writing about the Ryder Cup months in advance. It can seem like entire forests are decimated to publish the tens of millions of words on the Ryder Cup every two years—in the United States but also in Europe, Australia, Asia, South America, and everywhere else golf is a passion.

Radio pitches in, too. You might think that golf does not lend itself as well to radio description as the play-by-play of baseball, basketball, and football. However, for that portion of the international audience that has to rely on radio, the scoring updates, interviews, and various tidbits of information do go a long way toward offering a "feel" for the Match. Radio interviewers and listeners often find, too, that players are more relaxed on radio—just a couple of folks sharing a microphone away from the crowd, rather than in front of the glaring lights and background noise of TV spots.

Not to denigrate TV in any way, but the wave of the Ryder Cup broadcasting future may be the Internet, especially as live-action visuals are enhanced through technological advances. The Internet is a worldwide resource, and to some extent it is interactive, meaning you can choose the information you want. The Ryder Cup has its own Web site, which is continually updated and can be called up twenty-four hours a day.

For example, on Golf.Com, which is the NBC Sports golf Web site, we do scoring updates, course descriptions, and lots of statistics. Golfers seem to be particularly insightful about the enormous potential of the Internet. Certainly on Bob's show, *Outside the Ropes,* on Golf.Com, finding players to be interviewed has been no problem. When we did the Ryder Cup from Valderrama, the site received so many hits, we seriously wondered if the technology could accommodate them. As a journalist, knowing that one's interview or information is out there for someone in Fiji and New Delhi and Istanbul and Capetown and Moscow and Buenos Aires as well as in Dallas and Denver, San Francisco and New York, is a special experience.

The official Ryder Cup Web site in 1997, which was produced by IBM for Europe and the United States, offered more than 1,300 hours of information and coverage and received approximately 25 million hits. Some cyberspace experts anticipate that the number of hits this year could at least double.

In these days of proliferating computer access, there of course are other Web sites, all of which will be focused on the Ryder Cup Match of 1999 in the months leading up to September. They include www.golfweb.com, www.broadcast.com, www.igolf.com, and www.rcga.org. No doubt there will be more by September—

your best bet is to scan and find what's available. Keep in mind, though, that some of these sites will be second- or thirdhand reports without on-site action and information.

Obviously, through just about every form of media available, the Ryder Cup is a giant event. Thanks to the soaring media interest, the four majors, as wonderful as they are, are not quite keeping pace with the Cup's escalating *international* audience. The Ryder Cup perfectly represents how golf is going global.

Well, that's all very nice, but as in most endeavors, the bottom line here is still money. No matter how fantastic something is, if it keeps losing dough, it goes. No problem: The Ryder Cup has become golf's golden goose.

Oak Hill is a fabulous golf course and the event was attended by terrific, hardy people, but Rochester, New York, is not exactly a big-time metropolis and media center. Yet despite this, in 1995 the PGA of America raked in close to $30 million in hospitality tents, attendance, TV rights, and merchandise. Less than $10 million was collected in 1997, but that's pretty good considering the home site was Sotogrande, Spain. The total revenue outlook for Brookline? Get out your calculators.

Two years ago, as mentioned earlier in this chapter, the revenue from hospitality tents alone stood at almost $16 million. Let's conservatively say that the figure will be $25 by the end of this September. The event has pocketed $10 million for TV rights, so that's $35 million total. Attendance: Toss in 30,000 a day for three days, plus tickets for practice rounds and special tix that include a ton of amenities, and everything else you pay for to get through the gate, and we're talking around $5 million, for a total of $40 million. The other big gorilla is merchandise, all the stuff sold in connection with the Ryder Cup—easily another $10 million.

Now, $50 million may sound like a fine figure, but it may also be a low one. Keep in mind that we're four years after Oak Hill. Prices for everything having gone up, the Ryder Cup is bigger than ever, and it is being held right outside a major American city. It is not unreasonable to think that $70 million in Ryder Cup revenue is within reach. The fact is, no other golf major comes close to matching the Ryder Cup's earning power.

What does the PGA of America do with its portion of the Ryder Cup proceeds? Inevitably, some of it goes toward supporting the overall operations of the organization. But the PGA has also underwritten numerous programs for the betterment of the sport, which the Ryder Cup income helps pay for.

An example is the Ryder Cup outreach program announced by the PGA in October 1998. The organization is committing $13 million from each Ryder Cup Match to the program, which will create learning centers around the United States to teach newcomers, especially youngsters, about the game; it will also hold courses of instruction and education for golf professionals. The PGA of America has also pledged $2.5 million from each Ryder Cup Match to the PGA Tour, which means that players will see at least some indirect financial benefit from the Ryder Cup.

Given our PR-media-driven age, how does the Ryder Cup rank in hype? Very well, and it's getting even better.

In the golf world it is in everyone's best interest to promote the Ryder Cup to the max. This may sound like a cynical statement, and to some extent it is. More than a few of us have had our fill of excessively hyped events that turn out to have the substance and rot factor of cotton candy. However, by every measurement the Ryder Cup *is* the real thing in sports, so getting the message out there is a mission of pride, not crass materialism.

The media wants to plug the Ryder Cup because good buzz will get even more people to watch it, read about it, listen to it, and log on to it. The PGAs of America and Europe want to promote the event because the bigger it gets, the more revenue it generates. Players are quick to cite participating in a Ryder Cup as one of the biggest if not the biggest highlight of their career, not only because they believe it is (and they are right) but also because it gives them a higher profile in the golf community and among sports fans in general.

Golf equipment manufacturers on both sides of the Atlantic want their advertising to be involved not only because the Ryder Cup is a first-class event but because the players have endorsement contracts and whoever makes the Ryder Cup team is a walking billboard for that particular company. By this point in the history of the event, it's an advertiser's dream to do print ads and TV/radio/Internet ads offering "So-and-So is a member of the [U.S./Europe] Ryder Cup team, and he uses _____ clubs." Chi-ching!

While we're at it, let's talk travel. Just think—golf aficionados around the world with disposable income will want to be at golf's biggest international event, perhaps with their families and even extended families in tow. That's good for airlines, cruise lines, railroads, gas stations, restaurants, motels and hotels, and so on.

Just a glimpse at what the PGA Travel Service offers will give you an idea of the economic potential. In national and regional golf publications last year, PGA Travel advertised, "The world's premier golf event returns to the USA and the state of its birth, Massachusetts. As the official travel package provider, PGA Travel offers a wide variety of enticing options to witness this epic battle for the coveted cup."

The price tag? Well, one package included an eight-night trip on the luxury liner *Seabourn Pride* and tickets to the Ryder Cup Match for $8,750 to $14,315 per person. For the true golf fan, there were also packages to Scotland, Ireland, Arizona, and Florida.

Bottom line: The Ryder Cup today means big bucks. Be as idealistic as you want to be, but *that* may well be the strongest indicator—as it is for the Olympics, World Cup, Super Bowl, and World Series—of what constitutes a top-of-the-heap international sports event.

Of course, we don't have to be cynical and mercenary about this event. The joy of the Ryder Cup is the intensity of the competition and the team involvement, or spirit—and that those participating are really playing for their countries. Whatever the revenue, the hype, and any other material advantage, the players and their captains genuinely feel that they are competing to win honor, represented by the Ryder Cup.

"It has the special thrill of players going at it two-on-two and one-on-one—very different from a typical golf event," remarked Johnny Miller at Valderrama. "That has its own special tension."

In a September 1997 "Sports of the Times" column in *The New York Times*, Pulitzer prize–winner Dave Anderson wrote, "The Ryder Cup is golf's version of duty, honor and country. But that's the beauty of it. That's why it is different from all the money madness in sports. That's why it shouldn't be changed. . . . Without any prize money, the feeling of duty, honor and country increases the pressure. If one of America's best touring pros loses a payday by missing a putt in a weekly tournament, there is always another payday available next week. That missed putt is soon forgotten. But if the Ryder Cup turns on a golfer's missed putt, there is no opportunity for redemption for at least two years, if then. That missed putt might never be forgotten. . . . Ask Curtis Strange. . . . Ask Bernhard Langer."

As we've pointed out before, team play makes the Ryder Cup much bigger than the typical tournament and major. First, there is the effort to make the team. In the United States during Ryder Cup years, the months leading up to the PGA Championship are the golf equivalent of a pennant race in baseball—those below the top ten in points are trying desperately to break in, and those in the top ten do what they have to do to stay there.

Curtis Strange is among those who have criticized the urgency associated with the last week because, he contends, it detracts from the attention that should be focused on the fourth major of the year. There is some validity to this concern—at the PGA Championship in 1995, for example, as much or more attention was given to Brad Faxon's final-round 63, which put him into the top ten in Ryder Cup points, than to the tourney winner, Steve Elkington.

In fact, Faxon seemed more excited about making the Ryder Cup team than by the fact that he had shot the lowest-score final round in PGA Championship history. "I'll be playing with the best in the world," Faxon said after his scintillating round. "It means as much as anything I've ever done."

The individuality of golf is one of its unique features. Every player who tees off in a tournament is on his/her own, and how he/she performs on the course determines the result. Adding to the pro's personal pressure is that if he/she doesn't make the cut (except on the Senior PGA Tour, where there is no cut) there is no check—not a cent or shilling. You pack up and go home, or get an early start on practicing for the next tourney, with nothing to show for it. Compare this with other sports, where you can be in a slump, be injured, not feel like playing, whatever, and you still get paid.

The unusual nature of golfers pulling together as a team is one of the captivating aspects of the Ryder Cup. "Most successful golfers are loners. They like to golf alone and eat alone," said Bernard Gallacher. "But when the flags go up and the national anthem is played, they suddenly feel part of a team."

"The rest of the time we were always trying to beat each other's brains out," said Billy Casper. "But on the Ryder Cup there's nothing you want more than your rival the rest of the year to play his best. It's an unusual experience, but a very fine one."

"It's a special experience in golf, being a member of a team," Strange said. "For professionals who have been on the Tour for a while, it hearkens back to their college years, when it was all for one and one for all. Over time you really appreciate *that* opportunity the Ryder Cup represents."

It probably is no coincidence that just as in another major international sports event, the Olympics, the winners don't receive money. (These days players on the winning World Series team receive more than $100,000 each.) In fact, winners of Olympic events are better off because they get gold medals, whereas the victorious Ryder Cup team must take turns holding a seventeen-inch-high cup, which they can't each keep.

Instead, the players, captains, and respective PGAs compete for something symbolized by the cup that is abstract—to uphold the honor of their country, to assert their side's worthiness and merit, to come home with victory on display and the feeling deep in their minds and at the bottom of their hearts that they went out on this crusade and not only returned whole but with their opponent's shield.

In other sports when the final series or game is played, these feelings are inevitably mixed with coveting the money a team can win. In the Ryder Cup there are *only* these feelings. This is a purity rarely found elsewhere.

"Yes, the Ryder Cup is a great sports event because of the rivalry between the U.S. and European teams, and that can't help but be exciting every two years," said Tom Watson. "But I think the most beautiful thing about it—and I say 'beautiful' because you don't have this too much in professional sports—is that the players are in this event for the love of their country and for the love of the game.

"They're not playing for any type of financial reward at all," he continued. "And I think that's why the Ryder Cup is about the purest event in professional sport in the world."

We have to cite Tiger Woods again as a reason why the Ryder Cup is more of a popular event than ever. Yes, it's true, he's appeared in only one Match, and his record of 1–3–1 is nothing to be excited about. Certainly one of the motivations of his own professional life is to excel against Europe in September 1999 and erase his own Valderrama trauma.

But the fact is that any event Tiger enters immediately becomes a big deal, and for the Ryder Cup, Woods is the icing on the cake. Consider that Tiger was 22 in his first Ryder Cup; that's only two years older than Nick Faldo in his first Ryder Cup (okay, Faldo *did* start out 3–0), and the Ryder Cup record-holder has played in eleven Matches. Conceivably, if Woods has a career similar to (if not better than) Faldo's, he could be on U.S. Ryder Cup teams through 2017.

In fact, barring injury or other impediment, Tiger could be part of a quintet in their twenties—Justin Leonard, Phil Mickelson, Jim

Furyk, and David Duval—who form a strong Ryder Cup nucleus for the United States, perhaps rivaling the days of Palmer, Nicklaus, Casper, Trevino, and Littler that made America unbeatable. This should make for some especially thrilling Matches, more so if the United States is indeed able to reverse the recent European domination.

What also makes Woods's presence a high-profile one, at least for the near future, is that some other players who have consistently been in the top ten in the world rankings are not eligible for the Ryder Cup, such as Greg Norman and Steve Elkington of Australia, Vijay Singh of Fiji, Nick Price of Zimbabwe, and Ernie Els of South Africa. (Who knows what impact Gary Player could have had back in the 1960s?)

As we saw at Valderrama in 1997, though, the presence of Tiger Woods—nor, for that matter, Justin Leonard, Phil Mickelson, and any other rising star—does not guarantee a U.S. win. The Ryder Cup is ultimately a *team* competition, and the sum must be greater than a team's parts. As we approach the end of the century, it appears that the European players have been better at recognizing this and taking it to heart.

"Heart" is very crucial in the Ryder Cup. Certainly talent, timing, skill, luck, and other factors are important to winning a Match. But through the years, for the players on both sides of the Atlantic, heart and courage have often determined the Matches' outcomes. Participating in a Ryder Cup means harnessing a pumping heart, shaking hands and knees, twisting guts—and directing that energy toward winning.

Some succeed—and some don't.

Chapter 7

STRONG HEARTS, SHAKING HANDS

Talk to players from Ryder Cup teams of twenty or more years ago, and they are more likely to include the word *fun* when describing their experiences. Of course, the Matches were also fiercely competitive, the desire to win was very strong, and the team that didn't win was filled with disappointment. But there were enjoyable aspects to trying to beat each other on the course, and quite often the participants socialized after the day's last swing.

According to Brian Barnes, draining glasses after draining putts was a Ryder Cup tradition. "Oh bloody hell, we used to mix a few beers together at the end of the bloody day," said the player who is now successful on the Senior Tour and a teetotaler. "It was far more fun then."

But in recent years the word *fun* has been hard to find in interviews with players and captains. For better or worse, the Ryder Cup has become a very high-intensity event, and nerves can be stretched to the breaking point.

For example, after halving his singles match on the last day at the Belfry in 1989, Mark Calcavecchia, a veteran player who had won the British Open just two months earlier, was quoted as saying, "I never want to go through this again." (He did, though, in

1991.) And in 1995 at Oak Hill, Tom Lehman stated about his Ryder Cup debut: "I was so nervous, I could hardly breathe."

If you get to watch a video of the 1997 Match or can recall the televised images, take note of the players' faces: They are taut, pale, and much too serious. You get the feeling that they are expecting that at any moment one of the Valderrama olive trees is going to fall on them. And they do this for free?

Given the potential for disaster and humiliation, and that it is a stomach-churning experience, why does every Ryder Cup player consider being in the Matches an unforgettable experience that they wouldn't trade? Assuming they're not masochists, what is it about the Ryder Cup that makes it so special for a player?

Let us count the ways:

Honor

More than most other sports, the concept of honor—as when a player calls a penalty on himself at a crucial moment that he probably could have gotten away with—is still associated with golf. However, more recently there has been an emphasis on winning, establishing or breaking records, and money.

When the top pro golfers are listed in any publication, they are most often listed not by tournaments won or lowest average score or most top ten finishes but by total money earned. While last year was an exception, with Mark O'Meara on top of the voting thanks to his Masters and British Open victories, generally the person named Player of the Year is the one who has pocketed the most dough, such as Tiger Woods, who jumped past $2 million earned in 1997, and Hale Irwin on the Senior Tour, who broke the $2 million barrier in both '97 and '98.

Yet when it comes to the Ryder Cup, money doesn't matter. While there has to be a relationship between money earned and points accumulated—a player who earned $1.5 million each year leading up to the Ryder Cup most likely earned enough points to grab one of the ten spots on the team—only the points matter.

Conceivably, a player who earns $1.7 million in '98 could have fewer points than one who earned $1.4 million in '99, because there is a two-year total of points used, and victory points this year are counted double (quadruple for a major).

A player is selected for a Ryder Cup team based on merit, and this is true both for the United States and for Europe. So when we talk about honor, there are really two kinds in the Ryder Cup. One is the honor of making the team; the other is the honor of playing for your country.

It is a great honor to earn a berth on a Ryder Cup team because it is a recognition of consistent excellence over a fairly lengthy period of time—and because, other than expenses underwritten by the respective PGAs, you're not going to get a penny reward. It is not unreasonable to regard yourself as one of the ten best players in your country (U.S.) or on the Continent.

"I always took a very positive attitude toward the Ryder Cup," Arnold Palmer told us. "It was a great honor to have played well enough to be a member of the United States Ryder Cup team. I certainly never considered it a chore."

"I considered it an honor and a privilege to play in the Ryder Cup," agreed Billy Casper. "I always tried to make the team because I wanted to be on it every time. It was a symbol of achievement, and you really had to earn it—there were no shortcuts."

Being a captain's pick is a great honor, too. Most of the time the players picked didn't miss the top ten by much, so they have also put away a lot of points. For them there is the added bonus of knowing that the captain believes *you* are the guy whose game complements the rest of the team, and that at important moments your experience, skills, and/or courage will make a difference. In a way, being on a Ryder Cup team is the equivalent of making an all-star team in any of the other major sports.

"I never really thought of it like that, but I guess it is like an all-star team of professional golf," said Curtis Strange. "After almost two years of play, you have qualified for a team that has only ten spots. It has to mean that you are the best on our tour."

The other part of honor is that the players (and their captain) are representing their country. "The Ryder Cup format is unique, and the fact that you're representing your country is special," stated Jack Nicklaus.

"It wasn't just pride in your own performance, it was of course pride in trying to do your best for your country," said Brian Barnes. "This was true on both sides, America or the U.K. You never, ever forgot this aspect of it."

This feeling of pride should not be underestimated. Though money is extremely important in the sports world and every star would like to be known as the highest paid, there is something unique and fundamental in wanting to bring glory to one's birthplace. (The Ryder Cup rules state that you must be born in the United States or Europe to participate, not be a naturalized citizen.) There isn't enough money in the world to persuade a player to step aside from a Ryder Cup berth.

When you think about it, with all the criticism to which various sports and individuals have been subjected in recent years, doing something for the honor of it offers even more grandeur than ever. You do it for free, you do it for tradition, and you do it to represent your country—a combination that is very hard to find elsewhere.

Will competing for a Ryder Cup always be without financial compensation? Many observers hope so, but in the last few years, there have been calls to offer players more than expenses. Mark O'Meara has been one of those who has suggested that players be paid, and remember, we're talking about a veteran who is widely liked and respected and who clearly believes in the integrity of golf.

Those who advocate paying the players believe that since the Ryder Cup Matches generate huge amounts of revenue, the players should have a piece of the action.

"I know that for a long, long time, the PGA of America lost money putting on the Ryder Cup," according to Tom Lehman, another one of the most respected pros on tour. "I am sure they would take teams to England back then and would spend more than they would make. Times have changed, though, and it is a multimillion-dollar deal."

Lehman continued: "People are making serious amounts of money off this. Right now they give you a little bit to cover your expenses. But I know that both Ryder Cups that I have been in have ended up costing me money to play. But I am honored to play. I would do it for nothing because I feel it is an honor to be on the team. But you look at the PGA of America and realize they are making $15 million [probably an underestimate] off a Ryder Cup when it is in the States, yet they are not paying the players anything, and the players are really the biggest part of the show. Ethically it is probably not right."

However, the players on both sides are pretty well taken care of these days. On the European side, the treatment improved dramatically after Tony Jacklin became captain, and the Europeans have kept pace with the Americans ever since. At Valderrama in '97, each U.S. player received a $5,000 stipend, $15,000 worth of clothing, two round-trip seats on the Concorde, and ten free tickets to the Ryder Cup. Indirectly, members of the winning team—especially players who performed well on either side—receive higher-paying endorsement contracts from worldwide companies.

It's an interesting argument, and one that will no doubt receive more attention in the next few years as tournaments with growing international fields and soaring purses become more common and as the rigors of participating in the Ryder Cup become more demanding.

Being a Team Member

Talk to a baseball or football or soccer player, and sometimes he says he looks forward to being alone or being with family and friends for a while, taking a break from the team and the claustrophobic environment of playing and traveling and staying in hotels together week after week, month after month. However, in over 95 percent of golf, *team* is an alien concept.

It is true that despite a few changes in the cast of characters, players see and play with the same golfers every week on the PGA Tour. Some might stay in the same hotels or go out to dinner together. Some very strong friendships have been formed among players and their families on the Tour.

There is a strong feeling of fraternity among golfers—look at the way many players rallied around Stuart Appleby in 1998 after his wife's tragic death in a car accident, and how during a tournament that same year David Frost and Corey Pavin devoted extra time to comforting and encouraging John Daly, whose courageous battle against alcoholism continues. Years ago Jack Nicklaus and Gary Player tried to beat each other every week, giving no quarter, but off the course the two have been very close friends. Nicklaus and Arnold Palmer, too, have a great deal of affection and respect for each other.

There are, of course, rivalries, animosities, and feuds, but most players share the connection of a shared experience and mutual respect. Every golfer is a solo sports performer whose fortune and future depend on what happens week after week. Miss the cut, and they go home with nothing. There is no such thing, as there is in many other professional sports, as a minimum salary.

Still, this experience is far removed from being on a team. None of the regular PGA Tour events involve teams; you'll find teams in only a few of the "silly season" tournaments between the season-ending Tour Championship in October and the season-kickoff Mercedes-Benz Championship in January. In the Ryder Cup you are never playing just for yourself, not even in the Sunday singles matches. A player can go 4–0 in a Match, but if his team hasn't collected at least 14 or 14½ points, he doesn't end the big weekend feeling all that great.

"Golf is so different from other sports because we are individuals playing for ourselves, and all of a sudden we are on a Ryder Cup *team*," Strange said. "It's a completely different experience."

Being a member of a team and creating an atmosphere of mutual support is a special experience for a professional

golfer, one he might not have felt since his college and/or amateur days. It's refreshing after all the emphasis on money and
ranking. One of the most satisfying experiences a player can have
is pulling for a teammate to do well, and for a pro golfer the
highest level of that experience comes every two years during the
Ryder Cup.

"The Ryder Cup is a tournament like no other—it's really
something else," said Costantino Rocca, the Italian golfer who has
played on three European teams. "You are on a different planet,
there is a different atmosphere. The only thing that counts is beating the opponent, nothing else. While all the American players
compete under the same flag, we put together an Italian, a Dane,
a German, Swedes, Spaniards, and Englishmen.

"We needed to convince ourselves that we were their equals,
but it is still a difficult thing to do," Rocca continued. "In my
opinion it burns the Americans a lot—the fact that they lost the
Ryder Cup twice in a row. They are more attached to this cup than
we are, because they are from one nation."

It's also a bit of an adjustment for players to deal with the
reaction of the spectators. During the typical stroke-play tournament, a consistently partisan crowd is not usually a factor. During
a Ryder Cup Match, however, the home team is the hero from
Friday morning through Sunday afternoon.

This doesn't mean there isn't partisanship during a tournament.
During the 1989 U.S. Open at The Country Club in Brookline,
despite the respect for Nick Faldo, the vast majority of the
American crowd wanted Curtis Strange to win in the playoff (which
he did). Very few of the spectators weren't cheering enthusiastically
for Davis Love III as he closed in on his first win in a major, the
1997 PGA Championship. And of course there has been "Arnie's
Army," the adulation for Tiger Woods, and perennial crowd
favorites like Jack Nicklaus, Chi Chi Rodriguez, Fuzzy Zoeller,
Payne Stewart, Paul Azinger, and Craig Stadler.

What you often hear in a Ryder Cup are cheers or hisses for
misses, sympathetic groans, and the kind of spontaneous and very

emotional outburst that occurs at the conclusion of the match. The crowd is very much *into* a Ryder Cup Match, and so players have to adjust to that as well.

Adjusting to team play has helped make the European success so remarkable—meeting the challenge of becoming a fleet of many ships from many ports flying under one flag. This was a challenge the strictly British teams didn't have to face.

"I think I felt far more of a close-knit group in my first five Matches than I did in the sixth when Europe was involved," Brian Barnes said. "Nothing against the Europeans, but there was a different feeling."

Turned out to be the feeling of winning.

Sportsmanship/Gamesmanship

We're not going to be crabby and say that fair play is disappearing in many professional sports and these days can be found only in golf. But still we think you'll find more sportsmanship in a match-play round of golf than in any other sport, and traditionally the ultimate example of fair play and regard for opponents has been the Ryder Cup.

Match play allows for an opponent to concede a putt, which is something like okaying a basket after the ball has spun off the rim. Match play can even be likened to boxing—without the physical violence—in that even though each contestant is trying very hard to win, there will be no hitting below the belt. As badly as you want victory, the next-best thing is to lose with your head high and with no regrets.

There continues to be a debate over what Jack Nicklaus did in 1969, conceding a relatively short putt to Tony Jacklin that allowed the match to be halved and that Ryder Cup Match to end in a tie. (Nicklaus, of course, knew the U.S. would retain the cup.)

After that match the U.S. captain was asked what he thought of Jack's action. "We came here to win, not be good guys," Sam Snead barked.

Billy Casper told us, "We worked our tails off to win that Match. The least Jack should have done was make Tony earn the tie."

But in the overall scheme of things that the Ryder Cup represents, what Nicklaus did was dead solid perfect. And he doesn't regret it for a second. "I actually thought that was a very good ending," he told us. "Although the Ryder Cup is very competitive and every player wants to win, each player knows what a key element sportsmanship is in these events and golf in general."

Nicklaus has the full support of teammate Lee Trevino, a six-time Ryder Cupper and 1985 captain, who told us, "The whole place went mad, went absolutely crazy when Jack gave that putt to Tony Jacklin, but I loved it. You see, the British team had tied for the first time in Ryder Cup history, and while that wasn't a win, it was a big, big thrill for the home fans. So it might seem that Jack was giving something away, but in what the Ryder Cup is supposed to represent, I loved what he did and the reaction."

Even in the Ryder Cup there are sometimes problems. For example, the term *gamesmanship* and Seve Ballesteros go hand in hand. Despite the emphasis on sportsmanship in Ryder Cup competitions, over the years numerous players have tried to gain an edge over others. But Seve—well, let's say he wasn't reluctant to try a few small tricks to tip the scales a tad.

A much-used ploy has been for Seve to clear his throat "coincidentally," just as an American player is lining up his putt. He has also challenged opponents on the kind of golf balls they're using or the validity of a ruling. One of the most blatant examples of Seve's antics occurred during the 1989 Ryder Cup at the Belfry in England. Tipped by Curtis Strange that Ballesteros liked to try to cut corners and/or rattle opponents, Paul Azinger was ready when he drew Seve for the Sunday singles match.

Ballesteros wanted to take a ball out of play, and Azinger refused. On the eighteenth hole Ballesteros questioned whether Azinger had taken a proper drop after his ball had gone into water. Neither one conceded a putt to the other during the entire match, no matter how short it was, nor would they speak to each other. Azinger ended up winning, which was a crucial match because the Americans managed a tie.

It seems that Seve hasn't given up on his old tricks. In July 1998, just before the British Open, there was a mini–Ryder Cup Match in England: Ballesteros and Bernhard Langer took on the duo of Phil Mickelson and Corey Pavin.

On the par-5 fifteenth hole, the other three had laid up, and Mickelson wondered to his caddy if he should go for the green on his second shot. Immediately Seve said, "Sure, you can go there. Go on." Mickelson pulled his 3-wood into the right-hand bushes. He turned to the grinning Spaniard and said, "You told me to go for it." Seve responded, "It was your choice, not mine. Don't blame me."

By the way, the European team won when Ballesteros birdied the par-4 eighteenth, hitting a sand wedge to within three feet of the pin.

In spite of these occasional ploys, the Ryder Cup has remained an oasis in the desert of a win-at-all-costs philosophy in sports. Match after match, hole after hole, the mutual respect of the competitors is seen in conceded putts and behavior toward each other, distant at times but always respectful.

This has been true for seventy-two years. Gene Sarazen wanted to win as much as Ted Ray. Max Faulkner wanted to win as much as Ben Hogan. Tony Jacklin wanted to win as much as Billy Casper. Davis Love III wants to win as much as Nick Faldo, and Justin Leonard as much as Jose Maria Olazabal. But each could live with defeat if it meant the best qualities of sportsmanship were exhibited.

Fun and Camaraderie

Didn't we say earlier there was no such thing as fun in the Ryder Cup? If you believe that, then we deserve three whacks with a 9-iron. (Well, maybe just two.)

To be clear about it, in the last twenty years the Ryder Cup has become less fun for the participants because the competitive gap between the two teams has narrowed—the last six Matches decided by two points or less—and more worldwide attention has been focused on the Matches. *Fun* can be seen as a relative term then, because it was probably easier to relax when one team was routinely better than the other and the competition reflected that.

"I think things were more relaxed back in the 1960s and 1970s than they are now," Barnes said. "Okay, probably because the Americans knew they were going to beat the shit out of us all the time. But I think the attitude of the players was completely different from the way it is now."

"The Ryder Cup has taken me back to my college days," said Strange. "It's so much fun to hang out with twelve other guys for a whole week in really a fraternity-type atmosphere. We're a pretty close-knit group for that one week."

If there is a downside to the fun aspect, it's that the Ryder Cup week has become very social, filled with all kinds of events—autograph sessions, get-togethers with officials and dignitaries, media interviews, photo shoots, cocktail parties, and so on. The captains and players receive more requests than they can possibly handle while preparing for the Match. It may be getting too stressful for the already keyed-up teams, an issue Ben Crenshaw and Mark James will have to address this year.

"If someone asked, 'Did you have a great time at Valderrama?' I'd have to say no," reported O'Meara. "If you want us to win the Ryder Cup, you have to eliminate all the functions you force players to go to."

"I don't see us getting ready for majors by going to functions every night until midnight," Tiger Woods told *Golf Magazine*.

The Agony and the Ecstasy

To those who aren't familiar with the Ryder Cup, any mention of pressure might seem exaggerated. If it's just some guys putting around and the outcome doesn't result in a cent or a shilling, what's the big deal?

It is true of any sports event that is contested every so often—the World Series, World Cup, Olympics, Ryder Cup—that of course the outcome will be more crucial because in addition to pitting the best against the best, there is no tomorrow, or next week, or next month, or in the Ryder Cup's case no next year. So every win or loss is more dearly felt, whether it's celebrating or lamenting.

"There's nothing like winning your first Ryder Cup Match. It's like you've really arrived as a team player," recalled Lee Janzen. "That first day at Valderrama when Scott Hoch and I won our Match [defeating Costantino Rocca and Jose Maria Olazabal] was an experience I will never forget. Beating Olazabal in the singles on Sunday was wonderful too, but there's only one first Ryder Cup victory."

There are a lot of aspects to pressure in sports—individual competition, team versus team, the desire to excel (even to break previously held records), the personal challenge of exceeding prior performances or expectations, and the like. In this regard the Ryder Cup contains all that and more. While the players and captains are having it out on some of the most beautiful golf courses in the world, what most of the rest of us see is a nail-biting drama that takes place on a most intriguing stage.

It *is* great theater. "There is a deliberateness to the Ryder Cup," Johnny Miller said during the '97 Match at Valderrama. "It's almost a Shakespearean or Kabuki drama. Everything is sized up, and there is the feeling on any putt that everything depends on it."

According to Fred Couples, "Every hole of the Ryder Cup is like the eighteenth hole of the U.S. Open."

When you make a great shot, it's "Top o' the world, Ma!" If you make a bad shot or the golf gods cause a crucial putt to lip out, there is much wailing and gnashing of teeth. And even on only moderately important shots, not getting the result you want means evident irritation.

One example came during the 1997 Match, when on Saturday, playing with Mark O'Meara, Tiger Woods missed a makable six-footer on the thirteenth hole. Filled with frustration,

Woods dug at the errant ball, damaging the green—a faux pas rarely seen among pro players.

The pressure of such a huge international event can bend players in ways that don't really occur the rest of the year. Before the 1993 Match at the Belfry began, Tom Watson told his troops to be ready for a variety of feelings. The Ryder Cup, he said, was "the only event in the world that will make your legs shake."

Let's go back to Mark Calcavecchia's experience. Here is a fellow who was and remains one of the toughest competitors in golf. By Kiawah Island in 1991, he was no stranger to the Ryder Cup. During his first Match in 1987, he played only once the first two days and burned to show his stuff. When the captain, Jack Nicklaus, finally unleashed him on Sunday, Calcavecchia not only won his singles match, but the player he beat was Nick Faldo.

During the "War at the Shore," he was 2–1–1 going into Sunday, his two wins as a team member coming against Faldo and Woosnam and Steve Richardson and Mark James. For his singles match he drew Europe's emerging big gun, Colin Montgomerie.

No problem, said Mark. And indeed it didn't seem to be. He was 4-up with four holes to play, meaning Calcavecchia couldn't lose and needed just a halve a hole to win. (By the way, the British term *dormie* refers to a player who cannot lose a match. In the Calcavecchia-versus-Montgomerie match, starting the fifteenth hole, the American was dormie.)

Then through a combination of bad shots and bad luck, Mark's game fell apart, Monty won the last four holes, and the match was halved. Calcavecchia practically went into shock. He was taken to a medical tent where he was given oxygen for hyperventilation. He later told John Feinstein that he'd had "enough tension at Kiawah Island to last a lifetime" and that what happened to him "was damaging in a way. It was something I'll never forget."

"The pressure in a Ryder Cup Match is quite definitely different," said Neil Coles, who experienced it as a player eight times. "Effectively, you are playing for eleven other people for no financial gain and indeed the honor of representing your country. It is very hard to put into words the actual pressure experienced."

What is both funny and sad is that some of the pressure can occur after the Match, sometimes well after. The Ryder Cup has become such an international event and has invited so much more partisanship that what players do, good or bad, can linger. More than a few American players during the 1990s have had to cope with fans expressing their disappointment weeks, months, and even years after they performed poorly.

Ironically, the player who seems to have suffered the most in the United States, other than the unfairly maligned Curtis Strange, is Colin Montgomerie. Now, of course, one can say that after his pre-Match comments in 1997, he's made himself fair game for the catcalls and other heckling he has received during tourneys.

For example, it was tough going for Montgomerie during the 1998 U.S. Open at the Olympic in San Francisco. Monty was subjected to quite a bit of heckling during the championship, and perhaps this was due to his being in general an outspoken person. But on the last day, as he walked to the ninth hole, a fan shouted, "Go home, Monty!"

"Who said that?" the Scotsman demanded. "I did," a man replied. "Why?" the golfer queried. "Because of the Ryder Cup," the man explained.

Eyes gleaming, Montgomerie said, "There was nothing wrong with the Ryder Cup, except you lost."

After the U.S. Open, Monty said, "I seem to be blamed for winning the Ryder Cup, but I had eleven strong individuals with me as well. Yet I seem to bear the brunt of it."

"It's a disgrace, of course," Jesper Parnevik declared, defending his Ryder Cup comrade. "People don't realize that Colin is a very fascinating man with a good sense of humor off the course. But on the course, well, Colin is Colin, and if someone gives him a hard time, he won't just walk away—he'll confront the troublemaker, and it becomes news."

When the 1995 Match at Oak Hill was concluded, Bernard Gallacher said, "It's getting almost too much to bear, this Ryder Cup." And this from the *winning* captain!

"It's the most nervous you will ever be in golf," said Paul

Azinger. No stranger to challenges, this three-time Ryder Cupper has won a major, the PGA Championship, and even defeated cancer. "At a major, if you're in contention on the last day, it means you're playing well, which gives you confidence. But at the Ryder Cup there's pressure from the first tee. Even if you're playing terrible golf, the spotlight's still on you—you can't hide."

"I was paired with Davis Love at his first Ryder Cup," Tom Kite told *The New York Times,* referring to the 1993 Match at the Belfry. "There was a long fog delay in the morning, which gave us all a chance to get more nervous than we already were. By the time we teed off, Davis was a blithering idiot."

Has the European team handled the pressure better? Scott Hoch thinks that is possible. "They're better under pressure than we are, that's the only way I can explain it," Hoch told *Golf Digest.* "I think we've got the better players, we *definitely* do."

The Europeans don't seem to have an escape hatch from Ryder Cup pressure, either, however. "It feels like there is a million pounds on your back," said Jose Maria Canizares. "The pressure of your teammates, the pressure of your country, and the pressure of the collective countries of Europe—there is no medal-play tournament like this."

Does all this imply that things are getting out of hand and the Ryder Cup has actually become a traumatic experience for players? It's not unreasonable to think so, yet you would be hard-pressed to find a player who wouldn't jump at the chance to go through the mill. Many veteran Ryder Cuppers know that the pressure, no matter how intense, just goes with the territory.

"Because it's become so popular and people root for their own team, if you are a so-called 'goat,' you will hear about it—trust me on that one," said Curtis Strange. "But you know, if you think you're good enough to belong on the team, if you think you're good enough to handle the pressure, and if you think you're good enough to want to be in that swing match, then you better be good enough and strong enough and gutsy enough to handle it."

"Anybody who has played with Curtis knows what a great

competitor he is, and this is the same guy who saved the United States in the 1989 Ryder Cup by ensuring a tie," said Lee Janzen who, ironically, had to gracefully endure Curtis Strange being selected ahead of him by Lanny Wadkins for the 1995 U.S. team. "We all felt bad for the way Curtis was treated after the '95 Match, and we knew, too, that no one felt worse than he did.

"The Ryder Cup has almost become too personal," Janzen continued. "I don't know that the Americans dislike the Europeans as much as the Europeans dislike us. We feel like when they win they rub it in our faces."

Raymond Floyd echoes this sentiment. He has certainly seen it all, having been on eight Ryder Cup teams and been a captain of the U.S. squad in 1989 that went into the lion's den of the Belfry after two straight American defeats. In fact, he said that "being captain and my longevity is what I'm most proud of," pointing to having played on Ryder Cup teams in four different decades.

Floyd acknowledges that Ryder Cup players experience a great deal of pressure and that it has intensified since his first Match experience in 1969. Of all the players, he thinks the pressure is heaviest on the captain's picks because "you really go through the gauntlet" of having to prove that the captain's faith wasn't misplaced. (He, of course, did this in '93 when, as a captain's pick by Watson, the 51-year-old warrior downed Olazabal in the pivotal match.)

But like Strange, Floyd won't make excuses for the pressure. "There is no such thing as too much pressure," he stated firmly. "You are in a position to win with your peers and for your country, and that is an opportunity every player should strive for. Now, this might not be much consolation, but about the Ryder Cup pressure, I feel that if you can survive it, you can survive anything."

So most of the best players in the world keep coming back for more, doing what they can to make the Ryder Cup team and then trying their best to win for team and country. While more shaking hands and knees will be found in a Ryder Cup Match than at any other golf tournament, more courage and heart will be on display too. No Ryder Cup player can ignore the thrill and pride of doing well on golf's greatest stage.

After Christy O'Connor, Jr., won the eighteenth hole and his match against Fred Couples in 1989, he declared, "This has got to be the greatest and most emotional moment of my life."

"I didn't really know what it was all about," Davis Love III said about the Ryder Cup before he made the team. "All I saw was guys with golf bags alike and shirts alike and shoes alike. I never really watched it that much until I got on tour because it wasn't that interesting, really." Then when he made his first team in 1993? "It was a great experience—more of a grand experience."

"From watching the Ryder Cup and talking to the other players, I was expecting a lot of commotion surrounding the 1993 Match, but what happened was a lot more than I expected," recalled Lee Janzen about his first Ryder Cup experience. "And nothing prepared me for that moment during the opening ceremony when I stood with Tom Watson and the rest of the team watching the American flag be raised and hearing the national anthem. It's a moment that . . . well, you can't be more proud of representing your country."

"This is the finest experience I have had in the game of golf," said Tom Watson as he held the Ryder Cup at the conclusion of the 1993 Match.

Yes, the emphasis has been mostly on what the players feel and experience. Let's not forget the captains. They also serve who stand and wait—and as we'll see in the next chapter, in the modern-day Ryder Cup, the captains do a heck of a lot more than that.

Chapter 8

CAPTAINS COURAGEOUS . . . AND CRENSHAW

According to Lanny Wadkins, in the past "the American captain's performance was judged by how well he stocked the bar."

While that may or may not have been true—and we don't want to disagree with an eight-time Ryder Cup player with an eye-popping twenty wins and a former captain—the fact is that for both sides the role of the Ryder Cup team captain has changed significantly, especially during the last decade.

Having a team captain is another way that Ryder Cup competition differs from typical tournament golf. Most if not all pro players have a coach, and the higher-earning players can have coaches for various areas—swing coach, motivational coach, putting coach, physical conditioning coach, TV coach, and so on.

The very top players have their coaches travel with them, especially to important tournaments; for example, at one or more of the four majors (and the Ryder Cup), we have seen Butch Harmon, David Leadbetter, Jim Flick, Mac O'Grady, Dave Pelz, Dr. Richard Coop, and other teachers-coaches with their professional clients.

Being a *captain*, however, is a very different kettle of fish. A coach works with just one player at any given time, not a whole group of pros in a sort of classroom setting. The coaches at the top level get paid well for their expertise and communication skills, and Tiger Woods or Greg Norman or David Duval wants that coach's complete attention. Also, on the official PGA Tours there is no such thing as a team event, so there is no team to be the captain of—each week it's every man/woman for him/herself.

In the Ryder Cup it's one team against another, and each team has its captain. The position is not at all ceremonial, though as Wadkins implies, it may at one time have been little more than a formality for the U.S. teams that routinely won anyway. When you really did have the best golfers in the world, how much actual work did the captain have to do? Joe Torre said about managing the Yankees during their record-setting season in 1998 that the best thing to do with a talented team "is stay out of the way and let 'em play."

Like a lot of other things in the Ryder Cup, that hands-off philosophy began to change in the mid-1980s when Europe rebelled against American domination. The European captains—Jacklin, Gallacher, then Ballesteros—faced special challenges and ultimately faced them successfully.

One challenge was that unlike previous U.S. opponents from Great Britain, the European captain had to blend together players from half a dozen or more countries and languages, a difficult task.

"The fact is the Europeans, with good captaincy, have knitted together into a more potent force and a more potent team than the Americans have," said John Hopkins of *The London Times.* "Probably the U.S. in recent years has, man for man, had stronger teams, but Europe has developed this aggressive team spirit being skillfully led by inspiring captains—Jacklin, Gallacher, and Ballesteros. In professional golf, the virtues of teamwork will manifest themselves most in the Ryder Cup, and coordinating that teamwork is a big part of the captain's role."

This might seem like a breeze—stronger talent means more wins, right?—yet there are many examples in sports history of powerful teams that have lost to less-talented teams that just had better chemistry, cohesion, luck, whatever. It's no longer enough to simply show up and expect to win.

"Even in the years when we won Matches pretty easily, the captain never just showed up and said, 'Okay, go win now,'" said Billy Casper, who captained the 1979 team that won 17–11. "A lot of the matches could have gone either way, and suddenly you're faced with a tie or even a defeat. There was no relaxing as captain, and that's more true today than ever."

A special challenge for the European captain was the weight of history. When Jacklin became captain of the 1983 team, the Europeans had won only one Match in fifty years. It can't have been easy to motivate the players and make them believe that their day had finally arrived when their track record was so dismal.

But Jacklin did it. "I have played under some excellent captains, notably Tony Jacklin," said Nick Faldo. "He was a great motivator and a great tactician, and his results speak for themselves."

One more challenge is that as the European teams began to win, the ante was upped, meaning it was no longer as tolerable to lose to the Americans as it had been in the past. Whereas losing was once expected, and a good effort by the team was probably good enough, during the last decade or so the pressure has surged to win the Ryder Cup and keep it on just one side of the Atlantic. No wonder Gallacher said in 1995, "The only thing left in my stomach is acid."

Besides having to choose the best brands of booze for the victory celebration, the U.S. captains also faced a few challenges over the years, but of a very different sort. During the decades of one-sided results, it was at times difficult to keep the American players focused. Ben Hogan's irritation with the joyriding Arnold Palmer in 1967 is an example of that.

A more recent challenge is the risk of being a losing U.S. team captain, an experience shared by only Walter Hagen (twice, in '29 and '33); Jack Burke, Jr. ('57); Lee Trevino ('85); Jack Nicklaus ('87); Lanny Wadkins ('95); and Tom Kite ('97). (Conceivably, Raymond Floyd could join this list because the Ryder Cup Match in '89, when he was captain, was the only time that a U.S. opponent successfully defended the Cup with a tie.)

"Being the captain of a losing team is pitiful," Jack Burke, Jr., told us in his usual direct style. "There's all kinds of reasons, none of 'em happy ones. Hurts like hell, but you got to suck it up and hope you get another shot. I did, in 1973, and thanks to fellows like Nicklaus and Trevino, I was able to make the most of it."

With the U.S. consistently presenting "the best golfers in the world" into the 1980s, how does a captain keep them all happy? Anyone who sits out a match could feel slighted, and with players who are high up on leader boards, there are some big egos involved, especially among successful Ryder Cup veterans. The U.S. captain has to not only keep the players happy enough that they win but make sure that no unpleasantness develops that could carry over to the PGA Tour or infect the Ryder Cup team.

How are Ryder Cup captains chosen? It doesn't go by who the best golfers are, though it helps—Hagen was captain six times, Snead and Hogan three times each, and Burke, Palmer, and Nicklaus twice each. The selection process has been different on either side of the Atlantic, the respective PGAs have had different outlooks, and for the British/European team, some of the best players have not worn the captain's hat.

A way to see the difference is to look at who the captains have been for each team:

Year	U.S. Captain	British/Euro Captain
1927	Walter Hagen	Ted Ray
1929	Walter Hagen	George Duncan
1931	Walter Hagen	Charles Whitcombe
1933	Walter Hagen	J. H. Taylor
1935	Walter Hagen	Charles Whitcombe
1937	Walter Hagen	Charles Whitcombe
1947	Ben Hogan	Henry Cotton
1949	Ben Hogan	Charles Whitcombe
1951	Sam Snead	Arthur Lacey

Year	U.S. Captain	British/Euro Captain
1953	Lloyd Mangrum	Henry Cotton
1955	Chick Harbert	Dai Rees
1957	Jack Burke, Jr.	Dai Rees
1959	Sam Snead	Dai Rees
1961	Jerry Barber	Dai Rees
1963	Arnold Palmer	John Fallon
1965	Byron Nelson	Harry Weetman
1967	Ben Hogan	Dai Rees
1969	Sam Snead	Eric Brown
1971	Jay Hebert	Eric Brown
1973	Jack Burke, Jr.	Bernard Hunt
1975	Arnold Palmer	Bernard Hunt
1977	Dow Finsterwald	Brian Huggett
1979	Billy Casper	John Jacobs
1981	Dave Marr	John Jacobs
1983	Jack Nicklaus	Tony Jacklin
1985	Lee Trevino	Tony Jacklin
1987	Jack Nicklaus	Tony Jacklin
1989	Raymond Floyd	Tony Jacklin
1991	Dave Stockton	Bernard Gallacher
1993	Tom Watson	Bernard Gallacher
1995	Lanny Wadkins	Bernard Gallacher
1997	Tom Kite	Seve Ballesteros
1999	Ben Crenshaw	Mark James

As you can see, with the exception of Hagen's run as captain during the Ryder Cup's infancy, the British and then the Europeans have been more likely to keep their captains year after year, sometimes leaving the decision about whether to continue up to them. On the other hand, while the post-Hagen U.S. teams have had a few repeat captains—the last one being Nicklaus twelve years ago—the emphasis has been on rotation.

Look at the most recent Match: After the victory at Valderrama, Ballesteros could have stayed on, but he decided not to continue as captain. Essentially Tom Kite's captaincy was over as soon as Colin Montgomerie holed his last putt, and Crenshaw was picked for the '99 team less than a month later. Even the last winning U.S. captain, Tom Watson, knew it would be someone else's turn in '95, and he supported choosing Wadkins.

The difference is one not only of philosophy but of the selection process used by each PGA. For the PGA of America, a captain is chosen by an in-house committee that interviews candidates and makes its final recommendation to PGA executives.

Experience is a factor, but it is far from the only one. Arnold Palmer had been on only one Ryder Cup team before being named captain of the 1963 squad. Dave Stockton, who turned out to be a successful captain, had only limited Ryder Cup experience. It does seem, though, that the captains who have overcome the big hurdles are ones who have been on several Ryder Cup teams and kept their eyes and ears open.

"I learned from each captain I played for," said Raymond Floyd, who earned a stop-the-bleeding tie at the Belfry in 1989. "Each one was a different personality who had different experiences. You almost can't help but learn from that."

For the European PGA, the process of picking a captain is carried out by the Ryder Cup Committee, made up of representatives from different countries. Traditionally this committee has taken more of a hands-off approach. They will wait for the existing captain to make his decision about stepping down or staying and then, if he is leaving, often act on the departing captain's recommendation on his successor.

"The Ryder Cup Committee have a team of people from both the European Tour and the PGA heavily involved with the planning of the Matches, and that includes who is going to be captain," said Neil Coles, now chairman of the PGA European Tour. "While there has been some controversy, it has for the most part been an orderly process."

This doesn't necessarily mean that everything is hunky-dory between European captains. Indeed, things can get kind of testy.

In 1993, after Tony Jacklin was quoted criticizing Bernard Gallacher's selections to the team, the stolid Scotsman responded: "I don't even bother with Tony Jacklin. I mean, Tony Jacklin lives in America now. He's an American."

In fact, a somewhat entertaining subplot to the Ryder Cup is the occasionally abrasive relationship between captains on both sides, a relationship that spans the competition.

"After letting Hagen have it all those years, they finally offered it to me," growled Gene Sarazen. "I turned it down. This was well after I won the British Open and the American Open, in 1932. If they weren't going to make me captain when I was playing my best and deserved it, in 1933, I didn't want to accept it."

"They could at the very least have asked me," grumbled Ian Woosnam, eight-time Ryder Cupper, after the selection of Mark James in September 1998. "I've done as much as anybody. I've sure earned my stripes."

Down, boys. Being captain is a coveted prize, and it seems like Ryder Cup competition can be just as determined off the course.

"I would love to be Ryder Cup captain one day—what a honor!" Faldo told us. "But I still hope to play in two, maybe three more Ryder Cups, and I don't think you can combine the two, at least not effectively. Maybe 2005 would be a great time, in Ireland—imagine the atmosphere!"

Okay, now that we know how a Ryder Cup captain is selected, what exactly does he do? Without picking up a club in competition once during the three days, and with twenty-four of the best thirty or so players in the world having it out, can a captain really have a significant impact on the outcome?

Absolutely. This is especially the case since the Ryder Cup became truly competitive almost twenty years ago. It's plain common sense that if the Matches are going to be closer and if one match, player, or bit of strategy within each match can determine the outcome, the decisions the captain makes and how he conducts himself will have a direct bearing on who wins the Ryder Cup.

Of the many responsibilities a captain has, let's discuss what are probably the most important ones.

Long-Term Preparation

Though the Ryder Cup takes place every other year, a captain gets to work as soon as he is chosen. In this regard it might seem that the U.S. captain has the advantage because he is selected almost two years before the next Match. However, until recently this hasn't been the case because the European team didn't switch captains every two years, and Seve Ballesteros knew far in advance that he was going to take over for Bernard Gallacher. It is worth wondering if Mark James's selection as European captain only a year before the Battle of Brookline will be a disadvantage—it certainly would be if the '99 Match were being played in Europe.

Right away the captain pays special attention to who is playing well, or not playing well, on their respective tours, especially in the months leading up to the Ryder Cup. While the captain has no say about who the first ten players on the team will be because of the points system, he can pick two team members who can play as much or more than the others.

Sometimes the players who are number 11 and number 12 in points aren't automatically selected, because the captain will also look at who's had a strong overall year and is hot heading toward September, who has the kind of personality best suited to match play and Ryder Cup pressure, who might best complement the styles of a few players already on the team, and so on. For well over a year, a captain will read reams of computer printouts on players' performances in addition to trusting his own observations and instinct.

All this puts an extra burden on a captain who is still playing regularly on tour. On the one hand you're trying to win tournaments and lots more money. On the other, with the high stakes of the Ryder Cup, you can't set aside the many captain's responsibilities to focus on your own career. If captaining takes a toll on your game, so be it.

That's why, in addition to the captaincy being a symbol of gratitude and reverence, it has for the most part been bestowed on players whose best years are behind them. In that sense it can be a bittersweet honor, like a film actress or director receiving a lifetime achievement award—a fabulous honor, but the subtle reminder is that your career is past its peak.

As early and often as possible, the captain wants his probable team members to play the Ryder Cup course. Kite received some criticism that few team members had played Valderrama in 1997, and he stated that the criticism was justified. To be fair, though, it was a lot to ask that top players jet back and forth to Sotogrande, Spain, especially in the spring and summer, the peak of the PGA Tour season, when all four majors take place.

One other aspect of long-term preparation is making changes to the golf course upon which the next Match will be played. A visitor, of course, has no say, but the home captain has a big say. In the last decade this was an advantage Floyd, Watson, and Tom Kite didn't have. Lanny Wadkins had specific ideas in mind about the size of the rough, the restructuring of greens, and so on, for Oak Hill in '95. Ballesteros was very involved in making changes to Valderrama, not only with remodeling the seventeenth hole but with narrowing some of the fairways 250 yards or more from the tee, to counter the U.S. team's longest hitters—Davis Love III, Fred Couples, Tiger Woods, and Phil Mickelson.

It helps a lot if the captain has experience in golf course design. Ballesteros did, and Ben Crenshaw has a thriving course-design business. He and golf course architect Rees Jones have been conferring for well over a year to give the home team an edge or two in Brookline.

"As we get closer, Ben's going to start saying to these guys, 'Hey, you need to make a trip there and play,'" said Brendan Walsh of The Country Club in Brookline. "We'll do everything we can to accommodate them, and I can go out with these guys and give them a little local knowledge. Some of our members, too, have been around here for a very long time and are well versed in the golf course. This is a resource the U.S. captain can call upon."

Short-Term Preparation

Of course, long- and short-term preparation overlap a lot, but in the weeks leading up to a Ryder Cup Match, a captain finds that indeed the devil is in the details.

The captain has input in decisions involving everything from the transportation of players to the accommodations for players and their families to handling press conferences and other media-related tasks to supervising practices to the team dress code—and such chores are only the tip of the iceberg. A captain becomes a combination of den mother/scoutmaster, traveling secretary, corresponding secretary, treasurer, tourist guide, interviewee deluxe, swing coach, concierge, psychologist, and more.

Very, very short-term preparation involves being with the players during the days before the Ryder Cup officially begins. The captain is preoccupied with pairings; practices; the gala dinner; learning the habits, qualities, and preferences of each individual team member; and in many other respects getting the players mentally and emotionally ready for what could be the biggest event of their lives. The pressure is unbelievably intense for both captain and team. Golf fans tend to remember the players of winning Ryder Cup teams and the captains of losing teams.

Captain's Picks

With the player-selection process having changed many times during seven decades, the captain's ability to form the Ryder Cup team has ebbed and flowed because the number of picks he has has changed, too. "When Hagen was captain, he picked the people he liked to be on the team," Gene Sarazen told us. "He was the man in charge, and what he said goes. Fortunately, he was a very good captain."

The process is considerably more structured now for both teams, with the top ten players in points given Ryder berths. While in recent years a couple of captains have mentioned wanting more picks—Ballesteros actively lobbied for three (or more) selections in '97—it is likely that two captain's picks will be the norm, at least for the near future. To increase the picks would punish players who have earned their spots in the top ten on the PGA Tours over a two-year period. To eliminate the picks would unwisely reduce the captain's role and his expertise, experience, and instinct.

There is plenty of evidence from the past ten years that captain's picks do have an impact. Raymond Floyd couldn't have done better than to have Wadkins and Watson on his squad at the Belfry in '89, and during the furious 4–0 singles charge late on the last day that earned a tie, Watson beat Sam Torrance and Wadkins beat Nick Faldo. For Gallacher, it was a no-brainer to add Faldo, Jose Maria Olazabal, and Mark James to the European team in '91. Dave Stockton countered with Chip Beck and steely veteran Floyd, and Beck had a crucial win over Ian Woosnam that Sunday on Kiawah Island.

Gallacher again had three picks in '93, back at the Belfry, and no one could argue with his choice of Ballesteros and Olazabal, though Joakim Haeggman was a stretch. Watson went with Floyd and Wadkins, which turned out to be pivotal selections—Floyd, at 51, went 3–1, defeating Olazabal on the last day, and Wadkins became the heart and soul of the team by volunteering to go in the envelope.

For the '95 Match at Oak Hill, Wadkins selected Fred Couples and Curtis Strange, and he was most criticized for picking the two-time U.S. Open winner, because when push came to shove, Strange, Haas, and Faxon didn't get that crucial last win. Gallacher, with Europe having only two picks by this time, chose Faldo and Woosnam, both of whom helped the winning effort.

At Valderrama there was a great deal of controversy over the twelve players who made the European team. Faldo again was picked, this time by Ballesteros, and Jesper Parnevik, who had been second in the British Open that year, was also tapped. Tom Kite wanted Couples to be on the team again (which worked out fine, especially when he waxed Woosnam in the first singles match on Sunday), even though Couples was only seventeenth in Ryder Cup points, and he wanted Lee Janzen on the team, too, because he was not only a U.S. Open champion (as he would be again in '98) but a gritty player who thrived on tough golf courses (fifteenth in points). As it turned out, Janzen's gutsy singles win over Olazabal late on Sunday almost rescued the U.S. team.

Just as an aside: The all-time Ryder Cup leader in points has not had his best Matches as a captain's pick. Nick Faldo is 5–9 as a captain's pick but 18–10–4 as a player who qualified for the team. Does this mean anything? Probably not. As one American player, who asked not to be identified, said, "No matter how Nick is playing the rest of the year, he is still the most feared Ryder Cup player on the European side. No one wants to face him because he's a whole different player in the Ryder Cup—the pressure doesn't faze him, and he knows how to win."

We can only speculate what the outcome of some Matches would have been if captains of both teams had picked different players, but clearly the captains' choices have made a difference. No wonder they agonize over their picks and, until the Ryder Cup is decided, pray they made the right ones. Wadkins paid the price in '95 when he drew criticism for picking Curtis Strange, but he really shouldn't be faulted for his decision. Not only was Strange a hard-nosed competitor and Ryder Cup veteran, but one of his two Open Championships had been won at Oak Hill, and his experience there looked to be useful.

Pairings and Practice

Recently there has been a lot of noise about changing the way captains decide who will play whom during the three days of competition. Critics of the present system think it is not effective or exciting enough and that it limits each captain's ability to influence the Match.

The current system is that for each phase of competition—two fourballs, two foursomes, and the final full day of singles matches—

the captain decides whom he will pair together (fourballs and foursomes) and then in what order the members of the team will play singles. The captains then exchange this information, and only then does each discover what the other decided.

Figuring out the pairings is a much more complicated process than you might think. Among the captain's considerations:

Personalities

If two players are close friends, does this make for a stronger team, or will the friendship be a distraction? Is it best to pair players with different personalities, such as a confident player with a worrier, or will those personalities clash?

Styles

Will pairing players with similar styles make for a solid team, or is it better to pair players with differing styles that, taken as a whole, make for a better-rounded team? The conventional wisdom in alternate shot and best ball is to find combinations where the styles complement each other—for example, combining someone who is long off the tee with a teammate who is a very good iron player or a strong putter. Pairing Tiger Woods and Mark O'Meara, who are also close friends, at Valderrama seemed to be a perfect strategy on paper, but the results didn't support Kite's choice.

Experience

Usually the last thing a captain wants to do is pair two Ryder Cup rookies; preferably he would put together a veteran with a newcomer. This worked wonderfully for Jacklin when he teamed Ballesteros and Olazabal, and then in '97 Ballesteros as captain did the same with Faldo and Lee Westwood.

On the other hand, Couples and Davis Love III, both veterans, have been repeatedly paired successfully, and in '93 a big part of the American comeback was the victory of rookie John Cook and relative newcomer Chip Beck over Faldo and Colin Montgomerie. At Valderrama the pairing of Woods and Justin Leonard looked unbeatable, yet the best they could do was halve with Jesper Parnevik and Ignacio Garrido.

Who's Hot?

If during the weekend a particular pairing has won a couple of matches, do you keep them together for one or two more, or do you break them up so each can take his winning ways to two new pairings? This is sort of a bird-in-the-hand dilemma because the risk, of course, is that diluting a strong combo might give you two mediocre teams and no go-to guys.

What Do the Players Want?

Your initial reaction might be "The hell with what they want—they *have* to listen to the captain." Okay, ultimately that's true, it is a like-it-or-lump-it situation.

But the captain is dealing with twelve men who are, for the most part, instantly recognizable millionaires used to getting their way both on and off the golf course. While on the surface they may leave the decisions on pairings up to the captain, inevitably they do have preferences, and they communicate them in subtle (and sometimes not-so-subtle) ways. Hypothetically, if Phil Mickelson wants to play with Justin Leonard and Tiger Woods doesn't want to play with Mark O'Meara, the captain better find a way to create the pairing he thinks will be most effective without alienating and/or distracting his best players.

Singles

There is a lot of tossing and turning by the captain on Saturday night over this one. Do you send your best players out first so they can establish momentum that will carry through the entire day? If you do and it works, you're a genius. But if it doesn't work, you're left with lesser players trying to salvage the day, and even if it works fairly well, a very close Match might be decided in a late-day contest that doesn't include one of your best two or three players.

To some extent, the score at the end of Saturday could determine what to do. If your team is behind by a good margin, you'd better attack with your best players early, otherwise Sunday afternoon doesn't matter. Still, if you're ahead, why not launch the heavy artillery early, bury the other team, and spend Sunday practicing your victory speech? Obviously being saddled with these kinds of judgment calls can cause a captain to stock up on antacid.

In the last few years, several prominent golf writers and players have suggested an alternative to the current practice of pairings, believing that it would make each captain's strategy more intriguing and exciting. Instead of independently determining the pairings and order of singles, they'd like the captains to sit across from each other early on Friday, Saturday, and Sunday (or the evenings before) and take turns announcing who will play with whom and when.

Let's use as an example the Sunday two years ago at Valderrama. Say there was a coin flip, and Tom Kite won it. He picked Fred Couples (as he did in real life) to play the first singles match. The way it did work, Seve Ballesteros was committed to starting with Ian Woosnam, and he stacked his five big guns (Langer, Westwood, Olazabal, Faldo, and Montgomerie) for the final five-match barrage (though ironically they ended up going 1–3–1 those last few hours).

At that point, Woosie was 0–5–2 in previous Ryder Cup singles matches, while Couples had become a strong match-play performer. Ballesteros, rather than essentially conceding the point (Couples blew the Welshman out of the water, 8 and 7), might have countered with Langer or Faldo or Montgomerie. Then Seve would get to choose the second singles match player, Kite would counter, and back and forth in an intricate chess game instead of just letting the chips fall where they may.

Obviously this method gives the captain more direct input, and he has to be able to think on his feet. It can be fun, though, the way strategy and chance combine in the pairings. "I can still see the look of shock and horror on Jack's face after he and I exchanged evelopes," said Tony Jacklin about Nicklaus in 1983, when the American captain discovered his European counterpart was going to start off the singles matches with Seve Ballesteros, and Nicklaus was going with Fuzzy Zoeller (who did manage to halve the match).

As of this writing, the pairing and singles process will stay the same in Brookline, but with more former and future captains and journalists calling for a change, things might be different in the next century.

As far as practice is concerned, it's extremely rare that a captain has to coerce players out on the course. The players are well aware of how high the stakes are, especially during the 1990s, and no team member wants to leave the course with a loss. Visiting players in particular want to get in as much practice as they can so that they become familiar with the foreign golf course, weather conditions, spectators, "feel" of the environment, and the like.

For the most part, a captain's role includes trying to protect his players so they can practice with few distractions—media requests, special events, ceremonies, autograph seekers, and the like. Being a gatekeeper is more important than trying to be a coach, because while players will help each other during practice, most—if not all—of them have their own coaches on the course.

Another responsibility of the captain is to make sure the players don't overpractice. This can easily happen when the players feel a great deal of pressure and excitement and hitting balls becomes an obsession. The captain wants to ensure that the best performances are saved for Friday through Sunday.

Leadership

Ironically this has been more of an issue for the British and then European teams than for the U.S. because of the more formidable challenges they have faced over the years. Until the 1980s, though there wasn't an absence of leadership, the U.S. captain simply didn't have to worry too much about leading the charge because, with just a handful of surprising exceptions, his teams had no trouble dominating on either side of the ocean. While the best U.S. player-captains such as Arnold Palmer; Billy Casper; Jack Burke, Jr.; and Jack Nicklaus will insist that they never took their opponents lightly, the fact is there has to be a different outlook and approach when you win all of the time.

The Brits and Euros, however, like the Light Brigade, were being led into the valley of death every two years. Some captains responded to the challenge and tried to win in any way possible, while others just went through the motions.

All this changed for both teams beginning in the 1980s, when the talent levels were equalized. With the playing fields even, it became apparent that the leadership abilities of the captains could influence the outcome of the Matches.

There is no more striking example of this than Tony Jacklin. He not only displayed his own hard-earned Ryder Cup battle stripes, but he infused the European players with his own confidence and aggression and insisted that they receive the same respect and first-class treatment as that to which the U.S. teams were accustomed. He believed that his Davids could defeat the American Goliath, and as it turned out, Europe came close in 1983 and they won/kept the Cup in '85, '87, and '89.

While there are many components to being a good leader, certainly high on the list for a Ryder Cup captain is keeping all (or most) of his players happy. This has become more of a hurdle in recent Ryder Cup Matches. "Years ago you had two or three top players, then everyone else," said Bernard Gallacher. "Now every member of both teams is a superstar, or close to it, making millions, and there are bigger egos involved."

During a Match a captain has to make hard choices about who plays and how often and who sits. Every player wants to contribute and, even better, go home covered with Ryder Cup glory. But with twelve players and a total of twenty-eight matches, every player can't compete in every match—the most a player can do is participate in five matches (two fourball, two foursome, one single), and the least is just one match.

In Ryder Cup history the Americans have tended to spread play around, partly because they could afford to with the deeper talent, and perhaps because they were more democratically minded than the Brits, who are more devoted to a class system. Let's look at the contrasting styles of Tom Kite and Seve Ballesteros at Valderrama:

On Friday every U.S. team member played, but for Europe Thomas Bjorn, Darren Clarke, and Ian Woosnam sat out through the morning fourball and afternoon foursome matches. For a Masters champion and Ryder Cup veteran like Woosie, it had to hurt to be overlooked.

By the end of the Match, only Tiger Woods had played five times, and no American had competed fewer than three times. But for Seve's squad, Faldo, Montgomerie, Olazabal, and Westwood had hit the course five times—and Bjorn, Clarke, Per-Ulrik Johansson, and Woosnam only twice. The hell with democracy!

There was some grumbling about how Ballesteros had gone with his main guys, but he waved off any criticism. For him, the only goal was to win, and the players most likely to produce that result are the ones who will take the most swings. Perhaps this change in strategy and attitude, as much as anything, reflects the difference in U.S. opponents from previous decades.

During Ryder Cup play itself there isn't a great deal a captain can do. In other professional team sports, a manager or coach can set up plays, substitute players, and affect the dynamic of the contest in other hands-on ways. In the Ryder Cup once the captain turns in the pairings, his role becomes little more than determined spectator and supporter—he has to let the team play and hope for the best.

Coaching during a match is forbidden. The captain can clap and gesture and verbally encourage, but he can't jump on the course and help a player's swing or assist in lining up a putt. He zips around on a cart during the heat of action to spend time at every match, to lend support, and to see who is playing well and who is having a rough time.

"I never thought I was very fast on the course, but man, when I was captain, I was running all over that golf course," said Byron Nelson about his experience in 1965. "It got to be like I was going around so fast and so much, I was going to catch myself."

It has to be terribly frustrating to not be able to leap out, grab a club, and make something happen. Arnold Palmer faced this teeth-grinding dilemma, and thirty-five years after being a player-captain in 1963, he reflected on the difference.

"When I had the opportunity to be the playing captain, I suppose my ambitions and desires then were strongly in favor of a playing captain," he told us. "As time and the years slipped by, I found it intriguing to be a nonplaying captain. I suppose that, if I had my druthers, I would have chosen to be a playing captain. The alternative only comes with age and I suppose a little more maturity."

Probably the most important task for a captain on Friday through Sunday, other than pairings and strategy, is to help the players mentally and emotionally. Sure, this could mean a "rah-rah" speech, but depending on the composition of the team, that may not be what the players need. A captain might have to come off like George Patton to invigorate his players, or he might find more subtle ways to motivate. And with twelve fellows on the team, he may have to reach into his bag of tricks to come up with twelve ways to get each player to perform at his peak for three days.

Intangibles

By definition these are things that change with each captain, team, situation, and so on, and there's no rule or reason about them. Does a captain know when a particular player needs a pat on the shoulder or needs to be left alone? Is one captain a better chess player than the other? Does one captain have a greater record/ stature in golf than the other, and could that give his team the edge? Does he have an especially good tip for playing in a certain weather condition? Is he an effective communicator? Does he have good organizational skills? What has his relationship with the media been like?

In this category we should mention again the occasional role of the captain as psychologist. A good example is a story Byron Nelson told us about the 1965 Match. In the morning he had sent out the pairing of Arnold Palmer and Dave Marr, and they had gotten their butts kicked 6 and 5. But Byron had noticed that Palmer was seething about the embarrassing defeat and that Marr had played pretty well after the turn at the ninth hole.

"I didn't want my guys to sit around thinking about getting beat like that, and breaking 'em up could mean I had two teams with troubles," Nelson recalled. "Looking at Davy, I'd never seen a guy more nervous. So I made 'em my number-one team for the afternoon, figuring the British captain, Harry Weetman, would start off number one the guys who had beaten Palmer. Sure enough, that's what Weetman did. I went over to Arnie and Davy where they were having lunch and told 'em they had a second chance, if they were up for it. Well, I tell you they got right up from the table and went out on the course and crushed those other fellows 6 and 5, same score they lost at. These are the things a captain has to do, sometimes challenge or rile your players."

The approach to being at the helm has changed for every Ryder Cup captain since Walter Hagen and Ted Ray in 1927. With the intensity of play over a three-day period, all the shots and skills and luck involved, all the thinking and practicing and discussions over dinner, it is very possible that one intangible, one tiny variable and how it's handled, could decide the Ryder Cup.

The Ryder Cup captains of the last ten years have been as good examples as any of how the role is played and how a captain affects the outcome. They are probably even better examples than in the past because the competitive levels have never been so close for such a prolonged period of time and the pressure level of the Ryder Cup has never been so consistently high.

Let's look at the captain match-ups (home-team captain listed second):

Raymond Floyd v. Tony Jacklin, 1989, the Belfry

Floyd has been one of the best players ever to walk a course, with twenty-two PGA Tour victories, and he has had astonishing durability—he has won a major in each of three decades (PGA Championship in 1969, the Masters in 1976, and U.S. Open in 1986), and on the PGA Tour his first win was in 1963 and his last, at 50, was the Doral Ryder Open in 1992. He remains the only player to win on the PGA Tour and Senior PGA Tour in the same year (in '92), and to date he's added thirteen Senior Tour victories. And as we heard him tell it earlier, he is very proud of having been on Ryder Cup teams as a player in four different decades.

In 1989 he had played on five Ryder Cup teams and faced a tough task as captain: Europe had won twice in a row, the last time in the United States against a squad led by Jack Nicklaus, and Floyd's team was going to a course that was the headquarters of the British PGA. He laid down the gauntlet there by borrowing from Ben Hogan and declaring his team "the twelve greatest players in the world."

Jacklin, for his part, had to be brimming with confidence. A top-notch player and fierce competitor, he had led Europe to a near miss in 1983 and triumphs in '85 and '87. The Belfry gave him a big-time home-field advantage. Floyd was known for his steely stare and laserlike focus, but Jacklin was as pugnacious as they came, and he had a chance to make history.

Though Europe retained the Ryder Cup when the Match ended 14–14, and Jacklin ended his captaincy with an unequaled 2–1–1 record, in a way this was a win for Floyd and the U.S. players. They had gone into the unusual situation of having the odds stacked against them, and although they were down 14–10 on Sunday afternoon, they had courageously fought back via wins by Tom Watson, Mark McCumber, Lanny Wadkins, and Curtis

Strange. There was no quit in this team, and for better or worse, it led to the aggressive play of the '91 team.

Bernard Gallacher v. Dave Stockton, 1991, Kiawah Island

Gallacher's record of 13–13–5 is pretty amazing, considering that in eight attempts he had never played on a winning Ryder Cup team. He was known as a tough, determined, and resilient golfer. In '91, he was taking over a team that had turned the Ryder Cup Matches around and certainly had nothing to fear in South Carolina.

Stockton was relatively inexperienced in the Ryder Cup, having only a 3–1–1 record. He was a strong enough player on the PGA Tour, confident yet low-key, and had won two PGA Championships, but he was not on the same level as a Nicklaus, Palmer, Casper, Trevino, or Floyd. (As far as earnings were concerned, Stockton would outdistance all of them except Trevino on the Senior Tour.) On Kiawah Island he was leading a team that hadn't won in eight years and was facing a rowdy crowd energized by the American success in Desert Storm.

Europe should have kept the cup. They were up 13–12 and needed a total of just one point out of the last three matches. But Couples and Wadkins defeated Sam Torrance and Mark James, and in what many consider the most heartbreaking outcome in Ryder Cup history, Bernhard Langer missed a six-foot putt at the very last hole that would have beaten Hale Irwin and retained the cup for Europe with another tie.

In some ways Gallacher and Stockton were the wrong captains at the wrong time, and this is no judgment of their qualities as players and people. Gallacher had never tasted victory, and he was a rookie captain. Stockton had limited experience and was also a rookie captain, not a take-charge type. Neither was able to stop the Ryder Cup that year from becoming almost a sports epilogue to the Persian Gulf War, fueled by that event and by bitter feelings among American spectators over the United States not owning the Cup since 1983.

Perhaps no captain could have turned the tide on Kiawah Island, but clearly there was a need to right the Ryder Cup and return it to representing the virtues of international golf competition.

Tom Watson v. Bernard Gallacher, 1993, the Belfry

Looking at this match-up in the context of the entire history of the Ryder Cup, imagine if the United States had lost or tied again. After losing only three times in fifty-eight years, the United States would have had just one victory in a decade. As it was, the U.S. team hadn't won overseas since '81. It would have been very hard to argue against the contention that America, in golf, was a has-been.

That's some of the pressure Watson faced, in addition to testing if his strong 10–4–1 record as a player would translate into being a successful captain. A dilemma both he and Gallacher faced was trying to move the Ryder Cup Matches away from the aggressive, militaristic tone of the "War at the Shore" back to an emphasis on sportsmanship and mutual respect. To their credit, the two captains established this as a goal right away, and the result was not only one of the more exciting Ryder Cups ever but one that left both teams feeling that they had done their best and that both deserved to win.

Not that there weren't a few rough spots that year. During the Thursday evening gala dinner, Watson refused Torrance's request for an autograph, thinking that once one autograph was signed, he and his players would, instead of resting up for the next day's contest, spend hours signing for the hundreds of people in attendance. Torrance was insulted, and on the European team feathers were ruffled.

Gallacher had to be licking his chops at the prospect of taking on the Americans at the Belfry again, where they were 0–1–1. He had the home-field advantage, depth of talent, experience as captain, and the knowledge that he had been only a whisker away from winning in South Carolina.

He let go with his artillery, playing the combinations of Nick Faldo and Colin Montgomerie and Seve Ballesteros and Jose Maria Olazabal twice a day on both Friday and Saturday. Then on Sunday he saved for the final four singles matches the murderer's row of Ballesteros, Olazabal, Langer, and Faldo.

The competition was fierce and featured a big comeback—on Sunday with six matches yet to be determined, the United States was down 12½–9½. Watson's career-long example of being determined, steadfast, and fearless rubbed off on his talented players, and the Americans prevailed 15–13.

Bernard Gallacher v. Lanny Wadkins, 1995, Oak Hill Country Club

Well, Gallacher was in a bit of a pickle. After the '93 loss he announced he wouldn't stay on as captain. He later relented because many of the players wanted him back, his competitive spirit wouldn't let him quit, and he didn't want to leave behind an 0–9–1 Ryder Cup legacy. These considerations outweighed the facts that he would have to take his team to America to play on a tough Oak Hill course and that he would match up against Wadkins, second only to Palmer in wins among U.S. players (20–11–3 overall) and known as someone who never backed down.

Like the Europeans in '91, the U.S. team could look at the '95 match as one they should have won. Up 9–7 after two days and with Ballesteros and Langer both losing in singles, it should have been in the bag. But such unlikely heroes as Howard Clark, Mark James, David Gilford, and Philip Walton joined Faldo, Montgomerie, and Torrance to turn things around, and thanks to the 14½–13½ victory, the Ryder Cup sailed across the Atlantic for the first time since the 1980s.

It was vindication at last for Gallacher—and a crushing blow for Wadkins. At the closing ceremony late on Sunday, Wadkins was so overcome, he couldn't speak, and Gallacher, fully empathizing because of his own cruel past experiences, completed his counterpart's remarks for him. Gallacher could finally stand down, having led his team to only the second victory on American soil in the century.

Tom Kite v. Severiano Ballesteros, 1997, Valderrama

Kite was one of the most respected players around and second in the world in career earnings, and he had a 15–9–4 record as a Ryder Cup player. There was not a weak link among the twelve members of his team, and this could well have been Tiger Woods's shining moment on the grandest international stage. No wonder the United States was favored.

But Ballesteros didn't know the word for *underdog* in Spanish or any other language, and this match would be played on *his* turf. Not only were he and his players familiar with the Valderrama course, but being the first Ryder Cup contested in Spain was an enormous incentive for Ballesteros (and Olazabal and Ignacio Garrido) to win at all costs.

A potentially destructive hurdle had to be overcome, however, one that was indicative of Seve's personality. Fellow Spaniard Angel Miguel Martin, who had never made a Ryder Cup team before, was tenth in points. Ballesteros wanted Olazabal, Jesper Parnevik, and Faldo on his team but could pick only two of those three.

Martin had had wrist surgery that summer; Ballesteros got the British PGA to require Martin to play a round in early September to determine if he was well enough to perform. When he refused—Martin didn't want to risk injury by playing too soon and insisted he would be fully recovered in time for the Ryder Cup at the end of the month—Ballesteros booted him off the team. Olazabal, eleventh in points, moved up a notch, and the captain picked Parnevik and Faldo.

While Kite and the Americans, in their low-key way, watched the dramatics, Martin threatened to sue, and some of the European players thought Ballesteros had acted too rashly. The captain essentially told everyone to go jump in a water hazard—this was the team he wanted, and it was the team he got. Would the drama be too much of a distraction?

Apparently not. Europe jumped out to a 10½–5½ lead after two days and withstood the final furious rally on Sunday to keep the Ryder Cup. In his fiery, relentless way, Ballesteros was everywhere on the course, his cart like a magic carpet. Kite was more of a quiet, steady presence, which certainly had to help his players catch their breath on Saturday night and tap the resiliency that helped them mount a courageous charge the final day.

Kite and Ballesteros are very different people, players, and then captains, yet both have a burning will to win. (By the way, in head-to-head competition Seve is 4–2–1 against Kite.) At Valderrama the Match went to Seve—and they may never meet in such a way again. While Kite deserves a second shot (such as fellow Texan Jack Burke, Jr., got), according to Ballesteros, "I have had no second thoughts about giving up the job, and I don't think I will ever be captain again."

Courage is clearly one of the prerequisites to being a Ryder Cup team captain. You have to make and live with tough decisions, know or sense when a player needs a pat on the back or a kick in the butt, deal with the heavy demands of the media and spectators, and accept the consequences, whatever they are, as witnessed by hundreds of millions of people and move on.

For the United States the fellow now under the microscope is Ben Crenshaw; for Europe, it's Mark James. They will duel on the international golf scene's equivalent of Main Street in Massachusetts this year. Only one will be left standing.

Both know all too well how to battle—and win.

The 1999 Ryder Cup Captains

Mark James

First, because he will be a guest in the United States, let's take a look at the visiting captain. In the seventy-two-year history of the Ryder Cup, few British players have been so closely associated with it, yet James is not one of the world's best-known players, even though he has won twenty-three titles on the European PGA Tour.

The 45-year-old Englishman has plenty of international match-play experience. He has played in seven Ryder Cup Matches (spanning three decades), three Dunhill Cups, seven World Cups, five Hennessy Cups, and three Four Tours Championships. Unlike other recent European captains, if he had not been chosen for the top spot on the team, he might well have made it on points—still playing well, James wasn't very far from the top of the Order of Merit in 1998.

His first Ryder Cup team was in 1977 (with fellow rookie Nick Faldo), just two years after being on the Walker Cup team for Great Britain. It was a rude awakening to the Ryder Cup for James—in their first match, he and Tommy Horton were confronted by Jack Nicklaus and Tom Watson.

"When I stepped up to the first tee and saw those two standing there, I was so nervous I didn't think I could hit a fat cow's ass with a banjo," James said, recalling the scene twenty-one years later.

It would be nice to report that James recovered from the heavy jitters and he and Horton gave a good account of themselves—but they were dusted by the American duo 5 and 4. James didn't have it any easier in the singles matches, losing that Sunday to Raymond Floyd.

But James is a battler, and he kept coming back for more. In Brookline he might want to mention that in 1981, in an otherwise American rout, he and Sandy Lyle combined to defeat Jerry Pate—and Ben Crenshaw. As part of a duo, James has also been in matches that resulted in beating the likes of Fred Couples, Lanny Wadkins, Payne Stewart, Curtis Strange, Corey Pavin, and Mark Calcavecchia. His overall Ryder Cup record, however, is a less-than-sparkling 8–15–1.

His reaction to being chosen as captain? "I think you would have to be mental to want the job," James said. "But that's what twenty years on the Tour will do to you."

In addition to his participation as a player, Mark James was Ballesteros's assistant captain at Valderrama. Interestingly, Seve's recommendation for '99 captain was Bernhard Langer because of the German's distinguished playing record and solid-citizen reputation, but the European Ryder Cup Committee went with the homeboy because of the '97 experience. (Ever gracious, Langer said that he would like to be captain someday but for now will earn his way onto the team.)

Earlier in his career James certainly didn't look like captain material. Soon after he joined the tour in 1976, he became known as "Jesse James" because of his erratic, rowdy, and sometimes careless behavior. A member of the 1979 Ryder Cup team, he was fined for skipping meetings and declining to wear the team's uniform because he simply didn't find it attractive. James was not known for being very attentive to rules and to others early on. He enjoyed his reputation as a rebel and carouser.

"For whatever reason, in 1979 Mark James and Ken Brown acted like buffoons and did what they could to sabotage any chance the new European team had," Tony Jacklin recalled. "They wouldn't wear the right stuff, wouldn't stand at attention during the flag raising, wouldn't show up for meetings. If I'd been captain I'd have sent them home without a second thought, but John Jacobs was too much of a gentleman. It is rather interesting to see Mark as Ryder Cup captain now."

Now things have changed, and James has the respect of his peers. "That was just the attitude of the times," he said about his behavior of years ago. "I've reached the stage where I think I can do the job."

James expects that his style will contrast with that of Seve Ballesteros at Valderrama because the two captains have very different personalities. "Obviously, I won't be quite as excitable," James said. "Seve did a heck of a job, and I'll learn from other captains and try to pull it all together. I may talk to the players more, but jump up and down a bit less in the fairways."

Mark James will have to do the best he can, because the opposing captain he will face not only is a fierce and successful competitor on the course but has a genuine passion for the history and tradition of golf. Could there be a better U.S. captain to end the century of Ryder Cup competition than Ben Crenshaw?

Ben Crenshaw

He has occasionally been referred to as "Gentle Ben." Nothing could be further from the truth.

Oh yes, he is a polite and considerate person, a Texas gentleman who is loyal to his wife, Julie, their three children, and his friends. He knows how to win—two Masters and nineteen PGA Tour tournaments in total—yet he has borne the brunt of losing, even in the Ryder Cup, most recently as a member of the 1995 team that was defeated at Oak Hill. His devotion to the history of golf (Bobby Jones is his personal hero) and the intricacies of course design have earned him the respect of his peers, his elders, and his juniors.

But with a golf club in his hand, "Gentle Ben" is not gentle at all. He goes out there to win, and at this point in his life, Crenshaw badly wants to win the Ryder Cup, both because he admires its history and because, with his own game suffering from the responsibilities of being captain, a triumph at The Country Club will be cherished as much as, if not more than, the two green jackets he has earned.

Does this mean that Crenshaw may take the role of Ryder Cup captain too seriously and put additional pressure on the players? Probably not. When his appointment was announced on October 22, 1997, he said, "The best thing that I can possibly do is get the people who have a good sense of humor to inject that kind of tone." Crenshaw the Clown?

Let's not go that far. Though he certainly didn't intend to give up PGA Tour victories for Ryder Cup responsibilities, the fact is Crenshaw has unselfishly and painstakingly taken on the mantle of U.S. team leader and sacrificed a lot of money and a couple of more trophies because of it. That is very serious business. He also has made personal sacrifices—his youngest child isn't yet two, and his travels have not allowed him to spend nearly as much time with his wife and children as he would like to.

The Europeans will have to pay for this. Crenshaw knows a U.S. win is long overdue, and he badly wants it to happen in Massachusetts at the dawn of a new century—and only forty minutes east of the Worcester Country Club, where the Ryder Cup was first played seventy-two years ago.

Now here's an insider tidbit about the site of the 1999 Ryder Cup Match. It turns out there is a very close connection between Ben Crenshaw and The Country Club in Brookline, which has to further fuel Ben's desire to win. In 1968 Crenshaw, then 16, played in the U.S. Junior Amateur at The Country Club, his first national competition. He lost in the quarterfinals, but his experience there led to his "falling in love with [golf] history and architecture. From then on, I couldn't stop reading about them."

It didn't hurt that Ben learned that in 1913 what many consider to be the pivotal U.S. Open for the United States had been played there, when an American caddy, Francis Ouimet, defeated both the legendary Harry Vardon and Ted Ray (future Ryder Cup captain) in a playoff for the National Championship. That a native-born golfer had finally won the U.S. Open after two decades of British domination inspired a surge of interest in golf in the United States. It also doesn't hurt, for those who love golf and history, that The Country Club is indeed the first country club in the United States, constructed in 1894.

Clearly, the quest to bring the Ryder Cup back to the States with a victory in Brookline is both a professional and a personal odyssey for Ben Crenshaw.

He is 47, and this is his twenty-seventh year on the PGA Tour. His first victory came at the tender age of 21 when he won the San Antonio–Texas Open in 1973; his last victory was a very memorable Masters triumph in 1995 that he dedicated to his longtime teacher and mentor, Harvey Penick, who had died only the week before. Coming off the green after the emotional ending, Ben told Bob, "Harvey was with me . . . he was my fifteenth club in the

The British team, about to embark on their long journey to Worcester, Massachusetts, for the first official Ryder Cup Match in June 1927. In the center (with his dog) is Samuel Ryder. To his right, in the dark suit, is the team's captain, Ted Ray.

After their defeat in the first Ryder Cup Match, the British were ready to take on the Yanks again in 1929. This caricature was published in the May 3, 1929 issue of *Golf Illustrated*.

Gene Sarazen *(left)* and Walter Hagen, about to take on Percy Alliss and Charles Whitcombe in the first match of the 1933 Ryder Cup at Southport and Ainsdale in England. The match was halved, and though both Sarazen and Hagen (who was also captain) won their singles matches the next day, Great Britain won 6½–5½.

The 1933 British team, captained by J. H. Taylor *(center)*, was the last one to defeat the Americans until 1957. Seated on the right is Abe Mitchell, whose likeness stands atop the Ryder Cup.

Because of World War II, the Ryder Cup was not contested from 1939 to 1945, but an exhibition match benefiting the USO was held in Detroit in August 1941. A challenge team captained by Bobby Jones *(left)* defeated the PGA Ryder Cup team, despite the hex that honorary captain Walter Hagen seems to be placing on the Cup as PGA president Tom Walsh holds.

A large and enthusiastic crowd turned out for the Ryder Cup Match at the Lindrick Golf Club in Yorkshire, England, in October 1957. They are there to see Dai Rees's team defeat the Americans, the first British victory in twenty-four years.

Dai Rees was back as captain, but the outcome was very different in the 1959 Match. Captain Sam Snead holds the Ryder Cup after the Americans won 8½–3½ at the Eldorado Country Club in Palm Desert, California. From left to right: Joe Novak, Snead, Robert Hudson, Sr., Lord Brabazon of Tara (president of British PGA), Jimmy Hines, and Rees.

"The finest golfers in the world," is what U.S. captain Ben Hogan (center) called the 1967 team that crushed the British 23½–8½ at the Champions Golf Club in Houston. From left to right: Al Geiberger, Julius Boros, Arnold Palmer, Garnder Dickinson, Hogan, Gene Littler, Billy Casper, Johnny Pott, Bobby Nichols, Gay Brewer, and Doug Sanders.

However the match ends, sportsmanship prevails. In the 1973 Ryder Cup at Muirfield, Scotland, Arnold Palmer and Eddie Pollard shake hands after Jack Nicklaus and Palmer defeated Pollard and Maurice Bembridge 6–5 in a Friday morning foursome.

A longtime Ryder Cup tradition has been for the players and captains to sign the menu of the gala dinner held the evening before the Match begins, such as this one from 1973 in Scotland. Tom Watson's attempt to break with tradition caused quite a controversy twenty years later in England.

At the 1977 Match at Royal Lytham and St. Anne's in England, Jack Nicklaus is visited by two members of the 1927 Ryder Cup team, Johnny Farrell *(left)* and Bill Mehlhorn. After the 12½–7½ win by the Americans in the 1977 Match, Nicklaus urged the inclusion of players from all of Europe.

The formidable 1987 U.S. team was the first one to lose a Ryder Cup Match on American soil, victims of the rising talent level of the all-Europe teams. From left to right, standing: Curtis Strange, Hal Sutton, Andy Bean, Jack Nicklaus (captain), Dan Pohl, Mark Calcavecchia, Scott Simpson; kneeling: Lanny Wadkins (1995 captain), Larry Nelson, Tom Kite (1997 captain), Payne Stewart, Larry Mize, and Ben Crenshaw (1999 captain).

Jaime Ortiz-Patino, the proud owner of Valderrama in Sotogrande, Spain. Through his efforts, the Ryder Cup was contested for the first time on the Continent.

A dashing Tiger Woods was the center of attention when he arrived in Spain for the 1997 Ryder Cup Match, yet he and the other American "young guns" were unable to wrest the Ryder Cup from the Europeans' grasp.

Golf royalty meets real royalty: King Juan Carlos and Queen Sofia of Spain greet the European team *(left)* and the U.S. team at Valderrama in 1997.

bag." This line was picked up by the sports media all over the world.

Soon after winning the Masters for the first time, in 1984, Crenshaw was diagnosed with Graves' disease, a serious but not fatal thyroid disorder. But he fought back, step by step, and finally broke through with two tourney wins in 1986. He had foot surgery in September 1996 and again worked his way back to the links. *Quit* is not in the Crenshaw dictionary.

Ben is well aware of how much is at stake for the United States in Brookline, and that of all the Ryder Cup Matches since 1927, the 1999 match will likely be the most intense competition yet.

"The gravity of the Matches has certainly changed over the last five meetings," he told us. "For the captain there has to be an added importance to the Ryder Cup. And to some extent the Matches will take on the personalities of the captains involved. As far as the talent level, it's pretty much an evenly matched situation now. So the personalities and the decisions of the captains in a highly charged atmosphere can indeed be the difference."

One of the challenges Crenshaw faces is making sure that most if not all of the American players play The Country Club in advance of the September Match, preferably more than once. How big is this particular challenge? At the PGA Championship in 1998 the captain tried to organize a trip to Brookline for mid-September—and not one player accepted the invitation. The reasons ranged from commitments to other tournaments to wanting time off to players not feeling a sense of urgency a year before the next Match.

Crenshaw will have to correct this because no matter how strong the influence of the captains, the outcome of the Ryder Cup relies most on the performance of the players. No one could possibly knock the Ryder Cup experience, skills, and heart of Walter Hagen; Jack Burke, Jr.; Jack Nicklaus; Lanny Wadkins; and Tom Kite, yet their teams lost because their players simply didn't put the ball in the cup more times than the British and Europeans did.

Alas, that's little consolation for the captains, who have to bear the criticism, and there seems to have been more of it on the American side in recent years.

"In Tom Kite's case and in Lanny's case, they took a lot of criticism for losing, but you know, at the end of the day the captain is only as good as his team," said Curtis Strange, who would no doubt make an excellent U.S. captain because of his experience, intelligence, and competitive drive. "We're talking about adult, professional, veteran players. And if they lose the Ryder Cup, it's certainly not the captain's fault—you know he's going to do the best he can do. Somebody's going to win and somebody's going to lose. I find it disappointing that they even question the captain at the outcome of the Match."

"Being captain is the worst possible position," Davis Love III told *Golf Digest*. "I don't know if they have enough cigarettes for Ben Crenshaw, because he's going to be beside himself." However, Love added, "I think he's going to be great because he knows how to let guys go."

"In Ben's case I hope he realizes that all he can do is get the whip out and say, 'Go get 'em, boys,'" said Strange. "It's got to be, 'Go play hard for me and your country.' Other than that, once the horses have been let loose, it's hope for the best."

Raymond Floyd agreed: "The captain can't put the ball in the hole. There are things he can do right or wrong up to the start of play, but once the players are on the course, it is their responsibility to win the Ryder Cup. The captain doesn't have a club in his hands, which is just as well because his fingers are crossed most of the time."

"Raymond is so right," said Crenshaw. "No question it is how the team performs that determines if the captain is going to look wonderful or not. If they fail, there are going to be a lot of things that a lot of people will second-guess.

"It boils down to a three-day Match," he added. "It's match play, and your hope is that your players will be playing their best. It doesn't happen all the time. And sometimes in match play the best team doesn't win. A lot of those factors boil down, but Raymond is so right—if those players play well, you'll look great, but if they slip up, what happens won't be very nice."

Clearly, for Crenshaw the task at hand, other than helping to prepare the course for the '99 Match, is to prepare his players as best he can. Most of that preparation is psychological.

"Being captain was a great pleasure, and I had a lot of people to help me out, but I think the most important thing about the Ryder Cup is the attitude of the team going in," said Tom Watson, the last winning U.S. captain. "The attitude that you're going to win and nothing can stop you is one that the captain can instill in his players. With all the responsibilities involved, I think instilling the will to win and the belief in winning is the most important thing I did as captain in 1993."

"You've not only got to try to prepare your players mentally and emotionally, as best you can based on your own experience and personality, but you've got to prepare your players for a particular golf course," Crenshaw pointed out. "My players are going to have to be ready for The Country Club. Being ready in general is probably not enough."

Then, of course, there are the captain's picks. All the considerations offered earlier in this chapter and more are on Crenshaw's mind as he envisions filling out the '99 U.S. team. So far, he is leaving his options open, but he does have a guiding philosophy.

"One pick that you make might be on a lot of people's lists, but the other pick could go into the area where you may have a favorite for specific and not necessarily obvious reasons," Crenshaw said. "Most of all, what is going to be in my mind when decision time comes is how well a player has played recently, meaning the summer competitions, and, as important if not more important, how well I think that player will do at The Country Club, which I think is a very, very difficult course and requires a lot of thinking."

He continued: "That player should have his emotions under control, as much as possible, on a very difficult course and play sort of a steady game. Obviously, you want a well-rounded game, but you want a player who's going to play with a lot of thought and care."

A very valuable resource that Crenshaw can turn to when things get real tight are the experiences he has had with his own previous Ryder Cup captains. Ben, a very serious student of the game, certainly learned from some of the best.

"My first Ryder Cup, I had Dave Marr as captain, who was one of the finest people I ever knew in golf," Crenshaw said. "He was the most wonderful gentleman. Golf was his great passion, and it showed. Then I had Jack Nicklaus, in '83 and '87, and he sure doesn't back down from anybody or anything. Then Lanny [Wadkins] in '95, who was an excellent choice and a strong example of Ryder Cup focus and determination. I've been blessed in that regard."

And then there is Crenshaw's counterpart. While no actual coaching is allowed, during the three days of Ryder Cup '99, Mark James and Ben Crenshaw will try to be everywhere—encouraging players, developing strategy, studying the course, making mental notes of who is playing well and who appears shaky, and so on. Is knowing how James thinks and reacts going to be an advantage for the U.S. squad?

"I've known Mark as a competitor, and I've known him for a long time," Crenshaw said. "As a player he is very, very hard on himself with the way he has played in the past. He's had a lot of achievements and he's won a lot of tournaments, but he is very tough on himself. And I expect no less in his assessment of his team and how diligent he is going to be in preparing the players."

Though he describes James as "a wonderful friend," Crenshaw doesn't expect friendship to make for any less of a Ryder Cup rivalry. "No one has ever doubted Mark's toughness in competition," he said. "Mark will make it a priority to instill in his players a belief in themselves. He knows the nucleus of that team because he has been part of it for many years, and he will get them to play strong for those few days. I will be doing the same.

It's going to be a heck of a clash, and we'll see who is left standing come Sunday night."

This September, expect to see the fruits of maximum labor on the part of both captains. Mark James, a Ryder Cupper since the 1970s, wants to keep the European resurgence going and continue to exorcise the ghosts of past British losses. He also wouldn't mind joining the ranks of George Duncan, J. H. Taylor, Dai Rees, Tony Jacklin (twice), Bernard Gallacher, and Severiano Ballesteros as captains who have vanquished the Americans.

Good luck, Mark. Ben Crenshaw will be waiting for you with a lineup that may rival the best U.S. squads of the past. And he's going to expect the most from them.

"You know, a lot of times with the hype of the Matches themselves all the preparation you can do and all the mental jockeying and the pairings and this and that—those players still have to perform," said Crenshaw, perhaps offering a challenge to the '99 team. "I know it's a very difficult thing. These players are under immense pressure. But for your team, your country, and for yourself, you've got to get the ball in the hole before the other guy and more often than the other guy. And that's what wins the Ryder Cup."

Chapter 9
RYDER RELATIVES

The Ryder Cup over the years has spawned generations of inter-national golf events. With one big exception, these other events are not necessarily rivals but instead attempt to emulate the legacy of the Ryder Cup Matches, which took the concept of competition among countries on golf courses and brought it to the highest, most acclaimed level. If you're looking for more examples of fair play and hard-fought contests, these various children, grandchil-dren, and nieces and nephews of the Ryder Cup will fit the bill.

The amateur level has been the most active for the longest period of time in consistently offering opportunities to players of various countries to challenge each other using a team-versus-team structure. Such competitions constitute one of the most important functions of the United States Golf Association. The Ryder-like events it sponsors include:

Walker Cup

This event actually predates the Ryder Cup. It is named after George H. Walker, the fourteenth president of the USGA (and uncle of former U.S. President George Herbert Walker Bush), and involves male amateurs from the United States, Great Britain, and Ireland.

In the wake of World War I and after matches played between amateurs in the United States and Canada in 1919 and 1920, the USGA and the Royal and Ancient Golf Club in Great Britain discussed an event that would promote peace and international golf. In 1920 Walker donated the International Challenge Cup, which became known as the Walker Cup.

In 1921 there was an informal competition in Hoylake, England, with the United States winning 9–3. The following year the first official Match was held at the National Golf Links in Southampton, New York. Matches were held during each of the next two years, then the Walker Cup became an every-other-year event. The competition was not held from 1939 through 1946, then it resumed at St. Andrews in Scotland in 1947 and has continued ever since.

Jay Sigel, who is doing quite well now as a professional on the Senior PGA Tour, has been on the most U.S. Walker Cup teams (nine), and a British Ryder Cupper, Ronan Rafferty, was the youngest player ever to compete, at age 17 in 1981 at Pebble Beach, California. For any amateur, it is a great honor to make a Walker Cup team.

The United States leads the series 31–3–1, and the thirty-sixth Walker Cup is to be played this year in Scotland, two weeks before the Ryder Cup.

Curtis Cup

Margaret Curtis won the Women's Amateur Championship in 1907—defeating her older sister, Harriet, a year after Harriet had won the title—and again in 1911 and 1912. In 1958 she received the USGA's highest honor, the Bob Jones Award. The Curtis Cup, based on a design by Paul Revere, was created in 1927 and is inscribed, "To stimulate friendly rivalry among the women golfers of many lands."

The first Curtis Cup Match, with the cup officially donated by Margaret and Harriet Curtis, wasn't actually played until 1932, with the United States opposing Great Britain. It is held every other year during even-numbered years. The United States leads in the competition 21–6–3.

The most recent Match took place in August 1998 outside Minneapolis, Minnesota, and among the participants for the United States was Jenny Chuasiriporn, who the previous month had come within an eyelash of winning the U.S. Women's Open. The American amateurs tasted victory for the first time in eight years, defeating Great Britain and Ireland 10–8.

World Amateur Team Championship

In 1957 it was suggested that the USGA sponsor a team to compete against a team from Japan. The USGA instead promoted a competition that would involve teams of male amateurs from all over the world.

The following year President Dwight Eisenhower hosted the representatives of thirty-five countries who formed the World Amateur Golf Council. The first World Amateur Team Championship, with 115 players representing twenty-nine countries, was held at St. Andrews in October 1958, and Bobby Jones captained the first U.S. team. In a playoff Australia downed the United States.

The competition is held every two years, during even-numbered years, at sites around the world, with the winner receiving the Eisenhower Trophy.

Some familiar Ryder Cup names have done well in this event: Jack Nicklaus had the lowest individual seventy-two-hole score (269) and lowest individual first-round score (66) in 1960, Justin Leonard owns the lowest individual second-round score (66) from 1992, and David Duval (well, soon to be a familiar Ryder Cup name) has the lowest individual third-round score (65), also from 1992.

In November 1998, the fortieth anniversary of the event, the Eisenhower Trophy was won by Great Britain and Ireland in Santiago, Chile. They beat Australia by four strokes, and the surprising third-place finisher was Chinese Taipei, which edged out Japan and Sweden.

Women's World Amateur Team Championship

This was first played in October 1964—with twenty-five teams and seventy-five participants—and is also an every-other-year, even-numbered-year event. The winner receives the Espirito Santo Trophy, donated by the Ricardo Espirito Santo family of Portugal.

In 1964 France had invited the U.S. Curtis Cup team to have an informal match after its Match with Great Britain and Ireland. This invitation was then expanded to include other countries, and the St. Germain Golf Club outside Paris hosted the first Women's World Amateur Team Championship. Conveniently enough, it was won by France.

The eighteenth Women's World Team Amateur Championship was held in November 1998 in Santiago, Chile. There were thirty-two countries represented, and the winner, for the thirteenth time, was the United States. The champs set a record by compiling a total score of 18-under 558, easily beating the previous low score of 569 and twenty-one shots better than runners-up Germany and Italy.

The next event in this series is set for 2000 in Berlin.

Izzo Cup

This competition was held for the first time in June 1998 at the Legends at Chateau Elan in Braselton, Georgia, between the United States and Sweden. Each team has six girls and six boys, all amateurs between the ages of 16 and 19. The goal is to foster good relations between the junior golf programs in the two countries.

The Swedish team started very slowly out of the gate, down 0–6, then fought back. However, it couldn't climb completely out of the deep hole, and the United States won 18–12. The next Izzo Cup Match is set for 2000 in Stockholm.

* * *

Not all of the cup action has been on the amateur level. Professionals also have opportunities to participate in events that don't have the stature, excitement, and tradition of the Ryder Cup but are nonetheless fun to watch and are hotly contested.

Among the better-known events are:

Solheim Cup

This is the female version of the Ryder Cup, though it is not sponsored by the PGA of America. It was begun by golf manufacturer Karsten Solheim in 1990 to give women pros in the United States and Europe a chance to challenge each other.

The selection process is similar to that of the Ryder Cup. For the United States the top ten players in points during the previous two-year period make the team, and the team captain (who was Judy Rankin in 1998) has two picks. For Europe the top seven players in points are placed on the team, and the captain (Pia Nilsson in 1998) has a whopping five selections. Obviously, for professional female players the Solheim Cup, though without the long tradition of the Ryder Cup, is a mark of excellence.

In last year's Solheim Cup—it is played during even-numbered years—at Muirfield Village in Ohio, the U.S. team triumphed over the European squad 16–12. The Americans' record in the series now stands at 4–1.

Just as an aside, the Solheim Cup has to be one of the very, very few events in golf in which competitors can be pregnant. In the 1998 Match Tammie Green of the United States was six months along—she went 1–2 in the Match. Carin Koch of Sweden was also in the family way but elected to drop off the team before the Match began.

PGA Cup

This event was created by the PGA of America to be an equivalent of the Ryder Cup for PGA club professionals. The format is almost identical to that of the Ryder Cup, with the big difference that the U.S. opponent during even-numbered years is not Europe but Great Britain and Ireland. Brian Barnes, Tom Wargo, and the late Larry Gilbert are a few of the familiar names who have participated as club professionals.

The first PGA Cup Match was played at the Pinehurst Country Club in North Carolina in 1973, the site of the 1999 U.S. Open. There is no prize money; each team is after the Llandudno (clan-DUD-no) International Trophy, which was actually a trophy awarded to English club pros before World War II. It was kept in the personal collection of veteran Ryder Cupper Percy Alliss, and two years after he died, in 1973, his son, Peter (also a Ryder Cup veteran), donated the trophy to the PGA Cup Matches.

Teams of ten players compete every other September for a total of twenty-six points. In last year's event, held at the Broadmoor in Colorado Springs, the "Rout in the Rockies" took place, with the U.S. team winning easily 17–9. This may have made up for the 13–13 draw in 1996, but in any case the U.S. hasn't lost a PGA Cup Match since 1984, has never lost on American soil, and owns a 12–4–3 record.

Anderson Memorial

This is the oldest fourball tournament in the United States and is played every year.

The sixty-second version took place in July 1998 at the Winged Foot Golf Club in Mamaroneck, New York (site of Davis Love III's thrilling PGA Championship victory the year before). The two-man team of Walker Cupper Jody Flanagan and Noel Fox of Ireland downed Americans Jerry Courville and Matt Bernot 3–2.

Dunhill Cup

The Dunhill Cup International Advisory Committee oversees this event, which takes place annually among three-man teams representing fifteen countries. Up through last year the United States had had some rough going, winning only three times in the previous thirteen years.

Things looked brighter last October when, at St. Andrews in Scotland, the United States had a terrific trio of Mark O'Meara, Tiger Woods, and John Daly, who between them had collected two Masters, two British Opens, and a PGA Championship. Alas, this terrific trio came close, but not close enough. In the semifinal against Spain, the gutsy John Daly was the only winner, with Woods and O'Meara losing. The Dunhill Cup was eventually won by South Africa, which pitched a 3–0 shutout thanks to victories by Retief Goosen, David Frost, and Ernie Els.

World Cup of Golf

This tournament, sponsored by the PGA Tour, is usually held in November, but its days may be numbered because of the creation of "World Golf" events beginning in 1999 (more on this below).

The 1997 version was held on Kiawah Island, South Carolina, scene of the 1991 "War at the Shore," and was won by Ireland's Padraig Harrington and Paul McGinley. In this event each of thirty-two countries is represented by a two-man team of professionals who play four rounds of stroke play, and their total scores are added. Ireland's total of 545 beat Scotland (Raymond Russell and Colin Montgomerie) by five strokes and the United States (Justin Leonard and Davis Love III) by six strokes.

Harrington and McGinley earned $200,000 each, and Monty took $100,000 home for the lowest overall score (266).

The 1998 World Cup signaled what may be a comeback by Nick Faldo, who had struggled, especially with his putter, for most of the year. In Whangaparaoa, New Zealand, he combined with 26-year-old David Carter (shades of the happy work with Lee Westwood!) to produce England's first-ever victory in this event.

Heading into the back nine in the final round there was a five-team tie, then Faldo and Carter caught fire. They finished up with a 69 and 68, respectively, to capture the 1998 World Cup and left second-place Italy (Costantino Rocca and Massimo Florioli) in the Kiwi dust.

Given his recent success on international stages with youngsters Lee Westwood and David Carter, Faldo was asked why partnerships with him have proven so beneficial. With typical sly humor he replied, "I'm just a joy and a beautiful person to play with. All I want now is a percentage of their winnings."

The trophy for lowest individual score was won by Scott Verplank with a 279. He and John Daly teamed up for the United States to secure a three-way tie with Scotland and Argentina for third place.

World Match Play Championship

The most recent installment of this event was held in October 1998 in Wentworth, England, a week after the Dunhill Cup. The field included Tiger Woods, Mark O'Meara, Ernie Els, and Vijay Singh—between O'Meara and Singh there were the winners of three of the year's four majors.

The final draw couldn't have been more exciting. After all the other golfers from around the world fell by the wayside, only Tiger Woods and Mark O'Meara were left standing. There were all kinds of vibes to this match-up: the last two Masters champions, neighbors and practice partners, the last two Players of the Year, big-time money winners, and the young and brash gunslinger going up against the weathered veteran.

The outcome suggests that it's not Woods's town yet. O'Meara prevailed in the thirty-six-hole final (so much for young legs) 1-up. The increasing closeness of international golf suggests that these kind of duels will occur more frequently.

Caddies' Cup

We're not sure whether to place this in the amateur or professional category, and who knows how long it will last. For the first time, in late 1998, a group of caddies from the Pebble Beach Golf Links in California took on a cairn of caddies at St. Andrews in Scotland during two days of Ryder Cup–style matches.

"This is the workingman's Ryder Cup," said Mike Lahotte, the caddymaster at Pebble Beach.

More signs of how the entire world is embracing golf are still being nailed up as this book is being written.

The PGA Tour has joined with five other tours—PGA European Tour, Southern Africa PGA Tour, PGA Tour of Australasia, Tour de las Americas (South America), and the PGA Tour of Japan—to create the PGA Tours International Federation. This organization in turn is in the process of creating the World Golf Championships.

The outlook among the heads of the worldwide PGA Tours is that golf is inevitably going global anyway, and a way to spur that growth and attract a bigger audience is to pit the top international pros against each other. A major way that the cream of the pro crop will be lured to the newly developed events is through huge, unprecedented purses.

The World Golf Championships began earlier this year. The first one was the Andersen Consulting Match Play Championship (featuring the top sixty-four players in the official world golf ranking) in late February at the La Costa Resort and Spa in California. The NEC Invitational (featuring all members of the last Ryder and Presidents Cup teams) is to take place in August in Akron, Ohio, and the Stroke Play Championship (featuring the top fifty in the ranking and a few others) is set for Valderrama this November. Because Ryder Cup participation is factored into at least one of these big-purse tourneys, beginning in 1999 it really does pay to make a Ryder Cup team, which may quell the calls for players to be paid to play in a Ryder Cup Match.

On one hand, this looks like exciting stuff. The three World Golf Championships already in existence, plus those yet to be created, will have the most successful, best-known players in the world battling it out. However, there has been some criticism that this competition just helps the rich get richer, creating a financial gap between one tier of players and another, and that other tournaments that take place the same weeks—some of them decades old and with their own memorable legacies—will have to make do with a field of B-list players.

Perhaps you're thinking, "Maybe most of the top players will forget these newfangled events and stick with the longtime ones." A few probably will. But keep in mind that each of the World Golf Championships has a $5 million total purse, and that kind of green is hard to pass up.

"There's no question that golf has become much more worldwide and America does not dominate to the extent that it used to," said Jack Whitaker, the well-respected TV golf commentator (who now hosts *Shell's Wonderful World of Golf)* and writer. "The U.S. still has more good golfers, but it may not necessarily have the best golfers anymore—and they're not as driven as much as their international counterparts, it seems."

Aside from the tournaments attracting players from all over the world, the tours in various countries are doing better each year. There is a Japan Tour, an Asian Tour, an African Tour, and so on. They are attracting more spectators and broadcast outlets, are offering more prize money, and are producing more talented and skilled players.

An example is the Canadian Tour. Given its northern location and thus limited season, Canada certainly faces a big challenge in having a thriving tour, the same challenge seemingly overcome by the Scandinavian countries. Yet the Canadian Tour is going great guns.

In 1998 the total purse for Canadian Tour events leaped from $700,000 to $2 million (in Canadian dollars). The number of tournaments on the tour increased from ten to seventeen. In the tour's qualifying school, an unprecedented 265 players from fifteen countries tried to get their cards, which meant the previous one-day affair was held over two days.

Maybe the biggest boost is that in 1998 Canadian Tour graduates Trevor Dodds and Michael Bradley won tourneys on the PGA Tour: Dodds, the Greater Greensboro Chrysler Classic, and Bradley, the Doral Ryder Open. Among those who have crossed over from the Canadian Tour to play on the PGA Tour are Billy Ray Brown, Tim Herron, Dave Barr, Guy Boros, Steve Stricker, Grant Waite, and Stuart Appleby.

The Tour de las Americas demonstrates how another part of the world with a substantial population is embracing golf big-time. In 1998 it staged six official and two unofficial events with official prize money totaling $1.4 million. The season-ending Argentine Open (played last year opposite the Presidents Cup) sported a $350,000 purse and appearances by such world-ranked players as Craig Stadler and Dudley Hart from America and David Frost from South Africa.

This may not sound like the largest, most active tour, but the Tour de las Americas is undergoing a transition. The tour's operating budget went from $160,000 in 1997 to $1.5 million in 1998. In 1999 there will be a total of twelve events, with fifteen in 2000 and twenty in 2001. Tournaments have been staged in Venezuela, Peru, Brazil, and Argentina, and sites for the added tourneys will be in Chile, Ecuador, Jamaica, Cuba, Bahamas, Puerto Rico, and Mexico.

Certainly the creation of World Golf Village is a symbol of the international growth of golf. Developed by the PGA Tour near St. Augustine, Florida, it opened in the spring of 1998. It contains a 75,000-square-foot World Golf Hall of Fame, museum, hotel and resort complex, and an IMAX theater, and circling Village Lake is the Walk of Champions, filled with plaques commemorating the accomplishments of the game's best players.

Gene Sarazen and Sam Snead were the consultants of the design of the first golf course there, called "The Slammer [Snead] and the Squire [Sarazen]." A course dedicated to Arnold Palmer and Jack Nicklaus is being developed, with their input. The first international players elected to the World Golf Hall of Fame, inducted in 1998, were Seve Ballesteros and Nick Faldo.

Ryder Rival: The Presidents Cup

By far the Ryder Cup relative that has attracted the most attention is the Presidents Cup. It has also been a big point of contention between the PGA of America and the PGA Tour.

Since its founding in 1916, the Professional Golfers Association of America has been the dominant professional organization in the United States. However, friction developed between many of the players on the professional tournament tour and the PGA of America, much of it because the players felt that their best interests were not being adequately looked after.

A truce was declared when a separate organization, now known as the PGA Tour, was formed; it has the pro players and their interests as the top priority. For the most part the PGA of America and the PGA Tour cooperate and support each other because it's best for everyone involved. However, the creation of the Presidents Cup was probably the biggest source of friction between the two organizations since the PGA Tour began.

The concept behind this event surely seems reasonable—to give top players from the rest of the world an opportunity to compete in a match-play, team-versus-team format against the United States. It just seems to make sense that with golf becoming more popular in Asia, Australasia, South America, and so on, and with the Ryder Cup limited to only Europe and the United States, a contest that opens the door to the other prominent international players was needed.

You might even think that the existence of the Presidents Cup is good for the United States because if American players can play against the likes of Greg Norman, Ernie Els, Nick Price, Vijay Singh, Steve Elkington, and other topnotch non-Europeans and win both that and the Ryder Cup, wouldn't that show who truly is the best on the planet?

Of course it would. But that didn't mean the PGA of America was tickled pink by the Presidents Cup. The PGA feared that this newcomer could detract from the prestige of the Ryder Cup and burden players with another international event they didn't need.

"By being involved in two premier team events, the United States has risked the digestive overkill of heaping too much on its competitive plate," editorialized *Golfweek* in its October 17, 1998, issue. "Is it fair to expect Tiger Woods, David Duval, and Justin Leonard to tee it up every autumn—or the occasional winter—in each of the next fifteen years in defense of his country? It isn't, nor is it very realistic.

"At the same time," the editorial continued, "can you imagine the backlash awaiting the first player who politely declines to join up with his national team?"

Critics have claimed that the newer event was just a cheap imitation of its international granddaddy and could drain away some of the money that previously flowed into the Ryder Cup and the PGA of America. So the PGA would prefer to pretend that the Presidents Cup doesn't exist, and apparently the PGA Tour doesn't care what the older organization thinks.

Whichever group you agree with, the fact is that in its first outings the Presidents Cup has been pretty darn exciting. "It's not quite anything near like the Ryder Cup yet, but you still want to win," Fred Couples told *The New York Times*.

The selection process has some similarities and differences when compared with the Ryder Cup. Over a two-year period, first an odd year then an even year, through the season-ending Tour Championship (most recently in 1998), the players' earnings (not points) are accumulated, with the second year's earnings doubled. A player who collects $1 million in 1997 and $1 million in 1998 has actually accumulated $3 million in Presidents Cup dollars. The top ten money-earning players make the team, the captain has two picks, and the captain is chosen by the PGA Tour.

For the International team, for which Europeans are not eligible, the ten players are selected based on their positions in the official world ranking at the conclusion of their tour championship (in 1998). Conceivably, a player could have a strong odd-numbered year then a poor even-numbered year but still be in the top ten in the rankings and make the team. (There are also two captain's choices.) With the U.S. method of doubling second-year money, it's more likely that the players performing the strongest in the months preceding the Presidents Cup will make the team.

A Presidents Cup Match has a total of thirty-two points, because during the first two days there are ten fourball and ten foursome matches (as opposed to eight and eight in a Ryder Cup Match), followed by twelve singles matches on the third and final day. Every player on each of the twelve-man teams must compete every day, which makes the Presidents Cup a bit more democratic but takes some strategy out of the captains' hands.

There has been some criticism of having twenty matches played during the first two days. "It's daft, because that's just too much," said Tony Jacklin. "If one team gets on a roll, you can collect enough points by Saturday evening to make Sunday just about unnecessary, or at best not very interesting. That's exactly what happened in Australia [in 1998]."

There are two major differences in format from the Ryder Cup. Singles matches are played to their conclusions, meaning no matches are halved, until one team has earned 16½ points and thus has won the Presidents Cup; after that, singles matches can be halved. The other big difference is that if, after all thirty-two matches are concluded, the teams are at 16–16, there is no such thing as a tied Presidents Cup Match with the previous winner retaining the cup. Each team chooses a player who goes out, *mano a mano,* on the course for a sudden-death playoff. This hasn't happened yet, but if it ever does, the playoff will be a pressure-packed thrill ride—and we don't envy the fellow who comes up short.

The money is a different situation, too. First of all, the net revenue of the event is divided by the number of players and captains. However, the team members don't get the money; instead, each share is donated in the team member's name via PGA Tour Charities, Inc., to a charity for a golf-related project. Like the Ryder Cup, the players and captains are not paid, but their expenses are underwritten.

Second, the Ryder Cup and Presidents Cup are light-years apart in revenue. The 1996 Presidents Cup Match, for example, generated just over $800,000 in net revenue—nothing compared with the Ryder Cup's millions, but still a nice number for charity.

The Presidents Cup is in its infancy, so certainly there is room for growth. The first Match was held only in 1994, at the Robert Trent Jones Golf Club on Lake Manassas in Virginia. The U.S. team, steered by player-captain Hale Irwin (a good choice by the PGA Tour, considering that Irwin hasn't been and might never be a Ryder Cup captain), downed the David Graham–led International team 20–12. The honorary chairman of this Match was former President Gerald Ford.

Graham was all set to return for the 1996 Cup, held at the same course that September. But the players staged a coup and had Graham replaced with Australian Peter Thomson. The Americans, captained by Arnold Palmer, again prevailed, but this time the score was a nail-biting 16½–15½. Anyone who watched the final singles match probably won't forget the long putt by Fred Couples that sealed his win over Vijay Singh and the U.S. victory. The honorary chairman then was another former president, George Bush.

Last year's Match was half a world away, at the Royal Melbourne Golf Club in Australia and in December. This time the honorary chairman was the prime minister of Australia, John Howard. Did finally playing outside the United States reap benefits for the International team?

Well, going in, the U.S. captain, Jack Nicklaus, was confident. "I've got a pretty good selection [of players], don't I?" he said.

Yes he did. Representing the United States were (in order of Presidents Cup dollars accumulated) David Duval, Tiger Woods, Jim Furyk, Justin Leonard, Phil Mickelson, Davis Love III, Mark O'Meara, Scott Hoch, and Mark Calcavecchia. Nicklaus picked Fred Couples and John Huston to join the team, and after Hal Sutton, who had earned his way onto the team, dropped out because of his father-in-law's death a few days before the Match began, he was replaced by Lee Janzen. This was a powerhouse squad.

Peter Thomson was back as captain, and the 1998 Presidents Cup was on his home turf, the Royal Melbourne. In his arsenal were Ernie Els of South Africa, Nick Price of Zimbabwe, Vijay Singh of Fiji, Greg Norman of Australia, Steve Elkington of Australia, Stuart Appleby of Australia, Carlos Franco of Paraguay, Shigeki Maruyama of Japan, Craig Parry of Australia, Joe Ozaki of Japan, Frank Nobilo of New Zealand, and Greg Turner of New Zealand.

On the surface it would seem that the Americans had an advantage in depth, with players' familiarity with each other, and the weight of recent history. As it turned out, none of that mattered. The International team thoroughly thrashed the United States 20½–11½.

As Jacklin mentioned earlier, this Presidents Cup Match was essentially over by the end of play on Saturday, when at the conclusion of the twenty fourball and foursome matches the Internationals had a commanding 14½–5½ lead, meaning they needed to win only two of Sunday's twelve singles matches to take the cup. It would be nice to report that the Americans put up a valiant fight on Sunday, but in the very first two singles matches when Craig Parry downed Justin Leonard 5 and 3 and Nick Price got by David Duval 2 and 1, it was all over.

That Sunday the U.S. team won only half of the twelve singles matches and were no doubt already thinking about the long plane ride home. The only real excitement for U.S. fans was the day's second-to-last match, which had Greg "Shark" Norman versus Tiger Woods—these two "predators" had never competed against each other before nor played as a final pair in a tournament, each with a chance to win. Woods led for most of the match, Norman rallied on the back nine, then Tiger stretched at the finish line and won 1-up.

Why were the Americans beaten so badly? As was the case at Valderrama, the U.S. team was not familiar with the golf course in Melbourne nor the weather conditions, which included intense heat, gusting winds, and a constant swarm of large and mean-spirited flies. In contrast, Norman and Elkington combined had played that particular course close to two hundred times and Parry had grown up in Melbourne. (It was a very smart move on Peter Thomson's part to put Parry out there first in Sunday's singles matches, and he easily defeated Justin Leonard, whose record in professional match play doesn't reflect how successful he has been on the PGA Tour.)

Having a core group of players hailing from Australia—Norman, Elkington, Parry, and Stuart Appleby—and who were followed by enthusiastic crowds, had to be an advantage and an inspiration to the rest of the team. A big bonus was the inspired play of Shigeki Maruyama, who went 5–0 in the Match, topping it off with a 3 and 2 drubbing of Huston on Sunday.

Then there was the emotion factor. The Internationals simply wanted to win more than the U.S. team and earn their first Presidents Cup. Additionally, the home team had quietly dedicated the entire Match to Renay Appleby, Stuart's wife, who at only twenty-five had been killed in a freak car accident five months earlier. One of the most emotional sports scenes of the year was Stuart Appleby, given the honor of playing the last singles match of the 1998 Presidents Cup (against good friend Mark O'Meara), striding up to the eighteenth green with the huge crowd cheering and his teary-eyed teammates waiting to greet him.

The emotional and physical drain that was apparent with the American players—who were in the Presidents Cup at the very end of their competitive year as opposed to September—is something that will receive more attention. As the editorial in *Golfweek* pointed out, with both the Ryder Cup and the Presidents Cup the American players are now taking on a foreign all-star team every year.

"We're in a situation now where the Europeans have two years to prepare to take us on and the Internationals have two years to prepare," said Lee Janzen the Sunday of the last Presidents Cup. "We have just one year between international matches, and that may be taking its toll."

There was even some noise at the Presidents Cup about combining it with the Ryder Cup, perhaps a three-team round-robin tournament every two years. This is blasphemy as far as the PGA of America is concerned, but that hasn't prevented some people from considering the idea, especially if the Presidents Cup keeps growing.

"The potential of the Presidents Cup is larger than the Ryder Cup," Nicklaus said in Melbourne. "That's not to diminish the Ryder Cup, but the Presidents Cup scope is larger, with the rest of the world involved. It has a tremendous future."

"Give it another twenty years or so and take a look at the Presidents Cup and I think it will easily rival the Ryder Cup," said Tiger Woods. "I'm proud to be part of helping get it started."

"The baby's been born, and it's just going to get bigger and bigger," Greg Norman said.

It remains to be seen if, as with the Ryder Cup, the Americans' vulnerability increases interest in the Presidents Cup. The next one is set to be played in Virginia in September 2000.

Is the U.S. performance in the Presidents Cup an indicator of how it will fare in the Ryder Cup a year later? Well, yes and no. Certainly the Americans hope not, given the disaster at Royal Melbourne in December 1998.

Yes, in that there wouldn't normally be a dramatic difference between the Presidents Cup team of one year and the next year's Ryder Cup team. Whether it's by points or earnings, the core group of Tiger Woods, David Duval, Justin Leonard, Jim Furyk, Fred Couples, Mark O'Meara, Davis Love III, Phil Mickelson, and perhaps Lee Janzen and Scott Hoch will be on both rosters. For the 1999 Ryder Cup team, the roster will be determined by who has a strong season and the two men whom Ben Crenshaw picks.

The Presidents Cup is also an indicator because it uses teams, with a match-play format, and after a season of thirty or forty stroke-play tournaments, it's good to have each player giving their all in a Ryder-like contest. It's also the case that the U.S. team is going up against several of the best golfers in the world—those who happen to come from outside Europe. In this regard, with the parity of talent that exists today, the Presidents Cup is as much a challenge as the Ryder Cup, especially after what happened in Australia in 1998.

Among the significant differences:

1. Even though the Presidents Cup has been contested only since 1994, the Americans have essentially been fielding teams of professionals for international competition since the 1920s. The International team, on the other hand, has existed just five years.

2. Being in the Presidents Cup simply isn't the same for everyone involved on the American side as being in the Ryder Cup. There isn't that same sense of tradition, the ghosts of Hagen and Hogan aren't looking over players' shoulders, and while winning is always sweet, nothing beats holding *the* Ryder Cup aloft. Also, as far as fans are concerned, not as many people are interested in the Presidents Cup as in the Ryder Cup. This could change, however, considering the Asian population and if more Asian players (like the spark plug Maruyama) make the International team— and, as with the Ryder Cup, if the United States becomes chronically beatable.

3. So far the results of the Presidents Cup aren't really an accurate predictor of how the Ryder Cup will turn out and vice versa. In the Presidents Cup the United States won in 1994, then lost in the 1995 Ryder Cup. The United States won the Presidents Cup again in 1996, but lost the Ryder Cup again in 1997. Does the 1998 outcome of the Presidents Cup mean anything about the 1999 Ryder Cup? Ask us again at the end of September. The fact is, though, the United States has lost its last three international contests.

Up to December 1998, some American players have done very well in the Presidents Cup. The best was Mark O'Meara with a 5–0–0 record, followed closely by Fred Couples at 6–1–0, David

Duval at 4–0–0, and Davis Love III at 7–2–1. (On the other hand, Mark Brooks was 0–3–0, John Huston and Justin Leonard were 1–3–0, and Corey Pavin was 3–5–2.)

On the International side, with losses in 1994 and 1996, the records are not as shiny. Robert Allenby was 3–7–0, Bradley Hughes was 1–3–0, Frank Nobilo was 3–6–1, Craig Parry was 3–5–0, and Nick Price was 2–5–2. But on the bright side the team had gotten strong performances out of Steve Elkington (5–4–1), Ernie Els (3–1–1), Greg Norman (3–2–0), and Vijay Singh (5–4–1).

The International team actually came out of the 1996 event with momentum. On the final day the U.S. team was up 15½–11½ going into the last five matches and had Leonard, Mickelson, Pavin, Lehman, and Couples ready to go. A cakewalk? No way. Elkington downed Leonard, Els beat Mickelson, Norman dusted Pavin 3 and 1, and Nobilo sent Lehman packing. Only Couples's escape over Singh kept the Presidents Cup in the States.

Whatever the resentment of the PGA of America—and it is understandable—it is unlikely that there will be a halt to the Presidents Cup. It's good theater, brisk competition, offers world-wide audiences an opportunity to see the best non-European players teaming up, and there is money to be raised for charity and to reimburse vendors and other participants. The Presidents Cup is just the latest example of the growth of and enthusiasm for golf on an international stage.

What about that possible merger of the Presidents Cup and the Ryder Cup? Don't hold your breath, but some of the best-known figures in golf see it happening, among them Jack Nicklaus. "Ultimately, what will happen is we'll have tri-matches," he said. "The Ryder Cup is a great event for Europe, but now our guys play every year. That makes it harder to get our guys motivated. Someday, probably sooner than later, that merger will happen."

Chapter 10

RYDER CUP RECORDS

We're not going to drown you in statistics and page after page of Ryder Cup Match results. But since this book is about as much of the Ryder Cup as we can fit, there is lots of good stuff you not only want to have but should know to truly be part of the 1999 Ryder Cup and future ones.

First will be a list of the outcome of each Ryder Cup, then whatever general information seems worth including. After that we'll get more detailed with "The Best of the Best." Following that will be a category of material that—well, we couldn't quite categorize under anything else but "Ryder Tap-Ins and Other Tidbits." Please remember all this for when you're among golf fans and are stuck for conversation.

Ryder Cup Records

Results

1927	Worcester, Mass.	United States 9½, Great Britain 2½
1929	Leeds, England	G.B. 7, U.S. 5
1931	Columbus, Ohio	U.S. 9, G.B. 3
1933	Southport, England	G.B. 6½, U.S. 5½
1935	Ridgewood, N.J.	U.S. 9, G.B. 3

1937	Southport, England	U.S. 8, G.B. 4
1947	Portland, Ore.	U.S. 11, G.B. 1
1949	Scarborough, England	U.S. 7, G.B. 5
1951	Pinehurst, N.C.	U.S. 9½, G.B. 2½
1953	Wentworth, England	U.S. 6½, G.B. 5½
1955	Palm Springs, Calif.	U.S. 8, G.B. 4
1957	Yorkshire, England	G.B. 7½, U.S. 4½
1959	Palm Desert, Calif.	U.S. 8½, G.B. 3½
1961	St. Annes, England	U.S. 14½, G.B. 9½
1963	Atlanta, Ga.	U.S. 23, G.B. 9
1965	Southport, England	U.S. 19½, G.B. 12½
1967	Houston, Texas	U.S. 23½, G.B. 8½
1969	Southport, England	U.S. 16, G.B. 16
1971	St. Louis, Mo.	U.S. 18½, G.B. 13½
1973	Muirfield, Scotland	U.S. 19, G.B. & Ireland 13
1975	Ligonier, Pa.	U.S. 21, G.B.& I. 11
1977	St. Annes, England	U.S. 12½, G.B.& I. 7½
1979	White Sulphur Springs, W. Va.	U.S. 17, Europe 11
1981	Surrey, England	U.S. 18½, Europe 9½
1983	Palm Beach Gardens, Fla.	U.S. 14½, Europe 13½
1985	Sutton Coldfield, England	Europe 16½, U.S. 11½
1987	Dublin, Ohio	Europe 15, U.S. 13
1989	Sutton Coldfield, England	Europe 14, U.S. 14
1991	Kiawah Island, S.C.	U.S. 14½, Europe 13½
1993	Sutton Coldfield, England	U.S. 15, Europe 13
1995	Rochester, N.Y.	Europe 14½, U.S. 13½
1997	Sotogrande, Spain	Europe 14½, U.S. 13½
TOTAL:	32 Matches	U.S. 23, G.B./Europe 7 (2 ties)

Total Team Points

U.S.	413½
G.B./Europe	290½

Widest Victory Margin*

15	1967: U.S. 23½, G.B. 8½
14	1963: U.S. 23, G.B. 9
10	1947: U.S. 11, G.B. 1
	1975: U.S. 21, G.B. & I. 11
9	1981: U.S. 18½, Europe 9½
7	1927 & 1951: U.S. 9½, G.B. 2½
	1965: U.S. 19½, G.B. 12½
6	1931 & 1935: U.S. 9, G.B. 3
	1973: U.S. 19, G.B. & I. 13
	1979: U.S. 17, Europe 11
5	1959: U.S. 8½, G.B. 3½
	1961: U.S. 14½, G.B. 9½
	1971: U.S. 18½, G.B. 13½
	1977: U.S. 12½, G.B. & I. 7½
	1985: Europe 16½, U.S. 11½
4	1937 & 1955: U.S. 8, G.B. 4
3	1957: G.B. 7½, U.S. 4½

The Best of the Best

Most Matches Played

Nick Faldo (England)	46
Neil Coles (England)	40
Bernhard Langer (Germany)	38
Billy Casper (United States)	37
Seve Ballesteros (Spain)	37

*Since Europe's victory in 1985, no team has won the Ryder Cup by more than 2 points.

Christy O'Connor, Sr. (Ireland)	36
Tony Jacklin (England)	35
Lanny Wadkins (United States)	34
Arnold Palmer (United States)	32
Raymond Floyd (United States)	31

Most Ryder Cup Appearances

Nick Faldo (England)	11
Christy O'Connor, Sr. (Ireland)	10
Bernhard Langer (Germany)	9
Dai Rees (England)	9*
Lanny Wadkins (United States)	8
Raymond Floyd (United States)	8
Billy Casper (United States)	8

Raymond Floyd, 20 days past his fifty-first birthday in the '93 Ryder Cup, is the oldest player to participate, followed by Ted Ray in 1927 (50 years, 2 months, 5 days); Christy O'Connor, Sr.; in 1973 (48 years, 8 months, 30 days), and Don January of the United States in 1977 (47 years, 9 months, 26 days).

The youngest players thus far have been Nick Faldo in 1977 (20 years, 1 month, 28 days), Paul Way in 1983 (20 years, 7 months, 3 days), Bernard Gallacher in 1969 (20 years, 7 months, 9 days), Horton Smith in 1929 (21 years, 4 days), and Tiger Woods in 1997 (21 years, 8 months, 27 days).

Most Matches Won

Nick Faldo (England)	23
Arnold Palmer (United States)	22
Billy Casper (United States)	20
Lanny Wadkins (United States)	20

*We just want to point out that Dai Rees was on Ryder Cup teams from 1937 to 1961. Alas, there were no official teams from 1939 to 1945 because of the war, robbing Rees of as many as four more appearances.

Seve Ballesteros (Spain)	20
Bernhard Langer (Germany)	18
Lee Trevino (United States)	17
Jack Nicklaus (United States)	17
Tom Kite (United States)	15

Tied at 14 victories each are Jose Maria Olazabal, Ian Woosnam, Peter Oosterhuis, and Gene Littler.

Most Matches Halved

Gene Littler (United States)	8
Tony Jacklin (England)	8
Neil Coles (England)	7
Billy Casper (United States)	7
Brian Huggett (Wales)	6
Lee Trevino (United States)	6
Bernard Hunt (England)	6
Sam Torrance (Scotland)	6
Julius Boros (United States)	4
Tom Kite (United States)	4
Fred Couples (United States)	4

Most Matches Lost

Neil Coles (England)	21
Christy O'Connor, Sr. (Ireland)	21
Nick Faldo (England)	19
Raymond Floyd (United States)	16
Bernard Hunt (England)	16
Peter Alliss (England)	15
Bernhard Langer (Germany)	15
Sam Torrance (Scotland)	15
Mark James (England)	15
Tony Jacklin (England)	14
Brian Barnes (England)	14

Most Singles Matches Played

Neil Coles (England)	15
Christy O'Connor, Sr. (Ireland)	14
Peter Alliss (England)	12
Arnold Palmer (United States)	11
Tony Jacklin (England)	11
Bernard Gallacher (Scotland)	11
Nick Faldo (England)	11
Gene Littler (United States)	10
Billy Casper (United States)	10
Jack Nicklaus (United States)	10
Lee Trevino (United States)	10
Bernard Hunt (England)	10
Brian Barnes (England)	10

Most Singles Matches Won

Sam Snead (United States)	6
Arnold Palmer (United States)	6
Billy Casper (United States)	6
Peter Oosterhuis (England)	6
Lee Trevino (United States)	6
Nick Faldo (England)	6
Dai Rees (England)	5
Gene Littler (United States)	5
Peter Alliss (England)	5
Neil Coles (England)	5
Brian Barnes (England)	5
Tom Kite (United States)	5

Best Point Percentage
(Minimum Three Ryder Cup Matches)

Jimmy Demaret (United States)	6–0–0	100%
Jack Burke, Jr. (United States)	7–1–0	88%

Horton Smith (United States)	3–0–1	88%
Walter Hagen (United States)	7–1–1	83%
J. C. Snead (United States)	9–2–0	82%
Sam Snead (United States)	10–2–1	81%
Lloyd Mangrum (United States)	6–2–0	75%
Ed Dudley (United States)	3–1–0	75%
Ted Kroll (United States)	3–1–0	75%
Tommy Bolt (United States)	3–1–0	75%
Dow Finsterwald (United States)	9–3–1	73%
Larry Nelson (United States)	9–3–1	73%
Arnold Palmer (United States)	22–8–2	72%
Chip Beck (United States)	6–2–1	72%
Gene Sarazen (United States)	7–2–3	71%
Johnny Pott (United States)	5–2–0	71%
Tom Watson (United States)	10–4–1	70%
Hale Irwin (United States)	13–5–2	70%

The Great Britain/Europe players with the best winning percentages are Abe Mitchell of England (4–2–0, 67%), Jose Maria Olazabal of Spain (14–8–3, 62%), Seve Ballesteros of Spain (20–12–5, 61%), and Colin Montgomerie of Scotland (9–6–3, 58%).

Most Points Won

Nick Faldo (England)	25
Billy Casper (United States)	23½
Arnold Palmer (United States)	23
Seve Ballesteros (Spain)	22½
Lanny Wadkins (United States)	21½
Bernhard Langer (Germany)	20½
Lee Trevino (United States)	20
Jack Nicklaus (United States)	18½
Gene Littler (United States)	18
Tony Jacklin (England)	17

Tom Kite (United States)   17
Ian Woosnam (Wales)   16½

Dynamic Duos

Seve Ballesteros & Jose Maria Olazabal   11–2–2
Arnold Palmer & Gardner Dickinson   5–0
Jack Nicklaus & Tom Watson   4–0
Sam Snead & Lloyd Mangrum   3–1
Tony Lema & Julius Boros   3–1–1
Nick Faldo & Ian Woosnam   5–3–2
Lanny Wadkins & Larry Nelson   4–2
Bernard Gallacher & Brian Barnes   5–4–1
Tony Jacklin & Peter Oosterhuis   3–2–2
(No other duo has a winning record.)

Final-Day Comeback Wins

1929: Down 1 point, Great Britain scored 5½ points to win 7–5.
1949: Down 3–1, the U.S. team rallied with 6 points and won 7–5.
1957: Trailing 3–1, Great Britain went 6–1–1 in singles to win 7½–4½.
1995: Losing 9–7 at Oak Hill, Europe stormed back with 7½ points to take back the cup 14½–13½.

Most Consecutive Team Wins

7—United States, 1935–55
7—United States, 1971–83

Ryder Tap-Ins and Other Tidbits

In this section we offer a potpourri of information that may be interesting, curious, unusual, funny, ironic, or in any other way makes following the Ryder Cup more fascinating.

MORE RYDER CUP RELATIVES

There have been several sets of players who in some way were/are related to each other. They are:

- Percy Alliss and Peter Alliss, father and son
- Antonio Garrido and Ignacio Garrido, father and son
- Charles Whitcombe, Reg Whitcombe, and Ernest Whitcombe, brothers
- Bernard Hunt and Geoffrey Hunt, brothers
- Joe Turnesa and Jim Turnesa, brothers. (Amazingly, Joe was on the 1927 and '29 U.S. teams, Jim on the 1953 U.S. team.)
- Jay Hebert and Lionel Hebert, brothers
- Christy O'Connor, Sr., and Christy O'Connor, Jr., uncle and nephew. (We kid you not.)
- Sam Snead and J. C. Snead, uncle and nephew
- Bob Goalby and Jay Haas, uncle and nephew
- Jack Burke, Jr., and Dave Marr, cousins
- Max Faulkner and Brian Barnes, father and son-in-law
- Jerry Pate and Bruce Lietzke, brothers-in-law

STILL WAITING

Ian Woosnam has been on eight Ryder Cup teams through 1997 and has been one of Europe's steadiest performers—when teamed with someone. His record in singles is 0–6–2, meaning Woosie is still waiting for his first singles-match victory.

When he lost to Fred Couples 8 and 7 at Valderrama, the Welshman tied the record for the biggest losing margin for an eighteen-hole singles match (established by Tom Kite over Howard Clark in 1989).

BEST NOT TO DISCUSS IT IN THE DORM

Floyd and Gallacher on the same team? Such was the case on the Wake Forest golf team.

During the 1997–98 school year, Raymond Floyd, Jr., a senior, and Jamie Gallacher, a freshman, were members of that university's links squad. Jamie's father, of course, played on eight British-European Ryder Cup teams and captained three of them. Raymond Floyd, Sr., was on eight U.S. teams and captained the 1989 contingent. The two faced each other as competitors many times, but because Gallacher didn't become captain until '91, they never faced off in that role.

As adolescents, the junior Floyd and Gallacher were both at Kiawah Island in '91 to watch their fathers go toe to toe as opposing captains, but they didn't meet. As college teammates, they seemed to get along and to take the Ryder Cup rivalry in stride. "We'd watch reruns of the Ryder Cup on The Golf Channel and really get on each other," Floyd, Jr., said. "We kind of ribbed the U.S. guys after the last Ryder Cup," said young Gallacher, "but it's all in fun and we have a good time with it."

Until they meet in the real Ryder Cup, that is.

NO GOOD DEED GOES UNPUNISHED DEPT.

Ironically, Jamie Gallacher ended up at Wake Forest, because during the 1995 Match his father asked American captain Lanny Wadkins about colleges in the United States with strong golf programs. Wadkins urged Gallacher to enroll his son at his alma mater and offered to help any way he could.

To show his gratitude, Gallacher and his team bounced back and beat the United States at Oak Hill that year.

THE LONGEST DAYS

The U.S. team didn't win a match on the second day of the 1997 Ryder Cup. Only twice before had a team gone a whole day without a win—the British on the first day in 1947, and the British squad again on the second day in 1967.

TEAM PLAYER

Bernhard Langer has the distinction of having had the most playing partners (twelve) in Ryder Cup history. Assuming you can't name them and don't feel like looking them up right at this moment, Bernhard's buddies have been (in alphabetical order) Ken Brown, Jose Maria Canizares, Nick Faldo, David Gilford, Mark James, Per-Ulrik Johansson, Barry Lane, Sandy Lyle, Colin Montgomerie, Manuel Pinero, Ronan Rafferty, and Ian Woosnam.

MAYBE SOMEONE SHOULD INTRODUCE THEM

What may be even more remarkable is that Langer and Sam Torrance have been on eight Ryder Cup teams together yet have never played as a pair.

"BUT, HONEY, THIS IS THE *RYDER CUP*"

Tom Watson was on the U.S. Ryder Cup team in 1979—then he wasn't. Watson withdrew from the team before play began at the Greenbrier because his wife, Linda, was due to give birth any moment.

HUMBLE BEGINNINGS

In the spring of 1927, *Golf Illustrated* mounted a campaign to raise 3,000 pounds to send a team of British golfers to the first Ryder Cup Match, in Worcester, Massachusetts. The goal was realized with the help of golf clubs and associations, corporate donors, wealthy patrons, and eventually Samuel Ryder himself.

However, other contributors were less notable sorts who apparently just wanted to see the Ryder Cup become a reality. They included "A Boy Golfer," 2 shillings; "Anonymous," 1 pound; "Ten Handicap," 1 pound (third such donation); "Incog.," 2 pounds; Vaudeville Golfing Society, 3 pounds; and "18 Handicap," almost 7 pounds.

WHO SAYS MONEY DOESN'T MATTER

According to his club contract with MacGregor, if Darren Clarke had gone undefeated in the 1997 Ryder Cup at Valderrama, he would have received a brand-new Ferrari Testerossa worth $180,000.

Clarke was 1–0 going into Sunday, but the car slipped away in his singles match when he was downed by Phil Mickelson 2 and 1.

PROTECT THE WINDOWS

During the BBC's radio broadcast of the '97 Ryder Cup, announcers kept referring to the site of the '99 Match as "Brooklyn" instead of Brookline.

REMEMBER THE ALAMO

Texas has produced the most Ryder Cup captains, with eight. In alphabetical order they are Jack Burke, Jr.; Ben Crenshaw; Ben Hogan; Tom Kite; Lloyd Mangrum; Dave Marr; Byron Nelson; and Lee Trevino.

Which state is next in captains? Okay, we'll tell you. It's Ohio, where Dow Finsterwald, Chick Harbert, and Jack Nicklaus come from.

ACED OUT

There have been only four holes-in-one in Ryder Cup history, none by Americans. Peter Butler holed one at Muirfield in 1973, Nick Faldo at the Belfry in 1993, and both Costantino Rocca and Howard Clark at Oak Hill in 1995.

NICK'S NICE DEBUT

Speaking of Faldo, it's not enough that he was the youngest Ryder Cup player ever, two months past his twentieth birthday, when he participated in the 1977 Match. It's not even enough that he went 3–0 that year. Whom did he beat in singles on Sunday? Tom Watson, who that year was the reigning Masters *and* British Open champion.

EVENTUALLY, SIR NICK?

Oh heck, obviously Nick Faldo deserves his own category. Let's run down just a handful of his Ryder Cup accomplishments:

Youngest player	20 years, 1 month, 28 days
Most Ryder Cups	11
Most holes played	766
Most matches	46

Most wins	23
Most points	25
Most foursomes	18
Most foursomes won	10
Most fourballs	17
Most singles won	6

Is Faldo finished as a Ryder Cup player? The Americans hope so. As one U.S. player told us, "It doesn't matter how Nick is playing the rest of the year or if he fixes his putting problems. No one is more feared than Faldo. Put him on a Ryder Cup team, and he's on a different plane of existence." Look for Faldo to be a captain's pick again—you really think Mark James won't want him along?

THE BOBBY JONES FACTOR

Though the best amateur of all time never played in a Ryder Cup (he did captain an exhibition team during World War II), he still managed to have an impact on the event.

Having already won the British Open in 1926, Jones rallied to beat Joe Turnesa for the U.S. Open Championship at the Scioto Country Club in Ohio. One of the awed spectators was 16-year-old Louis Nicklaus, Jr. Five years later, the Ryder Cup was held at Scioto, attended by Nicklaus. To his surprise, because of a strong physical resemblance, the 21-year-old drugstore clerk was mistaken for Bobby Jones and was greeted by patrons and other players.

As Jack Nicklaus grew up, his father not only held up Jones as a shining example of golf's best but counted the 1931 Ryder Cup case of mistaken identity as one of his fondest memories. No doubt it made playing (and winning) in the Ryder Cup one of Jack's career goals.

As fun and exciting as records are, even the bad ones, they are made to be broken. As we saw during the 1998 baseball season with Mark McGwire and Sammy Sosa, nothing beats the thrill of seeing a performer approach greatness by challenging what seemed to be an unbreakable record.

This is also true in golf. Someday a pro player may shoot less than a 59 in a round. Someone might win the Masters by more than twelve strokes or win it seven times. It's even possible that someone will bypass Ben Hogan's three victories in majors in one year (1953) and win all four—the Grand Slam, the Holy Grail of golf.

The Ryder Cup has seen its share of records established, broken, and broken again. With each event the possibility of setting a new record becomes more exciting as the history, heritage, and legacy of the Ryder Cup continues. Seventy-two years is an awfully long time to carry on the best international golf competition there is.

The best of the best have gone after the Ryder Cup. As *the* ultimate test in golf, glory awaits the winner, bitter disappointment the loser. And as wonderful as all the past Ryder Cup Matches have been, 1999's promises to be the greatest golf competition of all time.

Chapter 11

THE BATTLE OF BROOKLINE

The Worcester Country Club has not changed much in seventy-two years. Seeing the rolling, green, treelined course on the last Friday of September, it is not only easy to envision the 1999 Ryder Cup Match that will take place nearby but to picture Walter Hagen, Gene Sarazen, Ted Ray, Charles Whitcombe, and Samuel Ryder himself strolling the fairways as they did here in 1927.

The Worcester Country Club was not an arbitrary choice to host the first Ryder Cup Match. Though there were other well-respected golf courses in the Northeast not far from a major city—Shinnecock Hills Golf Club on Long Island, for example—the Worcester course was fresh in the memories of players because it had hosted the U.S. Open only two years earlier, in 1925. The players and PGA officials had been impressed by the course's design and natural features and by the club's history, and there were international business relationships that the club members wanted to strengthen.

Club members granted the request to host this new international competition, the Ryder Cup, in Worcester. They didn't necessarily expect that it would turn out to be that big an event, and others involved didn't know what to expect.

"We were excited to be playing in the first official Ryder Cup Match," recalled Sarazen, "but that didn't mean many people would notice or that it would amount to anything."

"Most of us up around here didn't really know what this Ryder Cup thing was," said Francis Hickey, who at 16 caddied for Ted Ray, the British captain, in the 1927 Match and still lives only a mile from the Worcester Country Club. "Folks started showing up, Walter Hagen was there and many of us knew who he was, the players went at it, it was fun and exciting, and suddenly something big in golf had come into being, right here in Worcester."

The Worcester Country Club is in the hills above the manufacturing city in the central-east section of Massachusetts. The famed Scottish designer Donald Ross created the course. It opened in 1914, and the first shot off the tee was taken by former President William Howard Taft. Among the honored guests was Francis Ouimet, who had won the U.S. Open at The Country Club in Brookline, at only 19, the year before.

The 1925 National Championship really put the Worcester Country Club on the American golf map. It featured a playoff between the legendary amateur Bobby Jones and veteran pro Willie Macfarlane.

"What is very special to the membership of this club, who so value the tradition and principles of golf, is that not only was the Open in '25 an exciting one, but it exemplified true sportsmanship," said Paul Lazar, general manager of the Worcester Country Club. "It's the sort of heritage the Ryder Cup has, which began here."

As Lazar explained it, on the final day of the National Championship, Jones was one stroke ahead. He hit his tee shot at 11 into the left rough. Jones went down into it and was barely visible to the right-side gallery, and not even his caddy was with him. Suddenly Jones stepped away from the ball and called a one-stroke penalty on himself, contending that the ball had moved after he addressed it. Absolutely no one saw the ball move, and officials there tried to talk Jones out of the penalty, but he insisted the ball had moved, *he* saw it, and the rules call for a penalty.

As it turned out, at day's end Jones and Macfarlane ended up in a tie. There was an eighteen-hole playoff—tied again. The two played another eighteen holes, and Macfarlane won the U.S. Open by one stroke.

The Ryder Room and other parts of the club feature photographs of the first Match in 1927. Many of the shots include smiling and laughing players, some of them smoking pipes, all dressed neatly and soberly. One does get the sense that the Ryder Cup was meant to be a gentlemen's outing, with winning secondary to fair play and fun.

The newspapers of the time were quite intrigued by this new competition. They were even more excited when the United States won by a large margin. Both the Boston and Worcester papers featured the outcome in headlines almost as big as those given to Charles Lindbergh as he left France to return to the United States following his historic transatlantic flight the week before.

Going from the past to the present, a much-debated issue among golfers and golf fans is whether the Ryder Cup is indeed the "fifth major." Some people in broadcasting and print would have it so because such a distinction helps to build the Ryder Cup into a bigger event. And more than a few players and officials on both sides of the Atlantic believe that the Matches, after seventy-two years, have achieved that sort of status.

"I feel that within its playing year the Ryder Cup is effectively a fifth major championship," said Neil Coles, chairman of the European PGA Tour. "It brings an opportunity, on a biennial basis, to judge the relative playing skills of Europe and America. That is quite significant, considering the advances of players and the growth of the Matches."

"The Ryder Cup almost stands out more than winning a major championship," said U.S. Open winner Billy Casper. "But however you rate the Ryder Cup, there just is nothing else like it. It stands alone."

Some players, though, insist that the Ryder Cup should be viewed for what it is, an international match-play event restricted to two dozen players that, as Casper indicated, stands apart from the Masters, U.S. Open, British Open, and PGA Championship.

"I can't really rank the Ryder Cup up there with my twenty major championships," said Jack Nicklaus. "I can say that it's a special event that has been good to me. Do I think it's the fifth major? No. Do I think it deserves to be the fifth major? No."

"It's a different type of thing," said Byron Nelson. "It's so different that I wouldn't particularly say that it's like winning a major. It just isn't."

"I can't call the Ryder Cup a fifth major," said Lee Janzen, who has won the U.S. Open in 1993 and 1998. "The Ryder Cup is all about team; there's no room that week for individual accomplishment. If a guy goes out and ends up 5–0 but his team loses the Match, that guy's not going to feel that great."

"I'm proud of being the all-time leader in Ryder Cup points, but I can't really compare that achievement to winning six majors," said Nick Faldo. "It's impossible to compare the two. Let's just say that I think the Ryder Cup is the world's greatest team event—and the ultimate pressure situation."

Perhaps the best at putting it in perspective is Curtis Strange, who has had a lot of experience in majors (two-time U.S. Open winner) and in Ryder Cup Matches. He sees a difference between the Ryder Cup "event" and major-tournament play.

"I can only speak for myself, but also what I have read and heard other players say is that the Ryder Cup is bigger than life sometimes," said Strange. "Once you realize that it's not a do-or-die situation, that the sun will come up the next morning no matter what happens, it's an honor just to be on the team and obviously you want to win.

"But I view trying to win major championships as involving more pressure, because what you grow up dreaming about is winning a major, not the Ryder Cup," Strange continued. "It's different pressure from having teammates who are going to rely on you, and having a large audience pulling for you and your team. The Ryder Cup has become the biggest 'happening' in golf. It's not the biggest tournament. The four majors are the biggest tournaments, and the Ryder Cup is the biggest event. I see a clear difference, and thank goodness there is room in golf for both."

* * *

The immediate future of the Ryder Cup is, of course, the upcoming Battle of Brookline. On the last Friday in September 1999, the twenty-four American and European players who have performed the best during the previous twenty months or so will convene at The Country Club. By late Sunday afternoon, the Ryder Cup will either remain in Europe or will be brought to the United States for the first time in six years.

It would be hard to find a venue that more deserves the special and history-filled event that a Ryder Cup Match is than The Country Club in Brookline, a well-to-do suburb of Boston. Visiting it is like stepping into the past, when golf was new in America—come to think of it, much like visiting its younger cousin in Worcester.

It is called simply "The Country Club" because indeed it is credited with being the first country club in the United States. In 1894, for only fifty dollars, the club constructed six holes for the playing of golf, a relatively new game in the States. Golf was a bit of an afterthought, and obviously not a priority in the budget, because originally the club was dedicated to tennis, swimming, ice-skating, and other athletic and social pursuits.

By the beginning of the twentieth century, the course had eighteen holes over a total of 5,200 yards. Not long afterward the course was expanded to twenty-seven holes, consisting of the Clyde, Squirrel, and Primrose courses. It remained pretty much unchanged until Rees Jones was hired by the United States Golf Association to redesign the course in preparation for the 1988 U.S. Open.

A big badge of honor for The Country Club is that, while otherwise keeping to itself according to its members' wishes, it has hosted six different USGA tournaments, the only club in America to hold this distinction: U.S. Opens in 1913, 1963, and 1988; U.S. Amateur Championships in 1910, 1922, 1934, 1957, and 1982; U.S. Women's Amateur Championships in 1902, 1941, and 1995; Walker Cup Matches in 1932 and 1973; the U.S. Girls Junior Championship in 1953; and the U.S. Junior Amateur in 1968.

The Country Club, like the site of the first Ryder Cup seventy-two years ago, is awash in history, tradition, and pride. Photos adorn the wood-paneled walls (including the wet-bar-equipped "Gentlemen's Locker Room"), stunning in their clarity, of the great golf events that have been held here—the 1913 U.S. Open, 1932 Walker Cup, U.S. Opens of 1963 and 1988, the 1995 U.S. Women's Amateur, and many more. (All three U.S. Opens here were decided in playoffs.) A sure sign of the 1990s, though, is that in the locker room there is a TV always tuned to a cable business channel that offers nonstop stock-market updates.

One has the strong feeling that by visiting this place and other Valhallas of golf like Shinnecock Hills on Long Island, Pinehurst in North Carolina, Riviera in Los Angeles, Augusta in Georgia, Winged Foot in New York, Medinah in Illinois, Worcester, and Valhalla itself in Kentucky, just about the entire story of American golf is there to be told.

The Country Club is hallowed ground mainly because of the U.S. Open in 1913, which has an uncanny relationship to the 1999 Ryder Cup. Up to the 1913 National Championship, while golf was not unknown in the United States, it couldn't compete with other sports, especially baseball.

"Even a few years after the first Ryder Cup, when I was on the Holy Cross golf team and we were the best in the Northeast, all that people wanted to know was how our baseball team did," lamented Francis Hickey. "But we could see that things were changing, and much of it began with that kid winning the National Championship here in Massachusetts."

"That kid" was Francis Ouimet, a 19-year-old who in the 1913 U.S. Open (using a 10-year-old caddy, who wore a tie) beat Harry Vardon and Ted Ray in a playoff. The headlines raced from coast to coast: Not only had an American won America's National Championship in a very tough contest, but he had bested the British top guns Vardon and Ray. Thus began the wave that resulted—soon with the help of the barnstorming Walter Hagen— in the United States taking golf more seriously and wanting to knock off its British uncle.

What players, captains, respective PGA officials, spectators, and the worldwide media will find at The Country Club today is a golf course that is proud to be part of history and stay that way. Fittingly, the last Ryder Cup Match of the century will be contested at a course that shares the same respect for tradition and natural features with the course not far to the west where it all began in 1927.

In 1985 the PGA of America hired Rees Jones to redesign The Country Club. Jones is part of the second generation of the most famous American family of golf course architects, whose patriarch is Robert Trent Jones, now 92, who designed Valderrama in the 1970s. Rees Jones is much in demand these days, having done the redesigns for six U.S. Opens (including the Bethpage Black course for the one in 2002 on Long Island) and four PGA Championships.

Jones, a courtly, considerate man in his fifties, soft-spoken yet direct, has never prepared a Ryder Cup course. But his experience in preparing courses for the U.S. Open made him the perfect choice: He is responsible for much of what The Country Club course is today because he redid it for the 1988 U.S. Open.

In a May 1988 memo to the USGA and officials of The Country Club, Jones wrote: "I feel that all the participants in the U.S. Open will feel this is a great old golf course. In our restoration process all modern features were eliminated and restored to their original design style. The Country Club also has a visual contrast of grasses indicative of older courses, with high fescue grass as a secondary rough, bluegrass primary rough, and bentgrass fairways. As is the case with many vintage courses, the greens are relatively small with very testing designs."

After a specific hole-by-hole analysis, the memo concluded: "The variety of terrain, and hole layout, along with great putting surfaces make The Country Club a true test of golf for the world's best players."

That was then, this is now. Yet The Country Club is as much "a true test of golf" as ever.

"The Country Club is a perfect example of how some of the great golf courses are returning to their roots of undulating fairways, high rough, plenty of trees, and small greens," Jones told us. "The prospect of having it seen by as many as a billion people in 1999—well, I'm proud of that and proud to keep tradition alive and well."

Hosting a Ryder Cup is such a huge undertaking that it affects not only the club but the region. The LPGA had tried for over a year to find a site in the Boston area for a tournament. However, because so many corporations in eastern Massachusetts are pouring sponsorship dollars into the Ryder Cup, the LPGA couldn't find an underwriter in the area, plus no other country club in the region wanted to commit to hosting a tourney because of the exhausting Ryder Cup effort. They aren't hosting the Ryder Cup themselves, but surrounding clubs will be devoting their members and other resources to it.

"This is like taking your work to Broadway," said Jones. "I've been very fortunate that my work for majors has been well received, but in 1999 the lights will come on and that September the Ryder Cup will be center stage, for an international audience."

The Country Club in Brookline has never hosted a Ryder Cup. However, what isn't generally known is that it has been involved in an international golf competition—since 1898!

That year, over a century ago, the Royal Montreal Golf Club proposed a competition to members of The Country Club, and the invitation was accepted. For more than one hundred years, teams representing the two clubs have played every year, with the emphasis being camaraderie and goodwill between nations. "Not only was it a good match between the Americans and the Canadians, but it was, it is hoped, the first of a long line of international matches to be held in this and coming seasons," reported an almost clairvoyant *Boston Evening Transcript* in May 1898 after the first match. These contests have been held up to the present day.

The Country Club is thought of fondly, even enthusiastically, by players who have participated in tournaments there as amateurs or professionals.

"I think it's one of the best courses in this country," stated Jack Burke, Jr. "You don't hold three U.S. Opens at a course that doesn't meet very high standards. I was in that Open in 1963, and it was a tough, tough course. I remember taking bets that after the first two days nobody would break 146, and that's six over par. That course is especially hard if you put a wind across there."

Burke added: "That's why I expect the '99 Ryder Cup to be a classic. You've got a great course, the best players, and the wind forcing you to work pretty damn hard to play your best."

Curtis Strange also thinks highly of the course. "It's hard not to have good memories of a course on which you won the U.S. Open," he said, referring to his 1988 National Championship (which he repeated the following year at Oak Hill). "But this is a fine, challenging golf course that will require the best from the competitors."

Still, just the fact that the thirty-third Ryder Cup will be played on American soil doesn't necessarily mean the United States has an excellent chance of winning.

Many of the European players are used to tough courses in all sorts of locations and weather conditions. They are sure to be pumped with confidence after winning in the United States in 1995 and triumphing again in Spain two years later. And those players with a sense of history would no doubt love to close out the century with a European winning streak to balance the seventy-two-year-old scales a bit.

In a way, the Americans are in a backs-to-the-wall situation. They *have* to win, or there will be no escaping the verdict that Europe is now the international center of winning golf. A loss in the United States, the second in three Matches and the third in seven Matches, after losing none at home from 1927 through 1983, would be devastating. Even a tie wouldn't be welcome, because the twentieth century would end with the Ryder Cup still on the other side of the ocean.

The Americans know it won't be pretty if there is another loss and that much of the focus will be on the players. "You show me a losing player who walks away and says, 'That was fun. I really enjoyed playing in that,' and I'll show you a guy who shouldn't be doing what he's doing," Mark O'Meara told *Golf Magazine.*

It would appear that the United States will field a formidable team, and many veteran players believe this could well be America's year, but only by a slim margin.

"I think the U.S. has a really good shot at it," said Gene Littler. "We've got some awfully good players—but then, so do they. This thing has been so close for such a long time now, it may come down to where the ball bounces, for whom, and at what particular moment."

"I've been on both sides of it, the pain of losing and the euphoria of winning," said Ben Crenshaw. "I don't want to feel that pain again, and I don't intend to."

When asked by *Golf Digest* if the recent Ryder Cup losses prove that Europe's players are as good as or better than the Americans, Scott Hoch replied, "No. What it proves is they're better under pressure than we are, especially in the Ryder Cup. I think we've got the better players. We *definitely* have the better players.

"Valderrama was a perfect example. Our top players had a really tough Ryder Cup. Our major winners were 1–9–3, and yet we lost by only 1 point. That says a lot right there for our team— our top guys didn't play well, and we still barely lost."

"I think as a response to the increasing pressure, during the last Ryder Cup and Presidents Cup the U.S. players decided, 'Let's have some fun out there and maybe we'll win too,'" said Lee Janzen. "But if we've reached the point that for the United States the most important thing is to win the next Ryder Cup, then we have to realize that just making the team is not enough; winning is all that counts. That means it will be a more intense week in Brookline, less enjoyable, but we've got to do what it takes. I would never tell Ben Crenshaw what to do, but for me, being on those last two teams and getting shellacked, I would write everyone a letter to personally challenge them to be one or two percent better that week than any other week."

Then Janzen added with a laugh, "Of course, that doesn't make fifty-footers go in like we've seen our opponents do the last couple of years."

It is fun to speculate who will be on the U.S. and European Ryder Cup teams for the thirty-third Match. On the American side, barring injury, Tiger Woods, Mark O'Meara, Phil Mickelson, Justin Leonard, David Duval, and probably Davis Love III and Jim Furyk will make the cut. Continued good play in '99 will also put Fred Couples, Billy Mayfair, Payne Stewart, Hal Sutton, and Lee Janzen on the team. Other possibilities, especially someone able to capture a quadruple-points major in '99, include Steve Stricker and Mark Calcavecchia.

In a way, the composition of the European team will be more interesting because a few members of the longtime nucleus of the squad may not make the cut based on points. Locks are Colin Montgomerie, Lee Westwood, and Darren Clarke. Consistent play will probably put Miguel Angel Jiminez, Sven Struver of Germany, Robert Karlsson and Jarmo Sandelin of Sweden, and Costantino Rocca in the Match.

Hold on: What about Bernhard Langer, Ian Woosnam, Seve Ballesteros, Sam Torrance, Jose Maria Olazabal, and of course Nick Faldo? Ah, there's the rub. Except for Olazabal, the others are in their forties and are no longer winning European tournaments with regularity. For reasons of honor or anticipated effectiveness, they could be selected by colleague and now captain Mark James, but he has only two picks.

After winning at Valderrama, Ballesteros announced, "I will not be captain in 1999 for the simple reason that I would like to recover my game. I'd like to play in 1999." Memo to Seve: Not likely. After being his assistant in '97, it will be tough for James not to pick Ballesteros. But having spent most of the 1990s winless, the fact is that Seve's search for his lost game is like Don Quixote tilting at windmills—imaginary and elusive.

It will be hard to watch a Ryder Cup without the likes of Langer, Woosnam, Torrance, and the others—all great competitors and class acts. But the torch is being passed, a new generation of European golfer is ascending, and Monty, at 36, may well be the elder statesman. If James is focused on winning, he may have to go beyond the well-known names and far beyond Great Britain.

"There's some good chaps coming up, and not necessarily from Great Britain," said Max Faulkner, the Englishman who keeps a keen eye on golf developments. "These Swedes—you want to watch those chaps before long."

That time has arrived. As of February 1, 1999, aside from Jesper Parnevik, four of the ten players who are leaders in Ryder Cup points on the European PGA Tour hail from Sweden. As odd as it seems, given the golf-unfriendly climate of that country, Sweden seems to be emerging as the new powerhouse in European golf. This might have happened anyway, but one has to wonder about the influence and inspiration of the Ryder Cup on golf all across Europe.

It is quite possible that the Battle of Brookline, with all the youth involved, will provide a glimpse of the next two decades of Ryder Cup competition.

That sounds very exciting, but let's face it: Do any of us who love this event want to see it held without Nick Faldo, the all-time points leader and eleven-time competitor? Having joined the PGA Tour in the United States, to focus on winning more majors (and probably more money), he is not racking up European PGA Ryder Cup points, nor has he been playing at a level that promises plenty of points. Still, James could conceivably use one of his captain's picks on Faldo, who has continued to be a winner in the Ryder Cup and would no doubt be an inspirational leader.

And the weight of history can't be denied. "There's nothing I'm more proud of than having been on eleven straight Ryder Cup teams," Faldo told us. "That's a record hard to beat and may well last a very long time. But I want to make it twelve straight teams." (Memo to Mark James: It wouldn't hurt that Faldo is very familiar with the Country Club course, having lost the U.S. Open by a whisker there, in a playoff, to Curtis Strange in 1988.)

"What would be interesting and at the same time unforgivable is if the Americans have a tough time in Brookline because they don't know the golf course," said Tony Jacklin. "Just because the venue is in the United States doesn't mean that the American players will know it well enough. I expect that Ben [Crenshaw] will get the players to practice there and be fully prepared. Without that preparation, and with the high quality of European players, there may not be a home-field advantage. I do think Mark [James] and his team will have to work hard, and given the Ryder Cup history it's silly to expect the Americans to lose three in a row. The most important thing of all, though, for the Ryder Cup is that the Match be a close one."

One thing the Americans cannot count on is that the European players will be intimidated coming to Boston to defend the Ryder Cup. If anything, recent success has given the players a swagger, especially the younger ones.

"I think the Americans are very narrow-minded at times— they think U.S. golf is the be-all and end-all," Lee Westwood told *Golfweek*. "We have nothing to prove until 1999, and then we can prove we're the best again."

With the thirty-third Ryder Cup Match set to begin in September 1999, the players may not be quite ready yet, and the course will require more tweaking; there is a heck of a lot more business to conduct, and the members still have to brace themselves. But the shop at The Country Club is ready and waiting. Shelves are fully stocked with golf equipment and clothing, all featuring the Ryder Cup logo. Just sauntering around the shop and clubhouse and outbuildings, almost every overheard conversation seems to make reference to the Ryder Cup. In some ways September 24, 1999, has become the D-Day of golf.

Whatever the result of the thirty-third Ryder Cup Match, there is the hope that the event will continue to focus on its founding principles: competition among friends, fair play, sportsmanship, and pride in one's country.

"Being that it's back in Massachusetts where it began, I'd like to see the Ryder Cup return to its original spirit of a good competition between friends," said Jack Whitaker. "It's gotten pretty heated up lately, and some of the players have gone through a tough time. I'd like the future to be more like the past."

"The Ryder Cup has gotten kind of cutthroat, and I don't like to see where it's going," said Lee Trevino. "I'd like to see more fun back in it, because we used to have more of that. It used to be a competition among friends, and I'd like to see it go in that direction because that's what I think Mr. Ryder had in mind."

Whatever happens in Brookline in September '99, what is the likely future of the Ryder Cup? As an event, will it keep getting bigger and undergo further expansion?

What is clear is that the Ryder Cup reflects the growth of golf around the globe through the increasing level of play internationally. There are now simply more and better players than there were one, two, and three generations ago, which if nothing else bodes well for the competitive intensity of the Ryder Cup.

"When the PGAs of the world decided some years ago to conform to using the larger-size golf ball, to get maximum results from that ball you had to develop a better golf swing," Billy Casper explained. "So a better golf swing developed throughout the world, and therefore the caliber of play increased—it's now more equal than it's ever been in the game of golf. We're seeing that very directly in the international competitions involving professional players, and the best one of those is the Ryder Cup."

Concerning expansion, the possibility exists that before too long there will be a Senior Ryder Cup. The rapid growth of the Senior PGA Tour—in twenty years it has gone from two to forty-four tournaments and more than $70 million in total prize money—has opened a lot of eyes in America and in Europe to the financial potential of events featuring older golfers. A Senior Ryder Cup could be played in even-numbered years (take *that*, Presidents Cup!) and feature many familiar names.

"They're talking very seriously about it over here, and of course now it would have to include Europe," said Brian Barnes of England about a Senior Ryder Cup. "And in all honesty, it would still be exactly the same situation for probably another ten years as it was in the 1960s and 1970s, because there were very few European players who were really damn good in those days. So once again it would be down to the few playing against the many.

"Let's face it," Barnes continued. "In the next couple of years you've got Tom Watson, Tom Kite, Lanny Wadkins, Fuzzy Zoeller, Ben Crenshaw, and other excellent players coming through the senior ranks, and that's in addition to Hale Irwin, Gil Morgan, and Larry Nelson, who are there now. So once again it would be hold the line until Faldo and Seve and a few others came along to counterattack. But a few years after that, you could have a very competitive senior-level Ryder Cup."

Discussion of the future of the Ryder Cup has to include where the thirty-fourth, thirty-fifth, thirty-sixth, and subsequent Matches will be held. The areas that play host to them can expect an economic shot in the arm, plus clubs that host a Match increase exponentially in status.

Thus far, the first Match of the twenty-first century is set for the Belfry in England, familiar territory for the Ryder Cup. The PGA of America has decided for the most part to go with tradition in the next century. The 2003 match will be held at the Oakland Hill Country Club in Bloomfield, Michigan, where a World War II "Match" was held. Other sites are the Valhalla Golf Club in Louisville, Kentucky, in 2007 and the Medinah Country Club in Illinois in 2011. There no doubt is a connection that the PGA of America has awarded PGA Championships to Medinah in 1999, Valhalla in 2004, The Country Club in 2005, Medinah again in 2006, and Oakland Hills in 2008.

For 2005 the European PGA has pledged that the Ryder Cup will be held in the Republic of Ireland for the first time. Three sites were considered: Portmarnock Golf Club, founded in 1894 and twenty minutes north of Dublin ("The only place to play the Ryder Cup in Ireland," declared Christy O'Connor, Sr., last year); Kildare Hotel and Country Club, forty minutes west of Dublin, designed by Arnold Palmer and Ed Seay and opened in 1991; and

Druids Glen, another recently opened club, Irish designed and set in County Wicklow south of Dublin. Kildare was the chosen site.

One would think the European PGA would go with the older, more traditional course, but given the way the Ryder Cup has become a huge media and spectator event, it's equally important to consider a club and area's ability to handle traffic as well as quality of communications, availability and level of accommodations, and which facility can best afford upgrades and other changes.

Remarkably, an American businessman who owns the Loch Lomond Golf Club in Scotland has already put in a bid to host the 2009 Ryder Cup there. Having it in Scotland again would be wonderful, considering that that country is the birthplace of golf, but with the 2005 Match in Ireland pressure will be on to have the next venue in England or on the Continent a full twelve years after Valderrama.

Let's return to Worcester. With the Ryder Cup back in Massachusetts, shouldn't the Match be in Worcester instead of at The Country Club? Is the PGA of America snubbing the cup's birthplace?

Not at all. The fact is that at 6,422 yards, the Worcester course really couldn't host a major tournament. Its last national championship was the 1960 U.S. Women's Open. In addition, the three hundred members don't seem all that eager to open the club up to a huge event like the Ryder Cup. Still, none of them expects to feel left out.

"When an event of this caliber comes around, all the private clubs band together, so we'll be right in the mix," said Paul Lazar. "Some of our members will be marshals. Members will be hosting players and officials. And the whole region benefits economically."

The Worcester Country Club, seventy-two years after the Ryder Cup was first officially contested, is content with its place in history and the role it played to help nurture international golf. Looking out from the clubhouse on a mild autumn afternoon, one can almost see the horse-drawn lawn mowers and women in black dresses who kept the course manicured in preparation for the first Ryder Cup.

"The membership here guards history and tradition, they love it," Lazar said. "Every time you step out on the golf course you can sense it, and it's wonderful to have, just one of the old grand-daddies of golf courses. It very quietly sits here in the corner of Worcester and just keeps going."

Just like the Ryder Cup. Yes, concerns are expressed about the "event" it has become, the increasing intensity and pressure, the gamesmanship, and whether or not the spirit of Worcester and Royal Lytham and St. Annes and Pinehurst and the other old-time venues continues unabated today. That will all be sorted out in September and in the twenty-first century. There is an unlimited future to the friendly competition that Samuel Ryder, Walter Hagen, Abe Mitchell, Gene Sarazen, Ted Ray, and others began decades ago.

"This venue in Boston will have so much to do with the personality of the '99 Match," said Ben Crenshaw. "Boston is one of our most historic cities, and The Country Club has one of the most illustrious histories anywhere in American golf. In 1913 it gave us the real thought that we could compete with the best British players. The '99 Match has all the markings of a storybook occasion."

"The bottom line is that after almost three-quarters of a century, the Ryder Cup Matches will never be lopsided again," stated Billy Casper. "Time after time, indefinitely, I believe the awarding of that wonderful trophy is going to come down to what happens at the very last moment. Depending on what side you're on, you might want to look away—but you can't."

"The Ryder Cup is the greatest spectator event around," Lee Janzen said. "Just the electricity watching the Matches, it's either them or us, everybody's rooting for one side or the other. I encourage everybody I know to go to the Ryder Cup, because they will never see anything else like it."

When it was mentioned that it seemed appropriate that the last Ryder Cup of the twentieth century would be held back in

Massachusetts, where it all began seventy-two years ago, Francis Hickey said, "Isn't is exciting? Oh gosh, I can't wait."

Then the 88-year-old former caddy and lifelong golf enthusiast added, "I'm so looking forward to being there, if they'll have me. My whole life, just about, there's been the Ryder Cup. I was in the first one, and I sure don't intend to miss this one."

APPENDIX

Ryder Cup Players and Their Records

We've compiled here the records of all the players who have participated in the Ryder Cup Matches from the first one in 1927 through Valderrama in 1997, including the year or years they played. If you want to figure out the total points, award a point for each win and a half-point for each tie.

U.S. Team

Player	Year(s) Played	Won–Lost–Tied
Tommy Aaron	1969, 1973	1–4–1
Skip Alexander	1949, 1951	1–1–0
Paul Azinger	1989–93	5–7–2
Jerry Barber	1955, 1961	1–4–0
Miller Barber	1969, 1971	1–4–2
Herman Barron	1947	1–0–0
Andy Bean	1979, 1987	4–2–0
Frank Beard	1969, 1971	2–3–3
Chip Beck	1989–93	6–2–1
Homero Blancas	1973	2–1–1
Tommy Bolt	1955, 1957	3–1–0
Julius Boros	1950, 1959, 1963–67	9–3–4
Gay Brewer	1967, 1973	5–3–1
Billy Burke	1931, 1933	3–0–0

Player	Year(s) Played	Won–Lost–Tied
Jack Burke, Jr.	1951–59	7–1–0
Walter Burkemo	1953	0–1–0
Mark Calcavecchia	1987–91	5–5–1
Billy Casper	1961–75	20–10–7
Bill Collins	1961	1–2–0
Charles Coody	1971	0–2–1
John Cook	1993	1–1–0
Fred Couples	1989–97	7–9–4
Wilfred Cox	1931	2–0–0
Ben Crenshaw	1981–83, 1987, 1995	3–8–1
Jimmy Demaret	1947–51	6–0–0
Gardner Dickinson	1967, 1971	9–1–0
Leo Diegel	1927–33	3–3–0
Dave Douglas	1953	1–0–1
Dale Douglass	1969	0–2–0
Ed Dudley	1929, 1933, 1937	3–1–0
Olin Dutra	1933, 1935	1–3–0
Lee Elder	1979	1–3–0
Al Espinosa	1927–31	2–1–1
Johnny Farrell	1927–31	3–2–1
Brad Faxon	1995, 1997	2–4–0
Dow Finsterwald	1957–63	9–3–1
Raymond Floyd	1969, 1975–77, 1981–85, 1991–93	12–16–3
Doug Ford	1955–61	4–4–1
Ed Furgol	1957	0–1–0
Marty Furgol	1955	0–1–0

Jim Furyk	1997	1–2–0
Jim Gallagher, Jr.	1993	2–1–0
Al Geiberger	1967, 1975	5–1–3
Bob Gilder	1983	2–2–0
Bob Goalby	1963	3–1–1
Johnny Golden	1927, 1929	3–0–0
Lou Graham	1973–77	5–3–1
Hubert Green	1977, 1979, 1985	4–3–0
Ken Green	1989	2–2–0
Ralph Guldahl	1937	2–0–0
Jay Haas	1983, 1995	3–4–1
Fred Haas, Jr.	1953	0–1–0
Walter Hagen	1927–35	7–1–1
Bob Hamilton	1949	0–2–0
Chick Harbert	1949, 1955	2–0–0
Chandler Harper	1955	0–1–0
Dutch Harrison	1947–51	2–1–0
Fred Hawkins	1957	1–1–0
Mark Hayes	1979	1–2–0
Clayton Heafner	1949, 1951	3–0–1
Jay Hebert	1959, 1961	2–1–1
Lionel Hebert	1957	0–1–0
Dave Hill	1969, 1973, 1977	6–3–0
Scott Hoch	1997	2–0–1
Ben Hogan	1947, 1951	3–0–0
Hale Irwin	1975–81, 1991	13–5–2
Tommy Jacobs	1965	3–1–0
Peter Jacobsen	1985, 1995	2–4–0
Don January	1965, 1977	2–3–2
Lee Janzen	1993, 1997	2–3–0

Player	Year(s) Played	Won–Lost–Tied
Herman Keiser	1947	0–1–0
Tom Kite	1979–87, 1993	15–9–4
Ted Kroll	1953–57	3–1–0
Ky Laffoon	1935	0–1–0
Tom Lehman	1995, 1997	3–2–2
Tony Lema	1963, 1965	8–1–2
Justin Leonard	1997	0–2–2
Wayne Levi	1991	0–2–0
Bruce Lietzke	1981	0–2–1
Gene Littler	1963–71, 1975	14–5–8
Davis Love III	1993–97	5–8–0
Jeff Maggert	1995, 1997	4–3–0
John Mahaffey	1979	1–2–0
Tony Manero	1937	1–1–0
Lloyd Mangrum	1947–53	6–2–0
Dave Marr	1965	4–2–0
Billy Maxwell	1963	4–0–0
Dick Mayer	1957	1–0–1
Mark McCumber	1989	2–1–0
Jerry McGee	1977	1–1–0
Bill Mehlhorn	1927	1–1–0
Phil Mickelson	1995, 1997	4–1–2
Cary Middlecoff	1953, 1955, 1959	2–3–1
Johnny Miller	1975, 1981	2–2–2
Larry Mize	1987	1–1–2
Gil Morgan	1979, 1983	1–2–3
Bob Murphy	1975	2–1–1
Byron Nelson	1937, 1947	3–1–0
Larry Nelson	1979, 1981, 1987	9–3–1

Bobby Nichols	1967	4–0–1
Jack Nicklaus	1969–77, 1981	17–8–3
Andy North	1985	0–3–0
Ed Oliver	1947, 1951, 1953	3–2–0
Mark O'Meara	1985, 1989–91, 1997	4–7–1
Arnold Palmer	1961–67, 1971–73	22–8–2
Johnny Palmer	1949	0–2–0
Sam Parks	1935	0–0–1
Jerry Pate	1981	2–2–0
Steve Pate	1991	0–1–1
Corey Pavin	1991–95	8–5–0
Calvin Peete	1983, 1985	4–2–1
Henry Picard	1935, 1937	3–1–0
Dan Pohl	1987	1–2–0
Johnny Pott	1963–67	5–2–0
Dave Ragan	1963	2–1–1
Henry Ransom	1951	0–1–0
Johnny Revolta	1935, 1937	2–1–0
Loren Roberts	1995	3–1–0
Chi Chi Rodriguez	1973	0–1–1
Bill Rogers	1981	1–2–1
Bob Rosburg	1959	2–0–0
Mason Rudolph	1971	1–1–1
Paul Runyan	1933, 1935	2–2–0
Doug Sanders	1967	2–3–0
Gene Sarazen	1927–37	7–2–3
Denny Shute	1931, 1933, 1937	2–2–2

Player	Year(s) Played	Won–Lost–Tied
Dan Sikes	1969	2–1–0
Scott Simpson	1987	1–1–0
Horton Smith	1929–37	3–0–1
J. C. Snead	1971–75	9–2–0
Sam Snead	1937, 1947–55, 1959	10–2–1
Ed Sneed	1977	1–0–1
Mike Souchak	1959, 1961	5–1–0
Craig Stadler	1983, 1985	4–2–2
Payne Stewart	1987–93	8–7–1
Ken Still	1969	1–2–0
Dave Stockton	1971, 1977	3–1–1
Curtis Strange	1983–89, 1995	6–12–2
Hal Sutton	1985, 1987	3–3–3
Lee Trevino	1969–75, 1979, 1981	17–7–6
Jim Turnesa	1953	1–0–0
Joe Turnesa	1927, 1929	1–2–1
Ken Venturi	1965	1–3–0
Lanny Wadkins	1977–79, 1983–93	20–11–3
Art Wall	1957–61	4–2–0
Al Watrous	1927, 1929	2–1–0
Tom Watson	1977–83, 1989	10–4–1
Tom Weiskopf	1973, 1975	7–2–1
Craig Wood	1931–35	1–3–0
Tiger Woods	1997	1–3–1
Lew Worsham	1947	2–0–0
Fuzzy Zoeller	1979, 1983, 1985	1–8–1

Great Britain/Ireland/Europe Team

Player	Year(s) Played	Won–Lost–Tied
Jimmy Adams	1947–53	2–5–0
Percy Alliss	1929–37	3–2–1
Peter Alliss	1953, 1957–69	10–15–5
Peter Baker	1993	3–1–0
Seve Ballesteros	1979, 1983–95	20–12–5
Harry Bannerman	1971	2–2–1
Brian Barnes	1969–79	10–14–1
Maurice Bembridge	1969–75	6–8–3
Thomas Bjorn	1997	1–0–1
Aubrey Boomer	1927, 1929	2–2–0
Ken Bousfield	1949–51, 1955–61	5–5–0
Hugh Boyle	1967	0–3–0
Harry Bradshaw	1953–57	2–2–1
Gordon Brand, Sr.	1983	0–1–0
Gordon Brand, Jr.	1987, 1989	2–4–1
Paul Broadhurst	1991	2–0–0
Eric Brown	1953–59	4–4–0
Ken Brown	1977–79, 1983–87	4–9–0
Richard Burton	1935–37, 1949	2–3–0
Jack Busson	1935	0–2–0
Peter Butler	1965, 1969–73	3–9–2
Jose Maria Canizares	1981–85, 1989	5–4–2
Alex Caygill	1969	0–0–1
Clive Clark	1973	0–1–0
Howard Clark	1977, 1981, 1985–89, 1995	7–7–1
Darren Clarke	1997	1–1–0
Neil Coles	1961–73, 1977	12–21–7

Player	Year(s) Played	Won–Lost–Tied
Archie Compston	1927–31	1–4–1
Henry Cotton	1929, 1937, 1947	2–4–0
Bill Cox	1935, 1937	0–2–1
Fred Daly	1947–53	3–4–1
Eamonn Darcy	1975–77, 1981, 1987	1–8–2
William Davis	1931, 1933	2–2–0
Peter Dawson	1977	1–2–0
Norman Drew	1959	0–0–1
George Duncan	1927–31	2–3–0
Syd Easterbrook	1931, 1933	2–1–0
Nick Faldo	1977–97	23–19–4
John Fallon	1955	1–0–0
Max Faulkner	1947–53, 1957	1–7–0
David Feherty	1991	1–1–1
Bernard Gallacher	1969–83	13–13–5
John Garner	1971, 1973	0–1–0
Antonio Garrido	1979	1–4–0
Ignacio Garrido	1997	0–1–3
David Gilford	1991, 1995	3–3–1
Malcolm Gregson	1967	0–4–0
Joakim Haeggman	1993	1–1–0
Tom Haliburton	1961, 1963	0–6–0
Arthur Havers	1927, 1931–33	3–3–0
Jimmy Hitchcock	1965	0–3–0
Bert Hodson	1931	0–1–0
Tommy Horton	1975, 1977	1–6–1
Brian Huggett	1963, 1967–75	8–10–6

Bernard Hunt	1953, 1957–69	6–16–6
Geoffrey Hunt	1963	0–3–0
Guy Hunt	1975	0–2–1
Tony Jacklin	1967–79	13–14–8
John Jacobs	1955	2–0–0
Mark James	1977–81, 1989–95	8–15–1
Edward Jarman	1935	0–1–0
Per-Ulrik Johansson	1995, 1997	3–2–0
Herbert Jolly	1927	0–2–0
Michael King	1979	0–1–0
Arthur Lacey	1933, 1937	0–3–0
Barry Lane	1993	0–3–0
Bernhard Langer	1981–97	18–15–5
Arthur Lees	1947–51, 1955	4–5–0
Sandy Lyle	1979–87	7–9–2
Jimmy Martin	1965	0–1–0
Peter Mills	1957	1–0–0
Abe Mitchell	1929–33	4–2–0
Ralph Moffitt	1961	0–1–0
Colin Montgomerie	1991–97	9–6–3
Christy O'Connor, Sr.	1955–71	11–21–4
Christy O'Connor, Jr.	1975, 1989	1–3–0
Jose Maria Olazabal	1987–93, 1997	14–8–3
John O'Leary	1975	0–4–0
Peter Oosterhuis	1971–81	14–11–3
Alf Padgham	1933–37	0–7–0
John Panton	1951, 1953, 1961	0–5–0

Player	Year(s) Played	Won–Lost–Tied
Jesper Parnevik	1997	1–1–2
Alf Perry	1933–37	0–2–1
Manuel Pinero	1981, 1985	6–3–0
Lionel Platts	1965	1–2–2
Eddie Polland	1973	0–2–0
Ronan Rafferty	1989	1–2–0
Ted Ray	1927	0–2–0
Dai Rees	1937, 1947–61	7–9–1
Steven Richardson	1991	2–2–0
Jose Rivero	1985, 1987	2–3–0
Fred Robson	1927–31	2–4–0
Costantino Rocca	1993–97	6–5–0
Syd Scott	1955	0–2–0
Des Smyth	1979, 1981	2–5–0
Dave Thomas	1959, 1963–67	3–10–5
Sam Torrance	1981–95	7–15–6
Peter Townsend	1969, 1971	3–8–0
Brian Watts	1983	1–3–0
Philip Walton	1995	1–1–0
Charles Ward	1947–51	1–5–0
Paul Way	1983, 1985	6–2–1
Harry Weetman	1951–63	2–11–2
Lee Westwood	1997	2–3–0
Charles Whitcombe	1927–37	3–2–4
Ernest Whitcombe	1929–31, 1935	1–4–1
Reg Whitcombe	1935	0–1–0
George Will	1963–67	2–11–2
Norman Wood	1975	1–2–0
Ian Woosnam	1983–97	14–12–5

INDEX

Mehlhorn, Bill, 32
Meshiai, Hajime, 109
Mickelson, Phil, xvi, 124–25,
    195, 222
  and Presidents Cup, 192, 197
  as team member, 8, 14–18, 20,
    100–101, 135, 151, 208
Middlecoff, Cary, 51, 59
Miller, Johnny, 2, 18, 51, 69, 84,
    102, 122, 137
Mills, Mike, 112
Minoza, Frankie, 109
Mitchell, Abe, 28–29, 31, 204, 228
Mize, Larry, 86
Montgomerie, Colin, xvii, 74,
    184, 204, 208, 222–23
  as team member, xiv, 5–6,
    11–12, 16–18, 21–24, 85,
    89, 92–93, 95–97, 100–
    101, 138–39, 156, 160,
    166
Morgan, Gil, 74, 79, 226
Morgan, Walt, 110
Muirfield, Scotland, 66–68
Muirfield Village Golf Club, 83,
    85–87, 114
Murray, Bill, 112

NBC, 114–18
Nelson, Byron, 42, 45–46, 48–50,
    161–62, 209, 215
Nelson, Larry, 2, 68–70, 74, 83,
    86, 204–5, 226
Nicklaus, Jack, 59, 84, 129,
    131–32, 180, 188, 215
  and Presidents Cup, 192, 195,
    197

records and facts, 202–5, 210
  as team captain, 75, 78–80, 83,
    86–87, 114, 138, 145–47,
    158–59, 163, 173, 176,
    209
  as team member, 2, 51, 61,
    64–72, 125, 133–34, 169
Nicklaus, Louis, Jr., 210
Nilsson, Pia, 182
Nobilo, Frank, 109, 193, 197
Norman, Greg, 33, 84, 109, 125,
    189, 193–95, 197
North, Andy, 80

Oak Hill Country Club, 2, 8, 15,
    24, 99–102, 116–17, 119,
    153, 166–67
O'Connor, Christy, Jr., 89, 142,
    206
O'Connor, Christy, Sr., 51,
    201–3, 206, 226
O'Grady, Mac, 143
Olazabal, Jose Maria, xvii, 99,
    110, 202, 204–5, 222
  as team member, xiv, 6, 9–
    10, 14–16, 18, 20–22,
    24, 74, 81, 84–85, 87, 89,
    91–93, 95, 98, 135, 137,
    141, 153–55, 160, 166,
    167
O'Meara, Mark, xvi, 127, 129,
    184–85, 195, 221–22
  and Presidents Cup, 192, 194,
    196
  as team member, 1, 7, 12–13,
    16, 18, 20, 24, 80, 82, 87,
    90, 92–93, 136–37, 155

ABOUT THE AUTHORS

BOB BUBKA has been covering professional golf on radio for close to twenty years—having learned the art from the pioneer of golf on radio, Al Wester—and has covered football and basketball on WLNG radio for over thirty years. He lives in Springs, New York, with his wife, Donna, though most of his time is spent around the world toting a suitcase and a microphone.

TOM CLAVIN is coauthor of five previous books and has written about golf for various publications, including the *New York Times*. He lives in Sag Harbor, New York, with his wife, Nancy, and two children, Kathryn and Brendan, all of whom are now aspiring golfers.